Sexual Lifestyles in the Twentieth Century

Sexual Lifestyles in the Twentieth Century

A Research Study

Elina Haavio-Mannila, Osmo Kontula, Anna Rotkirch

Foreword by Jeffrey Weeks

palgrave

First published 2002 by
PALGRAVE
Houndmills, Basingstoke, Hampshire RG21 6XS and
175 Fifth Avenue, New York, N.Y. 10010
Companies and representatives throughout the world

PALGRAVE is the new global academic imprint of
St. Martin's Press LLC Scholarly and Reference Division and
Palgrave Publishers Ltd (formerly Macmillan Press Ltd).

ISBN 0-333-794184 hardback

This book is printed on paper suitable for recycling and made from fully managed and sustained forest sources.

A catalogue record for this book is available from the British Library.

Library of Congress Cataloging-in-Publication Data

Haavio-Mannila, Elina.
    Sexual lifestyles in the twentieth century : a research study/Elina Haavio-Mannila, Osmo Kontula, and Anna Rotkirch.
        p. cm
    Includes bibliographical references and index.
    ISBN 0-333-79418-4
    1. Sex customs–Finland. I. Kontula, Osmo. II. Rotkirch, Anna, 1996- III. Title.

HQ18.F5 H33 2001
306.7'094897–dc21   2001048208

10 9 8 7 6 5 4 3 2 1
11 10 09 08 07 06 05 04 03 02

Printed and bound in Great Britain by
Antony Rowe Ltd, Chippenham, Wiltshire

Consultant Editor, Jo Campling

Contents

List of Tables

Foreword by Jeffrey Weeks

Elina Haavio-Mannila and her colleagues have established themselves in the great tradition of sex researchers over the past century. Like their predecessors and contemporaries in Europe and America they have brought a social scientific zeal and a liberal imagination to bear on what is simultaneously the most intimately personal and the most publicly controversial of life's pleasures, passions and pains. The fundamental aim is always to understand before we condemn on the basis of prejudice or ignorance, to know in order to act (or not act), to tolerate rather than to excoriate. The sex research tradition has embodied many paradoxes and contradictions. Some of the earliest pioneers in the early 20th century now appear to us as old fashioned, mired in their own confusions and unwarranted assumptions. But they also offer a signal achievement: they have provided beams of light on what the forces of sexual regulation have often preferred to leave in obscurity, namely the vital importance of sexuality in shaping our sense of self, social identity and place in the wider society. The authors of this book embody the best of the tradition, while being alert to the wider debate about the history, meanings and shifting values of sexuality. The result is a fascinating and illuminating work that adds an important piece to the jigsaw which is contemporary sexuality.

Sex only acquires its meanings through the web of beliefs, values, norms and relationship patterns in which it is embedded. An important aspect of this book is that it locates its findings in a sense of great historical change which is transforming that web of meaning. Broadly, over the past couple of generations there has been a major shift from authoritarian patterns of erotic life, backed by tradition, church and state, to more highly individualised patterns, where sexuality has become increasingly a matter of negotiation between more or less equal, consenting partners.

Behind that shift are dramatic changes in family life and economic mobility, growing gender equality, and an awareness of sexual as well as cultural diversity. Of course, it is possible to exaggerate change. Inequalities between men and women persist. Prejudices and discrimination against sexual minorities remain potent. There are gross social and income differences. There are differences between cities, towns and villages, between regions. Value differences are growing rather than diminishing as we come to recognize the pluralism of even the apparently most homogeneous societies. We are still in the midst of a long, unfinished revolution. But no-one with a sense of history can doubt the importance of the transformations in intimate life that have taken place – and the transformations continue.

The result is a change in the western pattern of sexual life that is common across the highly industrialised world, and which this book documents. The details may be from Finland, but the pattern can be verified in many studies, from western Europe to North America and Australasia and beyond, even as different cultural histories give a distinct shading to each example. Marriage may not any longer be the only gateway to respectable sexual life, but committed relationships are the norm. Divorce may now be commonplace and easy, but serial monogamy shapes the lives of most couples. There are still unwanted pregnancies, but birth control and abortion are more freely available than ever before. Homosexuality is still encrusted by prejudice, but most jurisdictions are removing gross discriminations, and there is an international move towards the recognition of same sex partnerships. Sexual abuse, against children and adults, may persist, but everywhere there is a growing recognition that sexuality and power are inextricably linked, and that positive steps can be taken to check abuse. Sex may remain for many a source of fear, anxiety and disease, but by and large sex education is improving, sexual health is taken seriously, and the pleasures of sexual activity rather than the burdens are increasingly taken for granted. We live in a different world even from the one most of us were born into, and no doubt we will see yet further changes in the years ahead.

This book shows a world in the process of significant sexual change. It captures both a moment and a history. In its dispassionate presentation of the facts of contemporary life, it also gives us an opportunity. By understanding better, we can respond in more appropriate and sensitive ways to the processes of change. Sexuality is not a given. On the contrary it is a sensitive conductor of social change. By understanding what is happening to sexuality, we can better understand what is happening to our culture and society. As with the pioneers of the tradition of sex research, the authors of this book are casting light on the intricate processes of social change, as it is happening.

Acknowledgments

This book is a part in a series of research projects on sexuality in Finland (FINSEX) and its neighbouring countries. In the latter part of the 20th century, three representative surveys on sexuality have been conducted in Finland, one in St Petersburg, one in Sweden and one in Estonia (Kontula and Haavio-Mannila 1995a; Haavio-Mannila and Rotkirch 1997; Haavio-Mannila 2000; Haavio-Mannila et al. 2001; Haavio-Mannila and Kontula 2001). The results of the two first Finnish surveys were presented in English by Osmo Kontula and Elina Haavio-Mannila in 'Sexual Pleasures– Enhancement of Sex Life in Finland, 1971—1992' (1995b). Sexual autobiographies have been collected in Finland, Estonia, Lithuania and St Petersburg (Russia) using partly the same guidelines as in Finland. The Finnish autobiographies have been analyzed by Kontula and Haavio-Mannila (1995a, 1997) and Haavio-Mannila and Roos (1999). Anna Rotkirch has analyzed the St Petersburg autobiographies in 'The Man Question – Loves and Lives in Late 20th Century Russia' (2000). Comparisons between countries, combining autobiographical and survey research, are found in Haavio-Mannila and Rotkirch (1997, 2000) and Haavio-Mannila and Purhonen (2001). The third approach of the FINSEX study was to analyze how the way of presenting sexuality in certain Finnish newspapers and magazines had changed since 1961 (Kontula and Kosonen 1994).

We are grateful for the financial support of the Academy of Finland, which has made it possible to do broad and long-term empirical research in people's sexual lives. We also thank our Finnish publisher Werner Söderström Oy for paying for the English translation. Maija Mäkinen, a Finnish-born New-Yorker, translated the manuscript showing great flexibility and humour. Professor Tuula Gordon at the University of Tampere made detailed and useful comments on the English manuscript. Jo Campling was the wise adviser in our co-operation with Palgrave.

We have analysed the autobiographies while working as teachers and researchers at the Departments of Sociology and Social Policy at the University of Helsinki and at the Population Research Institute, The Family Federation of Finland. In these scientific environments several people have helped us. At the Department of Public Health Helena Suoknuuti and Päivi Penttilä typed or scanned the original, partly handwritten autobiographies into a computerised form. The thematic coding of the fragments by Osmo Kontula was transferred to the computer mainly by Peija Haaramo at the Department of Sociology. Peija also coded the data statistically and Elina Kuusi helped in the preparation of the index. At the Department of Social Policy, Professor J.P. Roos and docent Anni Vilkko have given us stimulating advice in the fine art of autobiographical research work. At the Department of Sociology, Marika Jalovaara commented on an earlier version of the manuscript and gave useful references to the theoretical part of the study. We warmly thank these colleagues for their kind support and assistance.

The writing of the book was divided as follows: Osmo Kontula wrote most of Part I (Sexuality in Early Age), Elina Haavio-Mannila most of Part II (Sexual Lifestyles in Different Types of Relationships) and Anna Rotkirch most of Part III (Remembering Sexuality). The Introduction, Chapter 1 and the Conclusion were written jointly. The book is based on empirical research conducted by Osmo Kontula and Elina Haavio-Mannila, reported in Finnish in Kontula and Haavio-Mannila (1995a and 1997). Our deepest gratitude goes to the many men and women who sent us their autobiographies and wanted to share their intimate experiences and reflections with us.

ELINA HAAVIO-MANNILA
OSMO KONTULA
ANNA ROTKIRCH
Helsinki

Introduction

How have people's love lives changed during the last century? This book will depict changes and continuities in the sexual lifestyles of three generations. We will analyse changes in sexual behaviour both statistically and through excerpts from autobiographies that present people's experiences and evaluations in their own words.

Both in a global perspective and on the microsocial level, many of the most drastic social changes in the 20th century were connected with sexuality. The beginning of that century witnessed declining birth rates and the spread of birth control in the industrialised world. A weakening of traditional morality and an increasing cultural detachment of sexuality accompanied this from reproduction. The sexual revolution in the 1960s continued to transform sexual behaviour and attitudes, especially with regard to women's sexuality, and to the public and commercial uses of sex. Finally, at the threshold of this century, sexuality assumed a leading role in identity politics and the increasing reflexivisation of everyday life.

Earlier research shows that as a result of these changes, sexual life has in general become more versatile, more gender equal and more satisfying (Kontula and Haavio-Mannila, 1995b). However, most sexological studies are either based on survey questionnaires or on studies of specific sexual subcultures, such as youth or homosexual sexual cultures. We were interested in how so-called ordinary adults remembered their sexual history. Which key events structured the sexual life course and which themes were seen as belonging to a sexual autobiography? Which problems and anxieties accompany the undeniable progress in family planning and sexual satisfaction?

In 1992, we collected a body of close to two hundred autobiographies about love and sexuality, written by adults in Finland. The rich experiences depicted in the autobiographies allow us to see how sexuality has evolved with time–in the life span of an individual as well as in the historical time of generations. The stories reveal how sexual experiences vary with gender and stage of the life course. They also describe the impact of major historical events – from war to economic crisis – and of the 'spirit of the times', from the emancipatory zeal of the 1960s to new age-influenced holistic ideals of total harmony of the 1980s.

While each life story is unique, the authors are ordinary in the sense that their education, working status and family relations are about the same as in the general population in Finland. The main exception is that young educated women are somewhat over represented among the writers. This generation of women, in which women are professionally autonomous and postpone child bearing into their thirties, clearly wanted to reflect on its experiences. Young women were also often those who sought to voice alternatives to conventional views of sexuality.

Here we will discuss Finland as one example of western European sexual culture. Some words should, however, be said about the specificity of Finnish sexual culture. Comparative research has shown that Finns share most of the western values and habits, which extends to sexual issues. Finnish legislation is based on full sexual self-determination unless the rights of other human beings are threatened. Finnish citizens usually have a favourable attitude toward sexual matters and believe that sexual health contributes to general well being. These opinions result in the general acceptance of an egalitarian gender ideology: Finland has longer traditions of gender equality than most other countries of the world, especially with regards to women's citizenship rights and their participation in the work force. Additionally, Finland does not have any influential religious or political forces that would oppose women's emancipation or sexual education. There has also been little prostitution in Finland (Järvinen 1990; Häkkinen 1995). Concerning sexuality, people receive free counselling on contraception and family planning at the communal health centres and the rates for unwanted pregnancies and abortions are among the lowest in the world. Finland has become a leader along with the Netherlands and other Nordic countries in providing high quality sexual health services and education.

Autobiographies can be quoted and analyzed in a number of ways. This book looks at key events in the sexual life course from the perspective of generational change and sexual lifestyles. We will talk about three generations: *the generation of sexual restraint, the generation of sexual revolution, and the generation of gender equalization.* The five sexual relationship types detected in the autobiographies are called monogamy, consecutive relations, searching, devitalised unions and parallel relations. These lifestyle groups describe people's ways of making choices or of repeatedly drifting into similar situations or circumstances.

Part I of the present book looks at sexuality at an early age, from children's sexual games to sexual initiation. Part II presents the rich variety of sexual lifestyles through an analysis of the five most typical sexual relationships in adult age. Part III analyzes the pleasures and disappointments voiced in the autobiographies and inquires into the changing meanings of sexuality. Our aim is to show in which respects sexual scripts and everyday morality have changed, as well as how surprisingly stable they have remained in other respects.

1
Research Material and Theoretical Perspectives

We approach sexuality as a specific social practice through the concepts of *sexual generations,* the *sexual life course* and *sexual scripts.*
Understanding sexuality as a social practice means that we do not
employ, say, the evolutionary, biological or psychoanalytical
approaches to human sexuality. The social realm of sexuality has
been characterized as 'the array of acts, expectations, narratives,
pleasures, identity formations and knowledge in both men and
women, that tends to cluster most densely around certain genital
sensations but is not adequately defined by them' (Costlow *et al.*
1993, 1). Human sexuality does appear to have some universal con-
stants – for instance, the intensity of sexual life usually diminishes
with age. The need to reproduce sexually is something we share with
other animals and also with most plant species. Many aspects of
human and animal behaviour can undoubtedly be explained by their
relevance for reproductive success. Yet, as Featherstone (1999, 1)
writes, animals always copulate in the same ways, whereas human
beings have woven into this act a wide range of practices, institutions, rites and representations.

Eroticism has an infinite variety of forms based upon constant inven-
tion, elaboration, taming and regulation of the sexual impulse. Sexuality
makes eroticism possible, but eroticism transcends reproduction
through its capacity to elaborate sexual experience and invent a separate
realm of associated pleasures. While erotic attraction to another person
is universal and appears in all societies, perceptions of sexual love are
culturally and historically specific. Eroticism is the 'cultural processing'
of sex. In the realm of sexuality, similar acts have also received a vast
array of cultural interpretations. With other social practices, such as

1

eating or dancing, it may be the other way around – practices differ drastically, but their interpretations are quite similar (Bozon 1999).

All over the world, two basic *types of love* have been distinguished: *passionate* and *companionate* love. Passionate love is a state of intense longing for union with another. It is a complex functional whole including appraisals or appreciations, subjective feelings, expressions, patterned physiological processes, action tendencies and instrumental behaviours. Reciprocated love (union with the other) is associated with fulfilment and ecstasy. Unrequited love (separation) is associated with emptiness, anxiety, or despair (Hatfield and Rapson 1993, 67; 1996, 3). Passionate love has also been called falling in love (Alberoni 1983), romantic love (Jallinoja 1984) and limerence (Tennov 1989). Companionate love, which is sometimes also called true or marital love, is a warm, less intense emotion than passionate love. It combines feelings of deep attachment, commitment and intimacy. It is the affection and tenderness people feel for those with whom their lives are deeply entwined.

In this book, we will mostly be concerned with love and sexuality in everyday life, although the autobiographies also describe sexuality as an *opposition* to the everyday. It is 'a realm in which the laws and identities governing everyday life can be suspended and the self be organised in ways that include aspects and qualities otherwise exiled' (Simon and Gagnon 1999, 32). But generally, we are interested in how sexuality governs everyday life, rather than suspends it.

A different approach sees sexuality as something larger than a 'social practice', as one of the many threads that constitute everyday life and the basic personal style of every human being. In such a phenomenological approach to the body, sexuality is a *constantly* present aspect of an individual's way of being, moving and talking. Sexuality is 'neither a separate sphere of life nor a separate order of significance but integrated in all behaviour. It is present in every act like a shade or a nuance.' (Heinämaa 1996, 160–1). This poetic description may be intuitively true, but it is too encompassing to be sociologically useful. Neither did the authors of the autobiographies we shall be quoting have any problem in limiting the topic of sexuality. Lay people seem to have a distinguishable – if not absolute, nor fixed – division between sexual and other human relations, or between sexually significant periods of life and other life stages. In the western world sexuality has developed into a separate life sphere, and the Finnish autobiographers clearly adhered to and reproduced this view.

True stories? Representativity and authenticity of the research material

The qualitative data this book uses in parallel with survey findings consists of self-solicited autobiographies that were gathered through a competition organised by sociologists in 1992.

The writing competition was called 'Sexuality as an Integral Part of Human Life' and yielded 166 stories fairly evenly from different parts of Finland. The integral text of the competition announcement is found in Appendix 1. The stories were, on average, 20 pages long, ranging from one to 60 pages (the maximum length in the guidelines was set at 50 pages). The age of the writers varied from 17 to 81. When quoted, the autobiographies are referred to by a code composed of a random running number (between 1 and 166), the sex of the autobiographical author (M for male and F for female) and the age of the author when she or he wrote her autobiography. Appendix 2 features the list of all codes and the year of birth, marital status and present professional level of the authors.

The social and demographic characteristics of the autobiographers have been compared with survey data, which we use to describe sexual patterns in the population as a whole. Comparative national population surveys of sexual issues were conducted in Finland in 1971, 1992 and 1999, in 1996 in St Petersburg and in Sweden, and in 2000 in Estonia (Sievers *et al.* 1974; Kontula and Haavio-Mannila 1995b; Haavio-Mannila and Rotkirch 1997; Lewin 1997; Haavio-Mannila and Kontula 2000; Haavio-Mannila *et al.* 2001).[1]

The autobiographers represented all types of social classes and professions. Among the women were, for example, teachers, artists, secretaries, librarians, journalists, pilots, cleaning and child-care women, kitchen workers, students, home-staying housewives and pensioners. The male authors included bank directors, production managers, building contractors, policemen, chauffeurs, travel guides, common labourers and unemployed people. In the same way as in the general population, women were more often white-collar and men blue-collar workers. The educational and occupational level of the autobiographers was slightly higher than in the population at large. However, people belonging to the highest professional strata had not bothered to write their sexual life stories.

The phase in the life course of the authors varied, too. Some were young single people searching for a partner, but the majority consisted of more or less happily married or cohabiting people. Many had secretly or openly had parallel sexual relationships in addition to their main relationship, which could be a vital or a devitalised union. The divorced and widowed authors were recalling with bitterness or love their former partners and they were often longing for a new relationship. Some middle-aged and older singles had said goodbye to all romance and sexuality in their life. Compared with the whole population, young, modern women were somewhat overrepresented among the autobiographers. The young women who sent in their autobiographies had also had more lifetime sexual partners than the statistical average. This bias in the data may cause women's sexual life to appear more liberated and sexually more active than average.

The men who sent in their autobiographies did not differ much from the men in the general population, although they appeared to be a bit more shy and withdrawn than men in general. The writers of the autobiographies had begun to date women and have sexual intercourse slightly later than the statistical average and had had fewer sexual partners. However, the special theme of this competition attracted sexually experienced men. In comparison with the men who participated in a general autobiography writing competition for men (Hänninen 1994), the male participants in our sexual autobiography competition were socially more affluent and sexually more active. In general, the autobiographers recorded their sexual lives according to the wishes expressed on the introductory sheet for the competition (see Appendix 1). The stories had mostly coherent contents and structures. The writers clearly chose events that have been significant to them in the course of their sexual life in its different phases. As is usual, painful and difficult events often receive more attention than happy and stable (but uneventful) periods of life.

But how should one read such autobiographical material? As autobiographies are still quite a novelty on the international social sciences scene, the use of them as research material often creates suspicions about reliability and authenticity. In our view, such doubts arise from every kind of data, whether statistical or qualitative. However, autobiographical research clearly has its own flavour and also its own methodological discussions. Do the autobiographies count as social facts, as testimony of actual experiences, or are they 'merely' stories and texts that bear no clear relation to the world outside the narratives?

The writing – as well as the reading – of autobiographies is guided by a wisdom that is rooted in emotions. Autobiographies can be understood as stories about 'how life should (or should not) be lived', as stories about the good life (Vilkko 1997, 52). To write one's autobiography is a way of dealing with the relation of the past to the present, and of using what took place in the past to understand and analyze what is experienced in the present. They are stories about individual choices and what these choices are based on. Autobiography appears as one of the tools of life control, self-reflection and identity work. They belong within the concept of life politics, at the core of the late modern project toward an increasingly reflective self. This view of autobiographies as a tool of identity helps to explain why the biographical genre has experienced such tremendous success from the 1980s and 1990s onwards, during an increasing reflexivisation and individualisation of society. Autobiographies also constitute one of the most democratic literary genres: most people are capable of writing or telling their autobiographies. According to J.P. Roos (1994, 11) '... anybody equipped with a functioning memory and ability to textualise/verbalise his or her life experiences can tell a life story. In other words, all that is needed is referentiality, the fact that I am telling about something that has happened to me, that I have experienced.'

At the same time, writing one's life story is not only a way of talking to oneself, but also of communicating with the reader. Anni Vilkko describes the autobiography that is permeated by self-awareness as quilt-like: it is a story that is aware of having been compiled: telling the autobiography is an act of sewing pieces together (Vilkko 1997, 54–5). One also feels more compelled to write one's biography at certain moments in life, often in connection with a turning point (Peltonen 1998).

The question of how such pieces relate to experienced events has been crucial in autobiographical studies. A realist position treats the related events as facts, while a poststructuralist position prefers to talk about limitless interpretations of a text, not necessarily referring to anything specific in the outside world. (For an overview of this debate, see Roos 1994.) In this heated scholarly debate we chose the middle road, albeit with our gaze turning to the realist side, where sociology in our understanding belongs. Autobiographies are both fact and fiction and it is exactly the interplay between 'facts' and 'stories', experiences and memories, that guarantee their appeal. They provide us with valuable, often unique, social information, but also with subjective and by definition biased accounts. We treat the autobiographies as essentially *reality-oriented narratives*. The truth is presented from a unique, concrete viewpoint – that of the author – and the task of the researchers is to verify and contextualize the related experiences (Roos 1994; Bertaux 1998). We have compared the sexual autobiographies with survey data and found that these two ways of data collection provide highly consistent results. We do not usually relate the whole life story of a person, but take key moments that highlight specific events, experiences or judgements.

But we also understand the autobiographies to be *stories*. This entails especially awareness that people forget, modify and leave things out, that they follow certain rhetorical conventions, and that they are prone to emphasizing themselves as positive agents. The autobiographical format in itself activates or develops a reflective and agency-oriented view of the self, what Pierre Bourdieu (1986) has called the 'autobiographical illusion'. The narrator usually presents him- or herself as an active agent and overlooks the social and economic constraints that actually shape and limit individual choices. It is even harder to deduce anything about the supposed actions of other personages in the autobiography. Obviously, a child's view of its parents behaviour or a husband's interpretations of his wife's motives do almost exclusively tell us something about the narrator.

Every autobiography has at least two 'I's: the 'I' who is writing the autobiography in 1992 and the younger 'I' who experienced the remembered events. We will use the present tense when referring to the first 'I', the one writing an autobiography and his or hers views and hopes at the moment of writing (for example: 'This man regrets he never asked his first wife ...'). When referring to the protagonist at the moment the events took place, we will use the past tense, for example: 'He regretted he had not asked his first wife and therefore tried to achieve an honest relationship in his second marriage ...'.

Three sexual generations

We discuss changes in sexual attitudes and behaviour using a three-generation model. The generations are constructed on the basis of sexual norms and practices that prevailed in their youth, that is, between 10 and 30 years of age. Our classification is based on Finnish data. For other western countries, the timing may vary, while the type of generation tends to be similar.

1. *The generation of sexual restraint* born in 1917–36. When this generation was young, sexual matters were taboo topics not to be discussed openly in front of other people, especially children. Patriarchal society strictly regulated sexual behaviour and sanctioned what was perceived to threaten the social order. This included non-reproductive sexual practices (such as same-sex intercourse or masturbation) and women's sexual autonomy. Double moral standards gave more sexual freedom to men than to most women, thus, on average, there was a wide gender gap in sexual

behaviour. Since safe contraception methods were rarely available, fear of pregnancy coloured many people's memories of sex.

2. *The generation of sexual revolution* born in 1937–56. The generation born in the 1940s stressed liberation as an ideal, and wanted to get rid of the traditions and authority their parents were supposed to represent. The formation and practice of this liberation ideal was partly due to the fact that the parents of this generation were not as authoritarian as their predecessors, and partly that liberation became a social and cultural possibility (Lyttkens 1989, 164). This generation had more sex before or outside marriage, employed more sexual techniques, and divorced and remarried more often. The new contraceptive methods made it possible to engage in pre- and extramarital relations without fear of pregnancy. Some feminists were critical of the increased pressure to have casual sex and felt that women were exploited against their will. At other times, sexual liberation joined the struggle for gender equality and other radical social movements in the 1960s and 1970s.

3. *The generation of gender equalisation* born in 1957–73. Until the mid-1980s when Aids entered the picture, people enjoyed more sexual freedom than ever before. Since then, a period of greater sexual caution and ambivalence has begun. Casual sex, while still practised by both sexes, is not favoured as much as commitment (cf. Janus and Janus 1993, 16). The gender gap in sexual behaviour is also much smaller. Double moral standards have not disappeared, but Finnish girls behave increasingly like Finnish boys – and the other way around. The age at first intercourse has ceased to decline after the mid-1980s. The attitudes of young people toward marital infidelity are less permissive than those of the young in the beginning of 1970s. The sexual attitudes and behaviour of young people are not very coherent – they seem to favour increasing individualisation and liberalisation while also stressing fidelity and long-term emotional investment (Kontula and Haavio-Mannila 1995b; Haavio-Mannila *et al.* 1996; Haavio-Mannila and Rotkirch 1997).

The liberalisation of sexual life during the last 30 years is a result of the improvements in birth control techniques, women's emancipation and a decline in traditional restrictive sexual values. In Finland, the liberation of sexual attitudes and behaviour began in the 1970s. The accelerating social and economic developments in society brought increasing numbers of people out of the agrarian community with its rigid social controls. The social norms restricting women's activity in sexual life changed. Sexual pleasure became separate from biological reproduction and sometimes also from intimate human relationships. The reformist and liberal spirit of the sixties and seventies led to legislative reforms and to livelier public debate on sexual behaviour. The contraceptive bill was approved in 1961, and cohabitation without marriage began to rise in 1968 (Aromaa *et al.* 1981). Women were entitled to choose to have an abortion (a physician's certificate is needed, but in practice it is a mere formality) in 1970 and the criminalization of homosexuality ended in 1971. The Evangelical-Lutheran church accepted family planning at the beginning of the 1970s.

In the Nordic countries, sexuality and eroticism are today looked upon as health producing 'welfare commodities' (Kontula 1989). Sexual behaviour is accepted when the adolescent individuals are mature enough for sex, and when they are in love with, care for and have tender feelings towards the partner. 'They are expected to be monogamous, faithful and sincere. It is the responsible sexuality that is idealized, and the sexual actors are expected to act as responsible citizens.' (Traeen 1993: 46; cf. Lewin 1987) A majority of Nordic adolescents have intercourse in accordance with the 'love ideology' (Helmius 1990).

The sexual life course

The *sexual life course* describes the general and typical way people of a certain society and generation have ordered the major events in their life course (Rodgers and White 1993). The general trend is for a 'prolonged youth': the transition to adult family life involving cohabitation, marriage, and/or children is increasingly postponed or altogether rejected. In old age, there is also an increasing use of 'second chances' with remarriages and new families. However, many features of the sexual life course have remained stable, such as the cycles of romantic and companionate love described above.

Nowadays it is often emphasized that there are no longer any normative expectations and that people can generally create their autobiographies on their own (Beck and Beck-Gernsheim 1995). Nevertheless, sexual key events are even now expected to follow one another in the traditional order: after falling in love, sexual relations can begin, and after that comes cohabitation, followed by getting pregnant and finally marriage. Today, key events in the script are getting married and becoming a parent at the age of 20–30, and the transformation of passionate love into real, companionate love a couple of years after falling in love. Part of the desirable life course is also that a possibly devitalised marital relationship is revitalised in later middle age. On the basis of the survey studies, it is possible to discern some typical features in the life course of Finns. The figures presented are statistical averages around which there is a lot of dispersion. Nevertheless, the averages with their standard deviations can be looked upon as some kind of indicators of generally accepted sexual scripts (see below).

Finnish people born in the 20th century have ordered the events in their sexual and family life course in the following way. According to our survey study, people had their first steady relationship at just under 18 and had sexual intercourse at just over 18 (Kontula and Haavio-Mannila 1997). Men began their first cohabitation or marital relationship at age 24 and women at age 22. Sexual relations began at a much later age for the older than the middle and younger generations. For the generation of sexual restraint, the periods between turning points were brief: women began to have relationships at age 19, had sexual intercourse for the first time at age 21, and entered into their first marital relationship at age 24. Women of the generation of gender equalisation had their first steady relationship already at age 16, sexual intercourse at 17, but did not marry until they were 28. In other words, they began having steady relationships 12 years before and experienced intercourse 11 years before getting married. The timing of having children in relation to the beginning of the marriage has also changed. Before, it was common to get married before the birth of a child, but nowadays these two turning points of a marital relationship occur at the same age.[2]

The probability of moving on to the next phase of sexual life is often determined by the duration of the preceding phase (Rodgers and White 1993, 240–1). For example, if a relationship goes on for a long time without sexual intercourse, it may fail. As a relationship progresses, there is a shift from the phase in which something is either allowed or not allowed, to a phase where something must take place. In a long-lasting relationship there is often not only the *permission*, but the *obligation* to have intercourse.

Increasingly often, a turning point in marriage comes in the form of divorce, which now occurs to one half of all married couples (OFS 1996:16, 15). For someone getting a divorce in the mid-1990s, the median for its occurrence was 14 years from the start of the marriage. At this point, the average man was 41 and the woman 39 years old

(OFS 1996: 16, 61). The incidence of divorce was clearly higher in groups that experienced social and economic problems (Jalovaara 1996).[3]

Manifold sexual scripts

The way we plan, act out and evaluate our sexual behaviour can be seen as being guided by *sexual scripts* (Simon and Gagnon 1984). Sexual scripts advise us with whom to have sexual relations with, when and where we should have sex and how we are to behave in the first place. The scripts also define what counts as 'sexual' – for instance, walking arm-in-arm can be defined as either a neutrally friendly act or as a sign of a quite intimate sensual relation, depending on the culture in question. In some cultures, such as that of the Finnish gypsies, any reference to the parental bond is indecent because it indirectly alludes to the sexual act. Instead of a script, it is also possible to talk about a *model or blueprint*, which guides people's actions. The script gets actualised in certain situations that involve choice – when one must decide, for instance, whether to go ahead with intercourse or not. Scripts are usually gender- and age-specific.

In studying the impact of the scripts on actual behaviour, it has been found that young Americans similarly act out a well-defined behaviour model in acquiring sexual experiences. They begin by kissing, move on to embracing and then to touching the breasts (first through clothing and then underneath). Next, there is touching of genitalia, first carried out by the man and then by the woman. This is followed by genital contact and vaginal intercourse. It is only after intercourse that young people begin to experiment with oral sex, first administered by the man, then the woman. Not all young people carry out the entire 'programme', or 'go all the way' (Laumann *et al.* 1994, 7). Part I of this book is structured to closely follow the beginning of the sexual life course, from childhood to young adulthood. It depicts the norms and the exceptions for dating, petting and first intercourse. When an individual, a relationship or a family is at a certain age, certain things are expected, and this is in fact reflected in practice. Tags such as 'in its own time' or 'too early' refer to such timing norms. It is not considered a good idea to enter a sexual relationship too young. Another timing norm has been that one should begin a steady relationship or at least have a few dates before proceeding from petting to intercourse.

Sexual scripts affect what is seen as the ideal *timing and order* of certain sexual turning points. According to these, a person of a certain age should have a dating or sexual relationship, preferably a steady couple relationship, children and even parallel relationships, because others have them too. Today especially, young people feel pressure to try out several partners. Those who married their first sexual partner are starting to appear odd. It is thought that they have not discovered their sexuality, because their experiences are so limited. Even those living in a marital relationship may feel that it is 'old-fashioned' to live with one and the same person all one's life, when all around a large number of people are in their second or third marital relationship.

Simon and Gagnon (1984) talked about three levels of scripts: cultural scenarios, interpersonal scripts and intrapsychic scripts. On the level of interpersonal scripts we will also talk about *everyday morality* (Rotkirch 2000). It stands for the possible, acceptable and typical (although not always the desired or ideal) developments of love and family life. Everyday morality represents the standard frame inside of which experiences are measured in life stories. It is not always clearly articulated into a coherent script. Instead, it represents the fascination, judgement, approvals and fears through which the articulated scripts eventually transform themselves.

There is an ongoing interplay between individual love maps, interpersonal scripts, everyday morality and the dominating cultural scripts. As everyday morality changes, it eventually influences the cultural scripts. Depending on the historical epoch, social situation and individual in question, the three levels may be in congruence or conflict with each other (Simon and Gagnon 1984; Laumann *et al.* 1994). One example of changing scripts concerns the timing of children. In the 1970s, couples in Finland started having children before getting formally married. However, no one declared that 'we want to have children first' or 'of course we'll get married once we have children'. The new pattern was something that emerged as a result of several economic and cultural factors, but was not immediately articulated culturally.

Serial monogamy is an example of everyday morality that is on its way to becoming an articulated cultural script. In the western world, about every second marriage ends in divorce and more than one in four people have had several marriages or cohabitations. Young people may get married thinking this will not be their last marital relationship. Still, this existing practice has not been generally acknowledged or approved of. It has not been acceptable to state that 'I want to get married many times and have several important love relationships in my life' (Jallinoja 1997). Wedding celebrations are still built around the

script of lasting monogamous love. Chapter 5 shows how the expectations of the sexual life course in the youngest generation are more and
more centred on the idea of consecutive loves. Also some Finnish
female celebrities have recently openly supported the script praising a
life with several important love affairs.

Scripting theory has been criticized for neglecting the body and
biology altogether (Connell and Dowsett 1999). The effects of biological instincts are understood as minor in comparison with the culturally
determined scripts (Laumann *et al.* 1994, 6). This view was a conscious,
and initially most radical, overturning of, for example, psychoanalytic
or biological reasoning, in which desires or instincts were the natural
point of departure. Simon and Gagnon emphasized how 'Desire is not
reducible to an appetite, a drive, an instinct; it does not create the self,
rather it is part of the process of the creation of the self' (Simon and
Gagnon 1984). Today such social constructionism has become commonplace in sexual studies. We, therefore, use scripting theory in a
limited way and together with the concept of the sexual life course.
Scripting theory aptly grasps many of the socio-cultural changes, and
we will derive some general types and prevailing sexual scripts from
our love stories. At the same time, the sexual life course is used to cover
the least changing aspects of sexual behaviour, including the influence
of biology through age, health, and so on.

The social scripts and expectations that shape love and sexual life
may be realized during the actual life of an individual or remain unre-
alized, in one of three ways: (1) people behave according to norms and
expectations, (2) they deviate from norms of their own volition by
rebelling, defying or searching for something new; they do not want
to act according to the script, or (3) a lack of external control on life
leads to people being forced against their will to deviate from the
timing of the turning points of a 'normal biography', and from the
duration of the phases. In the latter case the person is not able to
follow an internalized sexual script even though he/she would like to.
Adapting and following the norms of what is socially accepted as
appropriate is usually the easiest solution, and is rewarded by acceptance and social support.

The last decades have witnessed an increasing *plurality* of sexual
scripts. For instance, in certain milieus, it may be part of the script to
have sexual encounters without love, or to live together without any
intention of getting married or having children. Like religion, sexuality
has become *secularised* (Heiskala 1999). It is increasingly seen as a

matter of personal choice, not of unquestionable truth and custom. These days it is in fact more common that love and sex relationships break up after a few years and people engage in consecutive or parallel love and sex relationships. Deviating from traditional sexual scripts of one's own volition may lead to independence and creative solutions, 'being part of the new'. A person may also postpone or avoid certain turning points in the sexual life course, such as having a family or openly claiming a sexual identity that goes against the mainstream.

The scripts are also increasingly flexible with regard to sexual orientation. There are signs that people reject not only normative heterosexuality, but also a strict identification with any alternative sexual identity (Sipilä 1998). Hetero-, homo- or bisexuality are less and less exclusive categories and more catch words for a certain stage of life or lifestyle. Especially young heterosexual women seemed to be flexible in this respect, describing same-sex sexual relations without perceiving it as a major threat to their identity. Older men, by contrast, vehemently denied being 'homosexual' even if they in some cases repeatedly engaged in homosexual intercourse (Kaskisaari 1998; Ronkainen 1999).

Today's pluralisation of sexual scripts has not brought complete equality or ended gender and sexual discrimination. What it does mean is that there are several competing scripts in every social situation. This creates more freedom of choice, but also more confusion and ambivalence. Thus youngest autobiographers long for stable and clear rules, such as demands for lifelong fidelity. Memories of deviation from the sexual script as a result of external considerations such as studying, living, work or economic situation, unexpected pregnancy or miscarriage, betrayal by a partner, or the difficulty of finding a suitable partner, also still evoked negative feelings. People become embittered when they are unable to live according to those of the social scripts that they themselves have internalised. Someone who has deviated from the timing and order of the key events determined by the script will often make an effort to return to the 'correct' order as soon as possible.

During the last three generations, the gender gap between men and women has diminished. The double moral standards that have characterized the older generations are gradually disappearing. In Finland, the youngest generation is fairly equal where sexual behaviour and attitudes are concerned, although the sexual scripts of men and women continue to have clear differences. Especially young men and women are guided by different sexual morals, where women are judged for being sexually too 'available'. Research on girls and boys and young women and men indicate that girls are often called whores and boys homos or queer suggesting that boundaries of femininity, masculinity and (hetero)sexuality are still guarded and transgressions are often noted (Saarikoski 2001; Lehtonen 1999; Gordon and Lahelma 1996).

As a result of swift and permanent social changes, a clear gender script is missing in society (Hoikkala 1996, 3). Nevertheless, one can discern two basic, contrasting perspectives defining and interpreting people's social world. Gender and gender roles can be looked upon either as *polarised* or as *abolished*. This has been shown, for example, by Ken Plummer (1995, 158) who explored the rites of British sexual storytelling culture. On the basis of three kinds of stories – rape stories, coming out stories and recovery stories – in different media he sketched two contrasting sexual stories freely circulating at the end of the 20th century: a narrative of polarised gender and a narrative of abolished gender. In the first type of story, communities are found in the past and people draw upon them to assert the power of a dualistic gender in the life for the future. In the latter story people seek to provide new stories of the ways in which lives can be lived without the 'tyranny of gender'. In sexual relationships, the plurality of sexual scripts is mirrored by the existence of many possible parallel sexual lifestyles.

Five sexual lifestyles

Sexual relationships have their own life course and scripts in the same way as people do. Autobiographies offer the possibility of studying the development of sexual lifestyles and sexual relations from one phase in the life course to another. They may answer questions such as these: how do childhood sexual experiences and role models affect the sexual actions and related emotions and meanings at a later age? Are sexual lifestyles inherited from one generation to the next? To what extent do people appear to hold onto a certain sexual lifestyle their entire life or does it change, for example, when starting a new relationship? Depending on the phase in the life course, part of the fluctuation in sexual lifestyles is a result of biological ageing (for example, the effect of deteriorating health on sexual desire), but part is socially deter-mined. Hence, sexual scripts allow a young, uninvolved person significantly more versatile sexual actions than an older person who is in a relationship. The concept of 'single' denotes a new type of urban sexual lifestyle which is more generous with regards to biological age (Gordon 1994).

Several researchers have developed typologies of love and sex relationships (cf. Cuber and Harroff 1965; Jallinoja 1984; Giddens 1991, 1992; Hendrick and Hendrick, 1992, Kaskisaari 1995, 1998; Hatfield and Rapson 1996; Määttä 1999). On the basis of Finnish sexual autobiographies, J.P. Roos distinguished eleven types of relationships: (1) one great lifelong monogamous 'eternal' love, (2) several consecutive or serial loves one after the other, (3) searching for love, (4) devitalised love, and (5) parallel or complementary relationships with and without love, (6) love for an illusory man or woman, (7) love at a distance, (8) masochistic devotion, (9) loss of the loved one, (10) jealousy and (11) denial of love in life. (Haavio-Mannila and Roos 1995, 1999) These relationship or partnership types (or sexual lifestyles) will be used as a guiding thread throughout this book. However, we will focus on the most common types of relationships, that is, *monogamy, consecutive relations, searching, devitalised relations* and *parallel relations*.

These frequently occurring partnership types differ from each other in three respects. The first difference is the *number* of love and sex relationships, the second one is the *time dimension*, that is, whether the relationships are consecutive or parallel, and the third difference is the *quality* of the relationship, that is, whether it is based on love, still vital and happy or not. Our relationship types remind us of those identified by John F. Cuber and Peggy B. Harroff (1965), who distinguished between total, vital, devitalised and conflict-ridden couples. As the autobiographies describe sexual life in chronological terms, we are able to emphasize more than Cuber and Harroff, people's sexual trajectories, that is, stability and change in sexual lifestyles during the life course. Another difference between our typology and that made by Cuber and Harroff is the issue of faithfulness. Fidelity was not explicitly included in their typology as it is in our categorization.

Some demographic, social and sexual characteristics of the autobiographers belonging to the five types are presented in Table 1.1.

One-sixth of the autobiographies told about *one great, lifelong monogamous relationship.* These narratives of eternal love were about as common in the autobiographies of both genders and all generations, although the younger authors obviously had not experienced as long

Table 1.1 Demographic and social characteristics of people belonging to different relationship types. Per cent or mean.

Demographic and social characteristics of the autobiographers[1]	Mono-gamy	Conse-cutive relations	Searc-hing	Parallel relations and devitalised union	Total	Signi-ficance of differences between types
Number of stories[2]						
Men	10	8	10	25	53	
Women	16	34	26	34	110	
Average age, years						
Men	53	45	37	55	49	P<.000
Women	40	44	34	43	41	P<.000
Is working for pay %						
Men	40	62	40	56	51	ns
Women	37	47	42	79	54	P<.005
Married or cohabiting %						
Men	90	57	30	80	68	p<.009
Women	80	32	19	41	38	P<.003
Regular intercourse %						
Men	50	62	30	44	45	ns
Women	75	41	31	35	42	P<.027
Number of sexual partners, mean						
Men	3.3	5,9	7,6	16.2	10.4	P<.000
Women	2.6	6,0	8.4	11.7	7.9	P<.000
Lives in a happy couple relationship %						
Men	60	50	30	44	45	ns
Women	81	41	15	21	35	P<.000
Has divorced %						
Men	–	62	20	16	21	P<.010
Women	–	50	27	44	36	P<.003
Has had parallel relations %						
Men	30	37	30	56	43	ns
Women	12	29	15	59	33	P<.001
Has children %						
Men	80	62	30	72	64	ns
Women	69	59	27	73	57	P<.002

continued

Table 1.1   (continued)

Demographic and social characteristics of the autobiographers[1]	Mono-gamy	Conse-cutive relations	Searc-hing	Parallel relations and devitalised union	Total	Signi-ficance of differences between types
Homosexual feelings or experiences %						
Men	30	–	20	12	15	ns
Women	6	18	35	44	28	P<.015

Notes:
1. Type of childhood and present community, education, occupation, and number of infatuations were not significantly related to type of relationship.
2. Of men's stories 18 and of women's ones 23 belonged to the parallel relationship type, and 7 and 11, respectively, recorded devitalised unions.

relationships as the elder ones. Stories by men of the generation of equalization formed an exception, as none of their autobiographies were classified as this type.

One-fourth of the autobiographies were primarily classified as a story of *consecutive relations*. Women were more likely than men to report serial relations as the major style of their love life. Among women of the older generation, consecutive relations were common. The least number of stories about consecutive relations occurred in the auto-biographies of the oldest generation of men.

Every fifth story primarily belonged to the *searching* type. One-third of the narratives of the youngest generation were of this type, but less than one in six of the stories of the two older generations were in this category. There was no difference between men's and women's stories in this respect.

About one-tenth of the stories focused on a *devitalised union*. This relationship type was described equally in the autobiographies of both men and women. Every fifth story of the men of the young and old generations was classified as a devitalised union, but none of the autobiographies of men in the middle generation centred around the devitalisation of a relationship. One-fifth of the stories of middle generation women mainly described the devitalised state of a mar-riage, but only a few did so among women of the young and old generation.

Almost one in four sexual autobiographies was primarily classified as a story of *parallel relations*. One-third of the men but merely one-fifth of the women told a story about simultaneous sexual relationships. The story of parallel relations was particularly common in the autobiographies of men of the generations of sexual restraint and revolution. The same proportion of the autobiographies of women in all three generations focused on parallel relations.

The love stories in the sexual autobiographies were also classified on the basis of how the author described events and emotions *in different phases of his/her life course*: as a young person (under the age of 35, or before marriage), in middle age (ages 35–54) and in old age (roughly after age 55). Less than every second of all love stories featured the same major theme in all three life phases. Of the 68 stories of the middle generation, 28 belonged in the same type in both youth and middle age. Of the 35 stories of the oldest generation, ten were classified as of the same type in all three phases of life, ten were of the same type in middle and old age, seven were of the same type in youth and old age, and eight authors represented a different relationship type in the three phases of the sexual life course.

Initially, the events that occur in the life course of men and women take place in the same order, but this usually changes later. In the first phase of the sexual life course, it is typical for both genders to describe the search for a partner. After that, most women wrote about their consecutive relations while men described seeking parallel relations. In older age, men's stories often centre on a monogamous relationship and women on the other relationship styles, that is, loss of the beloved or having no love or sexual relationship.

Table 1.2 shows how getting older influences sexual life in different generations, that is, the *effects of age on the type of love*, when generation remains constant. Searching is clearly a phenomenon of youth in all three generations, especially in the older generation. Having only one great love is equally frequent throughout the life cycle in both the middle and older generations (as already mentioned, the 'only' loves of the youngest authors have not yet been tested by time). Stories of consecutive loves increase as people get older. Parallel relations are very rare in youth, but flourish in middle age and then decline. The effect of age on devitalised unions is minor.

We can also interpret the same results by looking at *generational differences*. The oldest generation usually cherishes faithful monogamy throughout the life cycle. Consecutive and parallel loves are characteristic of the middle generation of sexual revolution, which began to appreciate 'pure relationships' not determined by tradition (cf. Giddens 1991, 1992). Generation has no influence on the proportion

Table 1.2 Relationship types according to stage in the life course and sexual generation. Per cent.

Relationship Type	In youth				In mid life			In older age
	Equalisation	Revolution	Restraint	Total Youth	Revolution	Restraint	Total Midlife	Restraint
Monogamy	16	14	29	18	17	26	20	26
Consecutive relations	22	20	18	20	32	21	27	27
Searching	32	28	40	32	11	3	8	5
Devitalised union	7	16	8	11	7	13	9	13
Parallel relations	16	21	5	16	30	34	31	21
Other	7	1	–	3	3	3	3	8
Total	100	100	100	100	100	100	100	100
Number of stories	(56)	(71)	(38)	(165)	(71)	(38)	(109)	(38)

Sexual Generation

of people searching for love, which is common in the youth phase of all three generations. Stories about devitalised unions do not vary by generation.

There are some cases in which both age and generation independently influence the type of life story. Members of the generation of sexual revolution often take a second chance in mid life when they enter into consecutive love affairs. The generation of sexual restraint, which was very faithful in youth (only 5 per cent told about parallel relations), became more sexually liberated in mid life by engaging in parallel sexual relationships, but these decrease in older age.

Part I
Sexuality in Early Age

2
Childhood

The sexual morality of restraint

The morality of restraint characterised western sexual morals of the 1900s. According to moral rules, young people were to abstain from sexual intercourse until marriage or at least marry the partner in the case of an 'accident'. In actuality, this amounted to a script that restricted especially female sexuality: it was not 'proper' for women to 'put out' to men. The church and various government institutions co-operated to uphold these morals. Parents and relatives relayed the morals of sexual restraint to children and monitored to ensure that there were no deviations. The sexual morality of restraint has had a central role in shaping the scripts for dating and sexual interaction applied by men and women to their encounters even to this day.

As a result of the morality of restraint, the script of a faithful wife was assigned a much higher value than the script of an autonomous woman who enjoyed her sexuality. This partly changed in the 1960s, when women's economic survival was no longer dependent on marriage, and when the characteristics of a 'good woman' came to include being a skilful lover. A rational justification for the repressive morality was the significant risk of unwanted pregnancy, including the various social problems that the woman would have to bear. This justification gradually lost its potency as contraceptive techniques developed. To a remarkable extent, the introduction of the birth control pill to the market made the sexual revolution of the late 1960s and early 1970s possible. It became possible to initiate a discussion on the sexual rights of young people, women and sexual minorities, and to start providing organised sexual education.

The presence of the morality of sexual restraint was palpable in most stories about childhood and youth in the autobiographies. More than every second woman of the oldest generation wrote about the lessons of restraint she had received in childhood. These memories were a reason for calling this generation the generation of sexual restraint. A smaller number, about one-third, of the women of the middle generation wrote about being raised in the morality of restraint. When contrasting these typical accounts with the memories of the youngest generation, it was also apparent how this morality has now lost its dominating grip. Only one in ten women of the generation of gender equalisation wrote about being taught sexual restraint.

As introductory examples of this shift in sexual morality, we shall cite four sexual autobiographies. The first fragment is from a story of a retired cleaning woman of the generation of sexual restraint who received sex information from her cousin:

> When I was fourteen, an older cousin visited us. She was examining me ... about my knowledge on child birth. I knew that the stomachs of hags were bulging and that they stopped bulging when a new baby had emerged. There my information ended. But the cousin knew that a man first lies on top of his wife and his semen goes to the stomach of the woman, and then a baby starts growing. Thus take care of not letting men on top of you so that you do not get children, she said. Again I was stunned. Fortunately the boy [the author had been dating] from another village had not come on top of me but we had hugged each other standing on the road. That can't lead to children, I assumed. (25F57)

Also the autobiographies of the middle generation women feature horror stories about sexual morals. A secretary described her mother as repressive towards her own sexuality and as wanting to transfer that sexual attitude to her daughter:

> My childhood home was totally sex-negative because my mother's attitude to sexuality was distorted. ... She was 36 when she married with my father and before that she had not even fucked. She was a virgin until the wedding night; my father told me this. My mother, for example, despised the two sisters of my father who had been pregnant when getting married. My father has said that my mother had wanted to end their rare fucking after my birth at the age of 39, but in spite of this, my father had no other women. I believe that

also my father was a poor fucker. My mother taught me that sex is a sin and than one should be wary of men. She did not explain anything else and I did not ask. (144F35).

The author's use of expressions such as 'distorted' and 'not even' clearly reveal how she herself embraces quite another view of what is normal female sexuality. But there are also positive stories about sexual morals told by the middle generation – and often its male members. As a child, a retired computer operator received sex information from a psychiatrist at a hospital. The boy was very satisfied with it:

> At the age of nine I had already learnt everything. I was told how I would start to get pubic hair, have erections and begin to masturbate, which would bring me great joy and satisfaction. I would play sexual games first with boys before girls would join the sexual configurations. I was told how sexual intercourse between a man and a woman takes place and how children are conceived and born. In fact, I learnt the whole truth of the timing of human sexual life. (173M46)

Later, when this man went through any new developmental phases in his sexual life, he recognized the events, which the psychiatrist had told him about when he was a child.

The more open sexual morals in the childhood of the youngest generation are exemplified in the following narrative of a young academically educated women, who tells how she together with another girl explored the miracles of sexual life:

> The examination of the details of sexual life started with my cousin immediately when we had learnt the principle. Our correspondence was filled by detective observations of used condoms, contraceptive pill boxes of older sisters, and stories in Hymy [a semi-pornographic] magazine. When we met, we discussed the meaning of nodes in breasts and starting 'whites'. I was relieved to hear that my cousin's mother had told her that the knobs in her breast were not cancer but growing breasts. Later in our doctor games we were searching for the openings of each others' vaginas and watched through a mirror what the other had found. (146F33)

The parents of this woman did not forbid her sexual games and explorations. They also gave satisfactory answers to her inquiries about sexuality. In the childhood of several of the autobiographical authors of the generation of gender equalisation, sexuality was no longer considered to be sinful and dangerous.

This transition in everyday sexual morality is supported by survey results (Kontula and Haavio-Mannila 1995b). As recently as in the early 1970s, only one in five women over the age of 35 approved of sex in young people's relationships if the partners were not engaged or married. By the early 1990s, a great majority of the same age group approved of it. The great revolution thus had occurred among people who were young after the end of the 1960s.

Women aged over 55 had the most reserved attitude in the 1992 survey – only half of them approved of sexual relations among young people before engagement and marriage. The lessons of restraint they had learned in youth were still apparent in their attitudes. The same difference, but much diluted, was also detected among men. The morality of sexual restraint has not concerned male sexuality to the same extent as it influenced women's. The practical implications for men's sexual lives, however, have also been great, because during the hegemony of the sexually repressive moral script, it was difficult for men to find women who were willing to engage in sexual relations. In this sense, the morality of sexual restraint supported the institution of prostitution.

Childhood discoveries and sexual knowledge

Life's first major turning point is birth. The pleasurable post-partum closeness of mother and infant introduces intimacy into the new human being's life. Many of the satisfying sexual experiences in adult life stem from these early, pleasure-tinged emotions. A connection to these primary feelings is one basic model of sexual life. Sexual representations in culture are almost countless and children, too, are repeatedly the recipients of various sexual messages. Today's children witness sexual activity and nudity especially on television. Before, such messages were transmitted much more seldom in children's living environments.

Discoveries made as a child about the sexual life of the parents con-tribute to the shaping of a person's sexual script or love map. It is also influenced by the child's physical and emotional bonds to the parents. Approximately one-third of the autobiographical authors recalled something of their parents' sexual life. The main comment was how sexual matters between parents were kept secret. According to the survey, 35 per cent of the generation of equalisation, 58 per cent of the generation of sexual revolution and 75 per cent of the generation of sexual restraint felt that there was a secretiveness concerning sexual matters in their childhood home. Also among the middle generation, it was fairly common that children did not remember seeing any tenderness or physical closeness between their parents. This was the script that children had to extricate themselves from if they wanted to enjoy their own sex life.

> I grew up in a religious home. ... As a child I never saw my parents being affectionate towards each other or us children (I have one brother). (64F53)

Parents could not hide everything from their children, however. Because children and young people commonly slept in the same space or room with their parents, they acquired experiences of what adults possibly did during the night. Because it was never discussed, children could only guess at what their parents were up to in the dark or under the covers.

> The only observation was something I heard – sometimes at night I would hear panting from the next room, and extra creaking of the bed. As a child I just wondered about it, but when I got bigger, I guessed what was going on. (129M45)

In some cases children had the impression that their father was much more interested in intercourse than their mother.

> My mother's objections have stayed in my mind – 'Don't, behave yourself, let's go to sleep'. (172M46)

> The creaking of an old spring bed, or something, had awakened me. My father was working away somehow helplessly on top of my mother and repeating her name hysterically. My mother was silent, indifferent, probably disappointed. (51F46)

Children sometimes unwittingly witnessed their parents' sexual life during the day. These parents had tried to benefit from their children's presumed absence.

> I heard noises from the kitchen and tiptoed over to look: I only saw my mother's and my father's feet on top of each other – I must have

guessed what it was about, though I don't remember how I would have come about my 'knowledge.' (32F43)

For children, nudity is initially a natural matter entirely devoid of any sexual charge. Sexuality gradually enters the world of children more consciously when they come to understand that girls and boys are physically different. After the birth of a younger sister or brother a child may also start to wonder where babies come from. Especially in rural areas children have been able to witness animal births and the starting of new life. These situations pose new questions to occupy their minds. One in ten autobiographies featured childhood memories about watching animal breeding. Memories connected to such occasions were emphasized especially in the men's writings. These memories were most common among the oldest generation. Children of the generation of sexual restraint were often told not to watch animals' sexual acts.

> I was particularly fascinated with horse breeding and the studliness of the stallion. When it rose on the mare's back on two hooves, its gigantic pole pointed straight. And the men guided the pole in the right direction and it sank in there immediately. (34M61)

In some exceptional cases a child's relationships with a domestic animal became so sexual that the child got actual sexual pleasure through it. Two of the authors depicted such experiences with a horse and cat.

> We took an old, docile mare next to the fence so that by balancing on the fence, we could reach her pussy with our dicks. While one of us held still the mare, the other would get his pleasure in her soft pussy. (169M50)

> One night I woke up to a tremendous feeling of pleasure: the cat is licking my clitoris and labia. It was sucking me like I would be the mother cat, and I nearly fainted. (38F28)

Because of the sauna culture, Finland is a country with exceptional stimuli, in that it offers children the possibility of seeing their mother and father as well as other children without their clothes on. This made the children used to being among naked people without direct sexual connotations.

> When I was small, my father would lay me and my sister down, one after the other, on a bench in the sauna to wash us. First the backs

side and then the front. He also washed my penis, even under the foreskin. Later I washed myself, but I went to the sauna with my sister until I was twenty; neither she nor I had any sort of inhibition about it. In the sauna, I remember how I looked at my mother's labia as she bathed. (122M44)

Observing the opposite sex usually has to take place in secret and discreetly. Children quickly learn the boundary between propriety and impropriety. Some authors remembered how their parents covered their genital organs even in the sauna.

Men's stories, mother's warnings

Childhood is a time of sexual socialisation and of learning the related sexual scripts. Approximately half of the men of the generation of sexual restraint, but only a few of the women, talked about the kind of sexual education they received in childhood prior to adolescence and how this instruction was provided. Most of the men of the middle generation and about one-third of the women wrote about such memories. Among the youngest generation, half of both men and women wrote about it. Comparing the three generations, sexual matters seem to have entered girls' awareness at a constantly increasing rate. The quotations in the beginning of this chapter clearly revealed how earlier generations tried to keep sexual information from girls. Boys, on the other hand, were able to obtain trickles of information.

Men's recollections about what they saw and heard about sex-related matters typically focus on genitals, coitus or nudity. Over one-tenth of the men and women mentioned hearing stories as children about where babies come from. Many do not recall receiving any kind of instruction from any adult in sexual matters in their childhood. Based on the remembrances of some authors, the word 'sexuality' was not widely known at least in the 1930s. Even most of the middle generation authors reported that not a word was ever said in their childhood home about sexuality or 'hanky-panky' between men and women.

The first time I had an erection, I wondered aloud at the phenomenon to my mother, who I don't recall explaining anything really. (4M37)

Also many of the young authors tell that sex was never discussed in their homes. One boy recalled how his mother was in the habit of shaking and folding sheets in front of the television whenever there were scenes with kissing or anything referring to sex. One girl continued to be angry as an adult that she had not been taught properly how to wash her genital region. She had suffered from itching repeatedly. Another girl's story revealed that mothers might still find it difficult to accept their daughters' interest in sexual organs.

> When my mother realised what the object of my interest was (when I was three), she snapped something at me in a forbidding tone of voice. (167F22)

In many autobiographies, the mothers were blamed for having adopted the role of a warning beacon in all sexual matters. Sex was presented first and foremost as a threat. Since the 1970s, this controlling sexual morality has partly been included in the sexual education children receive in schools and through other public services. Sexual enlightenment has largely assumed the form of dealing with visions of impending danger and discussing risk factors.

> My stepfather's brutal jokes and openness were in direct opposition to my mother's religious, discreet disposition, which held that expressing sexuality was inappropriate. (44M53)

Fathers and the men in the village, on the other hand, sometimes told 'men's stories' without heeding the presence of boys in particular. These stories handed down the masculine script from one generation of men to another.

> ... In our living-room, men would talk rough and guffaw at risque jokes in front of the children, too. (74F31)

One woman remembered talk among adults that she did not understand as a child. She recalled the phrases: 'that maid was a one-woman whorehouse', 'he had a Gypsy girl at the fair', 'he gets a hard-on when he sees a woman' and 'sooner will the earth split than a whore feel shame'. The girl understood it all to be related to the lower end of the body in some way, but did not know how. In some cases, it was the father who voiced the moral warnings. In one family, the father's only instruction to his son was: 'Beware of disease, do you understand me?' 'I understand', the boy replied, even though he had no idea to what his father was referring. The same kind of advice was given by a mother to her daughter who was on her way to a dance: 'Don't go looking for misery for yourself.' In these cases, the parents were too embarrassed to tell their children what to watch out for.

Many in the middle generation also wrote that at school age, they still did not know how girls' and boys' organs were connected, how babies were born, or the basics of intimate hygiene. Also some children from the youngest generation had misconceptions about sex. One girl used to think that men wore a condom all the time and that they merely changed it once in a while. Often girlfriends educated each other.

> ... My best friend knew nothing about the whole process at thirteen, and I remember clearly how in simple terms I explained to her the principles of sexual intercourse and child birth. At first she would not believe any of it. (151F25)

Stories about sexual organs featured most prominently in recollections about childhood sexual matters. Over half of the men from the older and middle generations wrote about them. There has been a solid tradition among men of telling sexual stories that get handed down to young boys. Women did not write recollections about any similar traditions. Women's dreams and stories have usually been constructed according to a more romantic script. In the older generations, it was usually men who remembered and wrote about things which did not fit into the dominant feminine script, such as female exhibitionism.

> One well-known actress was checking out [in the 1930s] her surroundings (at a suntanning spot) through small binoculars attached to a little arm, and when she detected movement, she spread her legs and started stroking her 'slit' with a feather. (99M62)

Childhood sexual games

We have already mentioned the intense curiosity children feel toward the physical difference of the other sex. When children set off to investigate the differences in each other together, this is usually called playing house, playing doctor, or sexual games. On the basis of a youth study conducted in the 1980s such games, all of which include examining the sexual organs of another, were experienced sometime during childhood by approximately 40 per cent of the respondents (Kontula 1987). Over half of the men from the older and middle generations described some kind of childhood sexual games, compared to one-third of the women. Among the youngest generation, only one man but approximately half of the women describe childhood sexual games.

A typical game script is one in which a boy or girl hides somewhere with another child of the opposite sex of about the same age, and they show each other 'what they have underneath their pants'. Most children understand they are doing something forbidden. Some of them feel guilty afterwards. On the other hand, many had affectionate memories of these experiences as adults. Many autobiographies featured strongly positive memories of childhood games that the adults did not know about. Most games did not come to the attention of parents or other adults, although on the occasions they mostly resulted in unpleasant consequences and feelings of guilt for the children. Their parents' anguish and wrath often seem completely overblown to a modern reader.

Sexual touching between children was especially easy in the 1930s because it was common in agrarian Finland for women to walk about without briefs in the summer. For little girls, it was more a rule than an exception. Some boys especially liked hay-loft games if there were girls involved. One boy had enjoyed it tremendously when he had been able to touch a girl's bare skin. Some games among children surpassed the boundary of playing and turned into sexual harassment. One recurring example is older boys 'checking out' the genitals of smaller boys, accompanied by a tittering crowd of girls. For one man, this was a miserable and humiliating experience. Another man remembered how older schoolboys 'checked' the smaller boys to see if there was anything in their trousers, and sometimes threw snow, too. The worst memories were related to threats to cut off the genitals if the boy did not do what the bully wanted.

Playing house as a sexual game included practising child birth by stuffing a doll in a girl's pants. It also involved making babies, with dolls as babies. One writer remembers feeling frustrated at the sexlessness of their dolls: 'Some of them didn't even have a butt hole!'.

> Already before school-age we played a lot of sex games. I remember a 'coochie show' that was held inside a tent in the summertime, where one of us acted as judge while others lay there with legs spread. (151F25)

Playing doctor was different from actual sex games in that the intention was not to imitate adult sexual behaviour or to seek sexual satisfaction. Sometimes, though, you had to pay for 'a showing.'

When I was six years old, the neighbour's boy took me to the woods. He promised me a one-mark coin if I would show him my 'vee'. And sure I showed him; one mark got you a lot of salt liquorice back then. (16F25)

My boy cousins would flash their dick for a one-mark coin, I don't remember having to pay them that many times. You could feel the thickness too, and darn how it thickened there in your hand. (67F25)

Regardless of gender, an equal number of autobiographers wrote about sexual games proper as about doctor games. *Sexual games* refer to play that aimed to mimic the sexual behaviour of adults or to seek sexual satisfaction. A sex game was often a more daring 'upgrade' of the earlier doctor games. Some children even tried to imitate ejaculation by peeing. Others feared it would cause pregnancy.

It felt good when Pekka peed inside me. It was warm. We were about ten. (126F73)

Mirja remained on her back in the ditch and looked up at the sky ... Her slit was open right in front of my nose. I examined it with curiosity. Then I began touching that protrusion with the tip of my tongue. It made Mirja feel good and she asked me to lick, lick. It tasted salty and smelled of pee. But the licking felt pleasant to me. Then we came up with wanting to put my dick in there. I was pushing in utter desperation. Well, it didn't go in. (34M61)

These two people, as adults, shared their warm memories of these 'nudie games'.

Many games got their inspiration from observing the sex act among animals. Particularly the breeding of a cow with a bull was popular in the games of some children. Attempts were made to really insert the little penis. Some boys experienced their first erections during such a game. In this case, it it not clear whether the game was perceived as a sexual game by all participants, or how the girl reacted to being undressed by the author.

We were playing robbers, where one robber absconded with a younger girl cousin and took her somewhere in the woods that surrounded my home. I took the girl's pants off and looked at her 'vee'. I remember that it excited me and my dick was hard. I didn't know what to do besides touch and stare at my cousin's pussy. (172M46)

Sexual games between girls resemble that between girls and boys. At times they involved inserting various objects into the vagina. Sexual play between boys often focused on comparing penises and erections.

> The neighbour's girl and I were playing inside the tent again. We put various objects (for example, pens and clothe spins) between our labia and then we jumped about the tent and chanted something, though I no longer remember what. (16F25)

Pornographic magazines had inspired doctor games in the youngest generation of girls. Women in older generations made no mention of them. For example, one 25-year-old woman and her cousin found some porn magazines as children in the attic of an uncle, which the girls then eagerly leafed through. They came up with props similar to those used in the pictures and dressed up and struck poses like the ones in the magazines. Elderly women also wrote about sexual play between girls. Sometimes the girls managed to get their first orgasm while playing together.

> My friend was physically quite developed already at ten, and I felt pleasure-tinged envy as I stroked her big breasts and curly-haired pubis. We demonstrated sexual intercourse by using things like carrots and hairbrushes, and I in particular would coax Johanna to be bold and to experiment. (143F22)

Approximately one in four of the one-on-one sex games between children remembered in the autobiographies was discovered by parents or relatives. In most cases, the adults reacted very negatively.

> My mother had been watching our playing through the keyhole and gave me a horrible lecture after I woke up, about sin and the horrors that would result from such play. She spanked my bare bottom with a twig before I had time to pull my pants on. After that I didn't want to play doctor anymore. (6F50)

Some parents reacted with surprisingly strong distress to the quite innocent doctor games of their children.

> I befriended the neighbour's girl, Anja, who taught me a new game, playing doctor. We were playing it quietly in Anja's room, because she knew that it was forbidden. Despite that, her parents noticed,

and my mother dragged me to a real doctor who examined my vagina and hurt me very much. (157F63)

Following the examination, these children were not even allowed to see each other. As an after effect, the girl lost her appetite and suffered from feelings of guilt long into adulthood.

> 'In the end, I hated her, and even when I was of school age, I didn't say hello to her.'

Sometimes children's sexual games are played in groups. Descriptions of group games came from approximately one-fifth of all autobiography writers. Most stories dealt with playing in mixed groups of both girls and boys. Only about one-tenth of these group games came to the attention of adults. Group sex play was sometimes a continuation of earlier one-on-one experiments that others wanted to join as they found out about them.

> ... Then, Mirja told the other girls about how we had messed around. So, one time when we all went swimming, the others wanted to be with me like that too. In the sauna, each one spread her little slit for me to lick, one at a time, and of course I tried to put it in every time. The other girls looked on. (34M61)

For boys, group sex play sometimes led to learning about masturbation, not just to comparing penises. Through these group games, boys experienced friendship and positive experiences of being part of a group.

> Now that we were on the jetty, Jukka and Pekka said, let's try what the others did on the islet, and see if white liquid squirts out of anyone's dick. That's when I experienced masturbation and an orgasm for the first time in my life, at least I think that's what happened. (48M55)

This man thinks this experience has shaped his personality and sexuality radically. As a result of the incident, he would get sexually aroused fairly easily all his life when he saw naked boys of that same age.

Some boys tried to implement lessons on lovemaking learned from their fathers. One 62-year-old man told the story of how he and the neighbour's boy had tried to put their penis in the vagina of a girl who was willing to play. The other boy's devout grandmother intervened by swinging a broom. Playing with the 'kilkin' (penis) was an evil deed, according to her.

> As I was trying to push my dick into her 'coochie', this time we got it right and it went in and slid in deep. I can't be sure about remembering if it also felt good. However, I tried to pee inside Hilkka's thing without succeeding. No matter how I strained! See, we thought that's how babies were made! (65M44)

3
Sexuality in Youth

Obtaining sexual information

Many autobiographers described the sexual instruction and images they had received in youth. Men wrote frequently about obtaining sexual information from friends, books and magazines. Women were more likely to discuss school sexual education or the moral teachings they were given in their childhood home. Approximately one-third of the men and less than one-fifth of the women recalled receiving sexual images and information from *peer groups*. The focal points of these stories were pregnancy and lovemaking.

> I marvelled at how odd it must feel for a woman to have such a baton pushed inside her. It was wonderfully manly to know such things ... (118M48)

> One boy my age had his first experience with a woman paid for by some older boys ... . They had enjoyed her services as a group in some barn ... (159M55)

One boy recollected how one of his bunk mates during military service was a married man who kept talking about making love with his wife in the night time. His other bunk mates, too, strove to prove their virility.

Even though differences between men and women in sexual life have decreased, the practical expectations connected to relationships in the feminine script still differ from those of the masculine script. The vastly diverging activities of one group of girls and another group of boys gathered on a rooftop illustrate this.

> On one side, the girls were talking about love, life and their hopes. The boys were hanging out happily for a long time on the other side

of the ridge of the roof. As they came over to us girls, we asked them what they had been talking about. The boys had wanked off and competed about who shot off the farthest. (77F36)

But from the middle generation onwards, girls are under just as much pressure as boys to acquire experiences.

In our circle of friends you didn't get gold stars for sexual modesty. We kept a tally on how many kisses you got before confirmation school, and people tried to best each other in jeering at a sixteen-year-old girl who, as far as we knew, hadn't 'put out' yet. (55F41)

Books and magazines were named as a source of their information on sexuality significantly more often than talking with friends or adults. Approximately two out of five men and women made some mention of them. Quantitatively, various types of sex guides and pornographic publications were most often mentioned. Based on the number of mentions, pornography reigned as the no. 1 source of information among the youngest generation, women included. The autobiographies revealed Van de Velde's illustrated 'Ideal Marriage, its Physiology and Technique' as the most important source of information for the oldest generation. Some called it a forbidden book, and it was dog-eared from much use by both men and women. The friends of this man thought he was too fascinated with the book.

On one of those nights I got to borrow Van de Velde's book 'Ideal Marriage'. I was a fast reader, I read a lot in general, but this work enthralled me more powerfully than any novel. I didn't hurry to return it. I reread it many times and nearly knew it by heart, especially the different sexual positions. (19M59)

The booklet 'What Every Boy Should Know', according to one autobiographer, contained downright astounding, as well as false, stories about the harmful effects of masturbation.

There were horrible stories about the damage caused in people by self-contamination. The first symptoms resembled the initial stages of Aids today. Your posture would become hunched, skin turn yellow and the gaze becomes wandering. All this happens because that grey fluid that squirts out is really spinal fluid. The final result is a slow death. (34M61)

Medical manuals or encyclopaedias were not mentioned by any authors of the older generation as sources of sexual information. Younger people used these books actively.

> My feet took me to the library and to the encyclopaedia, and it opened to the letter 's' as if by itself. The pages on sexual matters were nearly black from countless, dirty boys' hands. (129M45)

Most writers reserved particular praise for the medical manual series as a source of sexual information.

> I read and wrote a lot as a child, and when I was in elementary school, one of my favourites reads was a fine, and at the time modern, series of medical manuals, from which I obtained correct information early on about the birth of children and sexual matters in general. I actually knew everything by the time I was nine and would secretly make Barbies have sex with each other. (144F35)

For the middle generation, the selection of guide books had grown and the level of information had improved. Fact books have been complemented, since the 1970s, by doctor's columns in various magazines, with their questions and replies. Systematically researched data on sexual matters also began to be published.

> The municipal library quenched my thirst for knowledge excellently. Among other things, the shelves boasted the wonderful work by Masters' & Johnson, 'Human Sexual Response'. The book was published in Finnish the same year. Of course you had to hide the books at home, and read them in secret ... . I had read a huge amount of all kind of books on serology. Kinsey, Morris, Masters-Johnson, and the last, Shere Hites [Shire Hite], were all familiar names. My head was bursting with theory, but I had no clue about the practice. (62M39)

The autobiographies mentioned pornographic products most frequently as sources of sexual information in youth. For the young generation, porn was clearly the main information source. In the youth of the oldest generation pornography was not widely available. Men in the middle generation were able to peruse sex magazines and could learn about sexual intercourse from foreign magazines.

At his house (a male cousin) there were piles of Playboys and other literature in the field; he himself had taken photos of his girlfriends from every angle. He had us read the cult book *Soya – seventeen*, which electrified me. We would even try and decipher the Kinsey Report one letter at a time. (4M37)

Sometimes young women devoured a stack of classics in this field.

On my parents' bookshelf, Henry Miller's books and *The Story of O* and *Marquis de Sade* were in heavy use when my parents were away. Soon I noticed that their glued backs were always broken at the 'action' spots. (5M25)

Now it was time for the Shere Hite reports, the Henry Millers, all the classics, *The Story of O*, *A Man with a Maid*, *The School of Venus*, Oscar Wilde's *Teeny* ... Knowledge is power. (57F25)

For many young women, porn magazines were tools for weaving sexual images, heightening arousal and for use in masturbation. At first, these magazines could be found in parents' stashes, obtained from a brother, or discovered somewhere else. Traditional romantic novels also influenced women's sexual expectations.

In them, girls were beautiful and innocent. Then they encountered a man who was handsome but oh so horrible, and then there was a conflict or two, and then they made love which meant a stoking of the embers, page after page (well, I'm sure you know). Then, in the end, the man turned out to be not so horrible after all, but actually fine and sensitive and at least damned wealthy and of fine birth, and they lived happily ever after, amen. It is terrible that the images girls receive about sexuality come from stories like that, and for boys it is wanking off with a porn magazine. But unfortunately, that is how it goes. (16F25)

Masturbation in childhood and adolescence

The script of sexual restraint and 'sex as a threat' have in recent decades been accompanied by the script of 'sexuality as pleasure'. This can be seen particularly clearly in the attitude toward masturbation. It became possible to discuss it and as a phenomenon masturbation has been given a positive interpretation. In the autobiographies, two-thirds of male and one-third of the female authors wrote about masturbation

in childhood and adolescence. Less than half of the men of the generation of sexual restraint described it, but of younger men, approximately four out of five did. Among women the gap was even more
noticeable, as only one-fifth of the women of the old and middle generations wrote about masturbation, compared to around 60 per cent of
the younger generation.

In earlier sexual scripts, enjoying sex was the prerogative of men, but
lately women's right to enjoy has become unquestioned. Alongside,
masturbation among women has increased greatly. Masturbation is
thought of as a good way to learn to know one's own body and its
sources of pleasure. Sexual satisfaction has become part of a woman's
life regardless of whether she has a partner or what kind of sexual relationships she shares with that partner. The autobiographies clearly
show that masturbation has become a much more significant issue for
young women. This is in line with the results of the survey: where a
third of the women belonging to the generation of sexual restraint
reported having masturbated at least once in their lifetime, while this
was reported to be the case for 85 per cent of the women belonging to
the generation of equalisation. The script 'sex is enjoyable' has spread
between women and has altered the interpretation of feminine sexuality, making the accompanying pleasure something acceptable.

One boy told about discovering sexual satisfaction already at the age
of three or four with the help of a radiator. Pressing his penis against
the radiator the boy experienced pleasure that would increase as he
moved back and forth. He experienced his first ejaculation this way,
and repeated it while bathing. He imagined that he was the only one
in the world to have discovered how to experience this satisfaction.
Later, he did it in bed using his hands. One important reason for masturbation being more common among boys was that boys were in a
better position to get practical instruction on the topic from friends.

At about age thirteen I learned to masturbate. We were hanging out
with some older boys when they started talking about 'jacking off'
and 'shooting a wad'. I was one of the boys who were begging them
to show how it was done and what would come out. One of the
bigger ones agreed, and started moving his foreskin over the head of
the penis. A clear droplet appeared on the tip. The movement of his
hand accelerated and the expression on the boy's face was of utter
pleasure. In a moment, his entire body stiffened and the movement
of his hand became jerky. Right then a light spray squirted out, and
then a second, a third ... and gently he pulled the foreskin over the

slowly softening penis. With a satisfied expression on his face, the boy said it felt really good. (44M53)

One middle generation man recalled how his best friend taught him to masturbate at school during class. The boys were sitting in the back row, so others did not notice how his friend would masturbate. A few weeks later the boy masturbated secretly in his own bed. He felt it had made him a man.

Sometimes girls, too, were instructed in how to masturbate. One 12-year-old girl learned from a male cousin six years her senior at her grandmother's house.

> I lay on my back with my knees bent and rotated my finger determinedly but carefully on that little nodule that was a little higher up, and I must have imagined something arousing, because before I knew it my lower abdomen exploded in an immense sensation of pleasure, my hips rose toward the heavens and my labia under my shaky hand throbbed, throbbed, throbbed … . It was an unbelievable sensation, and I did it over and over many times that night, I was tremendously exhausted, but happy, when the next morning I was able to whisper to Joni: 'It worked'. (143F22)

The arousal required to climax could be enhanced with sexual imaginings and fantasies.

> I would masturbate many times a day, fantasizing about romantic and exciting situations in which sex was always connected to danger and passions were intense. I also fantasized about sexual intercourse, even though I didn't know exactly how it was done. (3F29)

> In my fantasies I imagined being in a sheik's harem or in a brothel, half against my will. The thought that I could excite men aroused me. I masturbated by looking at myself in the mirror as if through a man's eyes. I felt I masturbated rather often, many times a week, sometimes several times in one day. (89F20)

Boys in particular often resorted to erotic or nude pictures to get sufficiently aroused to masturbate. Some read and reread the sexually exciting portions of their favourite books. Similar descriptions also surfaced among younger women.

> How many times I would sit with that picture in front of me and imagine making love with my beautiful classmate and huge crush!

I would masturbate at the same time, and as my semen squirted, I let it drip onto the photograph until the girl was completely covered. (12M65)

In some cases boys and, more frequently girls, used various objects or paraphernalia as aids for sexual arousal. These included a ball of yarn, the shower head and a carrot.

A very common and pleasant method was to place a large ball of woollen yarn under your 'vee' and when you lay on top of it on your stomach and rubbed your clitoris against that hard ball, you got a guaranteed orgasm. There were many balls of sock yarn that got to act as a man substitute. (25F57)

In the generations of restraint and sexual revolution, climaxing and orgasm as a result of masturbation was described mainly by men, but in the generation of equalisation, women wrote about it almost as frequently. The first orgasm from masturbation was a tremendously powerful experience for many men and could even frighten them with its violence. Children and young people who experienced it unexpectedly may have been very confused as to what had happened to them.

I was not aware of what was about to happen, but I felt an immense pleasurable sensation that kept growing. Suddenly my entire body flipped as if in a massive cramp – my toes spread as far away from each other as possible. I felt as if my toenails were coming loose and flying in all directions. I had experienced my first orgasm. (169M50)

Some girls had already masturbated for some time before experiencing their first orgasm.

I discovered parts of myself that produced pleasure when I touched them. That is, I learned the skill of masturbation. After doing this for a while, I had the first orgasm of my life. It was hot, scary, but oh so excitingly pleasurable. Every part of me throbbed inside and my legs were jelly. (128F25)

One girl in the young generation picked up the idea for masturbation from porn magazines, but did not know how to carry it out in practice. She tried all kinds of methods. At last, at age 13, she discovered that you could climax by rubbing the clitoris. She also passed this advice to her girlfriend.

Children and young people were frightened of the dangers of masturbation. They came to learn that it was a sinful and forbidden deed that could only be carried out in a safe place and even then, as quietly as possible. For many, this resulted in feelings of shame and guilt. For example, nearly all of the women in the young generation who described masturbation reported that it had made them feel guilty.

> I too was inspired, and every time I took a shower I tried to have ever-longer orgasms that I could feel ever-deeper inside my spine. Guilt and the fear of discovery weighed on me. But the water probably symbolically acted as a cleanser and in practice, as a good sound barrier for the noise. (77F36)

> ... At that time [age 12] I had already begun to masturbate and felt I was bad in spite of an article I had read that said 90% of young people were doing it. (89F20)

In part, young people's guilt feelings were caused by the observation that no-one talked about masturbation even though it gave them such important experiences. For some children and young people, warnings about the dangers of masturbation as well as the accompanying shame and guilt made them end this 'depraved' habit.

> I did everything I could to stop. Once, I even placed two fingers on an open Bible and swore to God the way you swear in a court of law that I would never masturbate again ... (48M55)

The times became less oppressive in this regard after the 1960s, because the younger generation did not report any attempts to make them stop masturbating in their autobiographies.

First love

Children and young people have infatuations and fall in love, but only sometimes are their feelings expressed to the subject of affection. Insecurity prevents or limits the expression of hopes and feelings. Some children will try to physically touch the subject of their infatuation under the guise of play or teasing. In many cases, a dating relationship will begin, accompanied by experiences of kissing and various caresses. Dating teaches the interactive scripts that are essential in later, more serious relationships. Nearly every autobiography describes the sweetness and at times misery of youthful infatuations and love. The sweetness is manifested either as pleasurable sensations or as physiological tremors, when the love object has gazed at, touched fleetingly or kissed the one in love. Misery has ensued if an outsider has interrupted the tender advances, the fear of pregnancy, or because plain inertia or commitment to another have prevented the expression of love. The worst memories concerned being abandoned because the other person's feelings have cooled.

Many authors did not tell others about their school day crushes, but kept them as secret loves.

> In elementary school I was infatuated with a girl in my class. However, I never talked to anyone about it. (35M34)

> I became interested in boys and I had a crush on this person and the other, but I didn't tell anyone about it; it was a form of self-protection. (72F42)

Teachers were often objects of long-distance love. The infatuation could be with a teacher of the same or opposite sex.

> Whereas the others were chasing boys, I would moon over the most beautiful girl in the class photo, and be infatuated with female teachers. (67F25)

Some men of the generation of sexual restraint had their first relationships with sexual overtones with servants.

> Vilma wanted to wash me and brought up the importance of keeping my penis clean. … She took my hand and brought it to her lips and from there slowly to her breasts. I was confused and embarrassed. I felt I was committing a sin, when she used my hands to rub the tips of her nipples, which were hard and sharp like pistol barrels. They aren't just for children, real men need these too (she said). I could feel something wonderfully strange taking place inside me. (99M62)

Part of drawing up a love map is pondering the characteristics of an ideal companion. Dreams, fancies and fantasies sometimes precede or replace concrete expressions of youthful love that would require physical proximity. Dreams also help one outline the criteria for selecting a partner in later dating relationships.

> This boy who only occasionally spent time at his father's, our neighbour, became 'The Prince of My Dreams' for many years. In addition to slips of paper, I wrote two notebooks about him. In the evenings I dreamt at the window gazing into the horizon. It seemed to me that he would ride his white horse to me from there, pull me onto the horse and into his arms, and then we would be together forever. (161F50)

In addition to romance, some dreamed of physical sex. The inspiration may have come from parental sex life and pornography.

> I believe that the sexually unhappy mood at home made me into a person who, on top of other anxieties, was overly interested in sex – not in deeds but in my thoughts. Even when I was small, I had sex dreams; all I remember is that some had to do with my parents, particularly my mother. (116F31)

Some recorded their daydreams or infatuations in diaries or wrote stories about them.

> My diaries from the first grades of secondary school are filled with notes about countless infatuations. Most of my crushes were in senior school, wonderful, unattainable, long-haired boys in maxi-coats, who would approach me in the school hallway, embracing and kissing me in dreams and daydreams. In reality we could only embrace boys in our own class under the guise of dancing at class parties. (146F33)

> My stories from middle school were very violent and sadistic. The main character was often raped and she was tortured. She was the most beautiful and desired (girl) in the world, every man competed to get her. (42F23)

Young men did their share of daydreaming and fantasising. Boys did not necessarily yet know what they wanted to do with a girl and felt guilty about their sexual fantasies. ' ... I was shy and awkward. I couldn't even talk to her about anything really.' (159M55)

The first grazing, trembling physical touching of the opposite sex may have produced huge sensations, sometimes akin to electric shocks.

> I greatly enjoyed walking hand in hand with a girl. Sometimes I felt a tremor in my arm. I can't really explain it, but it felt kind of the

same as when I've sometimes got an electric shock from a wall outlet. (81M47)

A conscious infatuation often included fleeting touches, looks, pulling the other's arm, or walking hand in hand.

> It was a big deal if we happened to lightly, semi-accidentally brush each other ... . We tried tickling each other, and in the end the three of them were tickling me and even grabbing me a bit, and I fought them happily. A few times we even played 'sandwich layers' where all of us piled on top of each other and the one in the middle had the best time. (89F20)

For many boys teasing was the way to express interest towards girls. Many girls approved of this, but some felt hurt by it. The sexual script of very young girls may have included publicly despising the physical advances of boys. Only when girls were a little older were they supposed to admit their interest in boys to their girlfriends.

Petting and dating

Half of the men and women who took part in the autobiography competition wrote about various kinds of sexual touching prior to their first intercourse. Such experiences included kissing on the mouth, petting and oral sex.

> All the way up to when I was nineteen, the gentle touch of a hand was enough. At that age a few boys even got to kiss me. That felt quite wild. (2F77)

Sometimes kissing and breast-touching awakened sexual desire.

> The neighbour's twenty-year-old boy. He stroked my breasts and kissed me. His mouth was wet, teeth knocking ... . It did feel very exciting. There was a nice burning sensation between my legs. (85F53)

Some girls of the generation of equalization were active in making sexual moves. They might seduce inexperienced boys while at the same time ensuring that coitus did not take place. The boys were often grateful that the girl had stuck to certain limits.

> Our teeth knocked against each other, there was a tickle feeling at the pit of my stomach, and my lips became sore, but once you got the taste of it, you couldn't stop. (96F20)

Sexual experiences were communicated to others with marks on the partner's neck. This kind of marking was often done without intercourse, and such markings were something to boast about to friends. Love and sexual experiences, along with marks, functioned as a measure of worth in the gangs of the youngest generation.

> Among girls, if inexperience had been revealed, everything would have been blamed on the boy by saying that he had just fondled. Among boys, the girl would have been labelled a prude if the inexperience had been revealed to the gang. (108M32)

Before the development of contraceptive methods, petting was almost used as an alternative to sexual intercourse. Sometimes lack of information bred confusion.

> He used 'finger sex' on me. I didn't like it and didn't really understand his intentions then. (39F45)

According to the survey, half of the generation of sexual restraint had never practiced manual sex. In the autobiographies, experiences of manual sex were already common among the generation of equalization.

> There was a sweaty, stiff organ inside his trousers, and it may be that I masturbated him all the way … . On the way home I smelled my hand and that sealed the decision for a final separation, because if men smelled that horrible, they could wait! (40F26)

Young women could be very adept in the various forms of petting. Some women found it particularly arousing to have their breasts stroked.

> … You can get me into a state of fierce arousal instantaneously by touching my breasts (this is still true today). (168F24)

Based on both the survey and the autobiographies, oral sex has become significantly more common in younger generations.

Boys entered my life when I was about thirteen. First I learned to satisfy boys with my hands and then with my mouth. (128F25)

His lips were soft and demanding, erotic. After the kiss I knew I was wet. ... His member was big and hard. I used my hands and mouth. The man was amazed at my skill ... (150F26)

Dances and movie theatres were stages for the petting that preceded first coitus for the older generation; for the middle generation, it was a car or a tent; and the younger generation used the parental home or summer cottage.

In rural areas, the love games occurred mainly in summertime, because at other times there was nowhere to go. Girls and boys too slept in outbuildings, most often in a cottage. Parents watched over daughters, so boys had to be poised and ready to make a run for it.

We were lying in bed naked in the intercourse position, but on her wishes I did not do it all the way. We were caressing each other. Aino was wet and I was pushing my finger inside her. (172M46)

A driver's licence and a car opened up new possibilities for finding places for loving. The car expanded the circle of friends and provided another, private 'lovemaking room'. Moreover, the 1960s was the golden age of hitchhiking and the younger generation has also used it as a way of getting to dances. For girls, arranging for a ride was exciting.

Hitchhiking had its own excitement. You never knew what kind of pervert was sitting behind the wheel ... . We were the weekend companions of some boys in the neighbouring village only because they had the use of a car. They were older than we, but still they didn't want to do anything beyond kissing or fondling. (151F25)

The youngest generation sometimes built huts in the woods, which could be used by members of the gang. Dating was still fairly innocent.

Girls used to say in these private sessions that you can do whatever you want. A girl expected the boy to make the moves, but what was a boy on the brink of adolescence able to do in that situation ... ? (108M32)

Sometimes a youth gang would fool around through common agreement. The circle of friends provided a safe framework for experimenting with physical intimacy.

> ... We played music on the boombox, turned out nearly all the lights, picked a 'partner' who was pleasing, settled comfortably in a reclining position, and then, without particularly caring about one another, started kissing and pressing up against each other ... (168F24)

Regular dating that preceded sexual intercourse in adolescence was described in some way by less than one-quarter of the autobiography writers. There was no difference shown between genders or generations in this regard. The fear of pregnancy was a common hindrance to sexual intercourse among those who dated regularly. The generation of sexual restraint often thought it normal to rein in their sexual urges.

> Sexual issues were foreign to us, and we did not hurry them. We still felt a natural attraction, but we let it take its own sweet time. (105F63).

> Perhaps we were momentarily astounded by the immense desire toward another person that came from kissing them ... . We came close – but something made us stop. (164F80)

Those in love and experiencing the awakening of sexual desire generally began plans for marriage so that the couple could begin sexual relations.

Men of the generation of the sexual revolution were often critical of dating where lovemaking only went 'half-way':

> Our petting often continued for so long and at such an intensity that at some point in the course of the evening I came. My girlfriend perhaps did not notice, and I didn't bring it up ... . Our dating consisted of night after night of petting that resulted in an orgasm. At first I was content, but gradually I felt increasing pressure. (88M39)

Women of the same generation on the contrary often enjoyed the time that elapsed from the beginning of dating to just the first kiss, not to mention sexual intercourse.

> We kissed, embraced, slept together and petted, but we did not have intercourse. I was also never away from home the whole night. That went on for a year, and it was beautiful. (72F42)

> Actually even today that is one of the best moments in the beginning of a new relationship: to approach that astonishingly

independent-minded living, moving organ. Penis, cock ... . The boy was ready to make love after six months of petting and kissing practise. I just wasn't ... mentally ready yet. (146F33)

When dating regularly, petting gave many people sexual satisfaction and an orgasm. The generation of sexual restraint often dated for rather a long while abstaining from sexual intercourse. The generation of sexual revolution was not decisively different in this regard. Only the youngest generation proceeded fairly quickly to sexual intercourse after the first date.

First intercourse

Most people consider themselves sexually experienced only after having intercourse for the first time. First intercourse is one of the most central turning points in the sexual life course, and is also felt to be a rite of initiation and symbol of becoming an adult. Most expect intercourse to occur in the youth's life phase. The ideal timing of the first intercourse depends on the type of reference group the young person belongs to. Once upon a time, marriage was generally seen as the ideal timing, but more recently the ideal is usually to acquire experiences approximately at the same paces as one's contemporaries.

Even when a young person has a strong motivation to experience first intercourse, there are usually many different obstacles in the way. These include fear of pregnancy, lack of self-confidence, shyness, lack of a safe place and so on. Before engaging in sexual intercourse, a particular situation and the interactive relationship (partner) should preferably fulfil the suitable script 'recorded' in the psyche. Stories about purely instrumental relationships in which the other person's task is to help oneself get the first sexual experience are rare.

First intercourse in Europe takes place now on average two years earlier than in recent decades (Bozon and Kontula 1998). In Finland the shift to a younger age occurred particularly among women who were in their youth phase in the early 1970s. After that, approximately 20–25 per cent had their first intercourse before the age of 16 and about half had it before the age of 18. Between 10 and 20 per cent experienced intercourse for the first time after turning 20. Prior to the 1970s the latter proportion was much higher. Furthermore, since the 1980s, regional and gender differences in the age of first intercourse have disappeared almost completely. Regional differences as a distinguishing factor have been replaced by education: young people who have a high level of education have begun having sexual intercourse significantly later than other young people.

Three out of four autobiographies mentioned their first intercourse. In certain cases, the first intercourse stood for several instances of intercourse. If the hymen did not seem to break the first time, intercourse was interpreted to have occurred only when the hymen no longer offered resistance. In earlier decades the majority of women married their first sexual partner. Starting in the 1970s, this became a rarity. Intercourse became part of dating with no goal-oriented aim to establish a lifelong relationship. Many people remembered seeking adventures and different kinds of experiences, thinking they would have regrets if they did not acquire enough experience before settling down.

One out of four men and women in the generation of sexual restraint had first intercourse with their future spouse or they were already married to the spouse (of those surveyed, 60 per cent of women and 25 per cent of the men in this age group married their first sexual partner). One in ten women of the generation of sexual revolution reported doing so, but none of the men. In the generation of equalization, only one woman wrote that her first intercourse occurred with her future husband; according to the survey this proportion is between 10 and 15 per cent. The writings of the generation of restraint often expressed the view that prior experience of intercourse ruined a woman's chances for a good marriage. Many writers believed that being sexually untouched was of utmost importance. There were some instances where the man had looked for evidence of blood on the sheets after first intercourse.

> Afterwards, he said: 'There has to be blood if the girl is pure', and wanted to look. Fortunately I had bled a little. I was surprised – had he trusted me so little? Had I known that he was so unsure about me, it would have never happened. (117F72)

For some women, sexuality had little significance in the marital relationship, or they had engaged in lovemaking only to please their husband. This could already be seen in the case of first intercourse.

> ... In any case, my future husband took my virginity, and to me, that pretty much amounted to a promise of marriage. What it was – a description? Fast, mechanical, go in, don't let 'that' in so there will be no be pregnancy. It didn't really feel like anything, I just wanted to please the man I imagined was my destiny. (39F45)

For many men, on the other hand, the first intercourse was a turning point towards sexual enjoyment.

> As if in a dream I rose to cover her with my body. My whole body was probably stiff. Trembling from desire, I went inside her. It was brief lovemaking, but so much more intense. Orgasm was approaching thanks to the experiences we had had from hand methods. I knew to be careful. It was interrupted intercourse, but a heavenly first experience of carnal love with a woman. (123M64)

Usually it was the woman who decided when intercourse took place. At that point, men had generally been waiting for her acquiescence for some time and were already eager for intercourse.

> I saw him sitting on the sofa in his new shirt and I thought: Today! … He was very gentle and took my inexperience into consideration, though he was sweating because he had a hard time getting inside me. I was probably so tense, even though I wanted nothing more in the world than to make love with him … . I also really wanted to get rid of my virginity … . I remember thinking as I went to shower that somehow I had become more a totality … . I felt much more secure, I had become a wanted woman, and I enjoyed the feeling. (106F39)

One-fifth of the generation of equalisation and one-tenth of those of the generation of sexual revolution wrote about coming under pressure, sometimes intense, to lose their virginity. Women of the generation of sexual restraint mentioned no such pressure.

> The condom felt disgusting, the intercourse didn't feel like anything, but for me the most important thing was that now I was no longer inexperienced. Virginity became a burden when, after R., my mother began to call me a hussy, a whore. (60F38)

> We went to bed and I decided it was now or never, because I was quite convinced that I was the only virgin in my class, and that embarrassed me. (16F25)

Some young women describe a more instrumental treatment of men. They gave a particular man the task of erasing their hymen. After that they could undertake to enjoy sex with other men.

> Before leaving for England I had met this guy Ari in my home town
> ... . Once he came to my house when my father was away some-
> where, and he fucked me. His cock did not go inside me properly
> and he asked kind of casually if I was still a virgin. I didn't reply, but
> I think he took care of the whole business very well. He wanted to
> fuck and got what he wanted. I got rid of my virginity ... I was
> happy that he did the 'dirty work' and 'punctured' me ... . To this
> day I cannot understand why the first time is considered so impor-
> tant, who cares how you do it. (144F35)

Intercourse with a previously unknown foreign partner had been easier
for some girls than having sex with a boy they know, who might even
tell his friends about it. It sheds light on the modern attitude that
some girls decide to terminate the relationship immediately if the boy's
skills as a lover do not prove to be satisfactory. In earlier times the lack
of contraception acted as a deterrent to intercourse. In more recent
times the issue has been whether contraception was available and
whether there was an ability or desire to put it to use.

> As I was pulling off Titu's panties, she was trying to stop me and was
> saying: Don't you know what it will lead to? I assured her that it
> would lead to nothing and dug out a condom. With shaking hands I
> was able to put it on and I rose on top of Titu. She didn't help me
> except by lifting up her knees, and let me do whatever and however
> I saw fit. (172M46)

Sometimes the intercourse took place in a drunken state, leaving the
narrator with very hazy and occasionally unpleasant memories. In
reality, this often amounted to sexual abuse or even rape.

> My girl friend left the tent with someone else. I was in a senseless
> state and it happened: I lost my virginity. When I woke up in the
> morning and realized what had happened, I headed home on foot
> with blood in my panties, and hated myself. It felt like all the
> passers-by could see on me what had happened. (72F42)

Forced intercourse or rape appear to be relatively uncommon in connection with the first intercourse. According to the survey, one in ten
women agreed reluctantly to intercourse. One in a hundred was
forced either by threats of physical force or through rape. Four women

(4 per cent) reported in their autobiographies that their first intercourse had been rape.

> I was the victim because I was more physically developed. I fought him as much as I could. It took some time. Sinikka also was not able to leave. I didn't have the strength to fight it. Four boys did it to me one after the other. I remember distinctly how it started to feel good. It took so long, maybe I even cried. I don't remember exactly.
>
> … At home I was made out to be a whore and a bad person, though in my own mind I was anything but: an ordinary girl, shyer than usual even. A real Gestapo type of discipline began. I had to be home by nine, and if I wasn't, I was 'out whoring'. (36F52)

Of those surveyed, 70 per cent of men and 25 per cent of women considered first intercourse a pleasant experience. Approximately one-fifth of all authors considered first intercourse very good and approximately the same proportion had found it to be a bad (and frequently painful) experience. Only one woman mentioned having an orgasm in her first intercourse. Men, on the other hand, generally described their ejaculations and the eruption of their pleasure in an orgasm.

> I was sixteen when I first fell in love. The mystical first time came also. Luckily, the boy was several years older and experienced. I was afraid of the pain and my inexperience. He knew I was a virgin and because of that, guided me gently, with care, from a girl to a woman. He kissed me, licked and fingered me so I was ready for him, and made sure that I had an orgasm too. It was perfect, though not lasting, but I learned to trust, to abandon myself, and to experience pleasure. (120F30)

One girl had her first sexual experiences in a group of friends in which boys and girls were with each other. For her, this arrangement was very safe and instructive.

> We were not dating anyone in particular, but would each time select new pairs so that in the end everyone had been with everyone. I remember being amazed at how different every boy's penis was. It could be narrow, thick, long, short, curved … . The boys taught me how good it felt to them to have the tip of the penis touched. Girls instructed the boys, all of whom were too rough-handed at first, it was probably the way they touched themselves. (77F36)

The stories mainly described first intercourse as a rather meaningless experience, and less often about particularly good or bad intercourse.

> I didn't really feel anything when we were in bed. But now I knew at least what 'all men wanted'. (140F55)

While the narrator did not feel a particular desire to have intercourse, she also did not consider it to be significant. Actual experiences were often a far cry from the romantic expectations thought to be connected to love.

> Fingers are being pushed inside me, and a penis goes in. First time. Nothing romantic, nothing that is beautiful. Woo-hoo, that was it? On the top bunk, the object of my love, a quickie from behind. Someone even came in the room during the proceedings. Not a thought to contraception. (57F25)

> ... 'It' happened in the back of a car right by my home. I did not feel much, just hurt a little. I didn't even have time to get excited ... . It was quite primitive. (151F25)

In many cases the experience of intercourse was unsatisfactory because the man ejaculated so quickly. This was mentioned by both men and women. Sometimes the problem was that the man did not properly know how to have intercourse. Two men said that in otherwise successful intercourse, they had not ejaculated.

Some men of the generation of sexual restraint had their first intercourse with a prostitute. Many men found these experiences disappointing. One boy had to continue by masturbating in order to get some pleasure out of the experience.

> There were five soldiers waiting in a queue for that drunken woman, and I was number three, and that experience was a momentous disappointment, because it did not resemble in any way what I had imagined when masturbating ... . My cock didn't get squeezed as tightly as it used to do in my own hand. The woman's pussy was slippery from the sperm of the previous two men and it felt unbelievably wide. (171M71)

The initiation rite of the first intercourse was a measure of the nerve and skill of a young man. The pressures related to intercourse were in many cases relieved too quickly in a manner typical of young people.

She dug a condom out of her bag and skilfully put it on me. She took off her panties. That was the sign that I could go in. I got on top of her and she guided my rock-hard penis inside. It was an extremely arousing situation. I began to slowly move in and out, but I could already feel the rhythmic contractions advancing and I came. I hadn't even properly begun the lovemaking itself, when it was already embarrassingly over! (88M39)

Young men experienced various kinds of pressure to succeed in first intercourse. It is not surprising, then, that one in ten men talks about a difficulty in achieving an erection. These erection problems often appeared well before attempting actual intercourse.

... When S. finally opened my zipper the first time to feel what I was like 'there', I did not have a hard-on. The same thing happened the next few times too. Only after several weeks had I calmed down enough for the long-awaited stiffening to happen, and S. was able to take a good hold of me. I came after a few yanks, and it is pointless to try to explain how amazing it felt ... (13M25)

In our population survey, approximately 40 per cent of women and 5 per cent of men reported that their first intercourse experience was painful. One-fifth of the women felt it was very painful. This equals the share of women authors who reported painful first intercourse.

Pekka entered me quickly to abbreviate the pain, but it was tearing me apart like a knife. I dug my teeth in his shoulder and bit like a rabid mutt, gnawed on his skin and wailed from the pain that would not let off. – 'Stop moving', I moaned. Pekka obeyed. – 'Does it hurt that much?', he asked frightened, and smoothed my hair. 'Yes it does', I replied dejectedly. 'You're the first girl I've deflowered. I didn't know it could hurt so much'. (166F30)

Intercourse is occasionally painful for men, too.

It was not just an erection issue, but intercourse gave me real, physical pain, as if my body wanted to tell me that sex with a woman was unnatural. (54M36)

One female writer believes that the pain of intercourse is the reason for her smouldering grudge against men, and the reason for her interest in women perceived as softness, touching and a yearning for tenderness.

Concluding remarks: childhood experiences and adulthood

Childhood sexual experiences among autobiographies changed greatly from generation to generation, particularly with regard to moral scripts. Binding sex and marriage together and the subsequent requirement that young people should be sexually abstentious was a fairly unconditional script for the patriarchal culture of the oldest generation. Mothers often took it upon themselves to pass down this set of morals to their daughters and to frighten them with being labelled a whore. Attitudes towards dating and even sexual relations had become more liberal in the generation of equalisation. Young people have gradually been given permission to enjoy each other, especially in the context of a steady relationship.

The writings conveyed a masculine subculture that passed down the 'sex is enjoyable' script from one generation to the next in the form of 'men's stories.' Through their stories, adult men stimulated the interest of boys toward sexual matters, and emphasized the pleasurable aspects in particular. Girls only told about hearing these stories or lessons incidentally, because mothers did not speak of sex in a similar manner. Usually, girls primarily connected sex with a romantic script without attaching many expectations of pleasure to it. In this respect, however, the youngest generation is moving in the direction of equality. Today, also women use pornography as the most common source of information and reinforce the script of 'a woman who enjoys her sexuality'. Sexual experience has become something to strive for among young women, too, regardless of their dating or relationship status. At the same time, young men appeared to value the emotional side of a stable relationship more and boys' sexual initiation takes less often place with a prostitute or a in a purely sexual relationship.

We mentioned in the previous chapter that the writers of autobiographies were divided into five basic relationship types: monogamous, consecutive, searching, devitalised and parallel relations. Many writers belonged to different types in different life phases. These types are used as a basis for analysis in the next chapter. Here we shortly examine whether certain events in childhood and youth are connected to certain types of sexual lifestyles in adulthood. The primary observation was that various childhood experiences did not have a strong or logical connection to the adult sexual type. The only systematic conclusion drawn was that negative adult reactions to sexual play among children usually caused distress in those people as children, and that in many cases this continued into adult age.

In Finland's quite homogenous society, people in all relationship types had fairly similar experiences in youth. Gender and generation determined the experiences most. However, some events in childhood and youth seemed to have a tendency to be connected to certain adult types. Men who were classified as the parallel relationship type as adults were more likely than others to discuss the sex-related information they acquired, or observations they made in childhood, for example lovemaking situations between adults and animal breeding. Women with parallel relations, on the other hand, often described childhood sexual games and parents' negative reactions to them. These women had been popular among boys and their first experiences of intercourse were good. It would seem that, compared to others, people of the parallel relation type often had a more powerful interest in sex, already developed in childhood, that continued through life. Some women who were later classified as searcher types felt a lot of pressure in youth to get rid of their virginity. They wrote a fair amount about youthful infatuations. Sometimes their own curiosity was in dire conflict with the repressive lessons of their parents. Such people often had difficulties forming the desired relationship with the object of their infatuation – difficulties that could continue into adult life.

Most of the women who experienced first intercourse with their future spouse had consecutive relations as adults. In some cases their first intercourse was a bad or particularly painful experience. These women also generally wrote about parents' lessons concerning sexual abstinence. While this affected the choice of their first sexual partner, later they have deviated from the ideal of monogamous sexual morality and engaged in consecutive relations. Their own feelings and hopes have partially replaced the morality of restraint learned in childhood.

Part II
Sexual Lifestyles in Different Types of Relationships

This part will present the most common types of sexual relationships found in the autobiographies, that is, *monogamy, consecutive relations, searching, devitalised relations* and *parallel relations*. In the Introduction, we have already discussed the general relationship between sexual lifestyle, generations, gender and the stage of the life course. The effects of age or life stages on central aspects of the love story can be summarized as follows: people search for love when they are young and they develop consecutive and parallel relations as they mature. Having only one great love in a lifetime and living in a devitalised union is not related to age when the influence of generation is taken into account.

The main generational difference in the life stories is that people of the generation of sexual restraint describe one great 'eternal' love more often than those who belong to the generations of sexual revolution and gender equalisation. Consecutive and parallel relations are also most common in the generation of sexual revolution. As we shall see, memories of individual experiences both illustrate and subvert these general patterns. In each chapter, we will present examples of this lifestyle by preceding from the oldest generation towards the youngest.

4
Faithful Monogamy – Eternal Love

Western, Judeo-Christian culture has long upheld the ideal of one, life-long love and sexual relationship. In the survey, every second Finn considered marriage without other sexual relations the ideal lifestyle in the current phase of his or her life course. One-third of all men and half of women have also lived accordingly. However, the sexual life entailed by this ideal has become increasingly rare. The change has been particularly great among women. Seventy per cent of the women of the oldest generation live in a monogamous union, while of the middle generation women approximately half and of the youngest generation a full one-third live in a monogamous union. The corresponding figures for men are 41, 36 and 23 per cent.

People who were classified as faithful and monogamous in their primary relationship type make-up close to one-fifth of all the sexual autobiographies. The monogamous authors are approximately of the same age as on average but they are less often working for pay. A large majority of monogamists are married or cohabiting at present and most of them have children. Most of the monogamous women have a regular sexual life and live in a happy couple relationship. Comparatively few of the monogamous persons have had many sexual partners, parallel relations or homosexual feelings or experiences.

Following our definition, the monogamous authors have one important, life-long love in their life, perhaps preceded by a searching phase. In this chapter, we will present three lengthy examples of a monogamous lifestyle. The man in the first story (123M64) is of the generation of sexual restraint and is an exemplary case of a *traditional, religion-based, monogamous lifestyle*. The other two autobiographies represent typical women (106F39 and 40F26) of the generations of sexual revolution and gender equalisation. Both are sexually independent women who *chose the monogamous lifestyle based on reflection,* emphasizing the quality of the current relationship rather than the principle. This does not, of course, exclude the possibility that they might not alter their sexual lifestyle at a later point in life. For example, a new relationship following divorce or widowhood might transfer them to the type of consecutive relations type. In addition to these three main stories, we will briefly examine other sexual autobiographies of the monogamous type.

Marrying one's first love: a 'one-woman man'

The life story we use as our first example was written by a man of the oldest generation, born in 1928. He has had three important women in his life, but has had sexual relations only with his wife. In his text he calls himself a 'one-woman man'. This is why we have placed him in the monogamous type even though his life course has included elements of consecutive, devitalised and parallel relations.

This man was the shy son of a share cropper and his life's work was as a warehouse manager. During the Second World War his mother sent the young teenager to work on a farm in order to help him survive (access to food was more easily guaranteed in the countryside). He learned to plough, sow, operate a horse-drawn harvester, make fences, thresh corn, bale hay, harvest, manure, chap straw, foresting, all kinds of repairs around the farm, help birth animals, geld hogs and butcher animals. The farmer was old and sick and his old wife was so devout that 'the day's toils were finished by praying on our knees'. The man remembers how he, as a young man, used to suffer guilt as a result of masturbation. His sexual awakening occurred when he met the daughter of the house, a woman in her early twenties. The young people did all the farm work and toiled from morning till night. Living a closed-in, monotonous life and spending virtually all their time together, the adult, mature daughter began to view the boy as her equal and invited him to her room.

> We kissed each other endlessly, passionately. The passionate French kisses were new to me. ... The awareness of sex and love flourished in me simultaneously ... . I started to take off her underpants. It was troublesome because at that time there were belts and garters. She did not resist except by saying that I should not make a ruckus, or her mother would come. I was able to extract one leg out of her underpants and was already putting it in when the door opened. It

was the old, devout farm wife, earlier than usual because of the rain
... everything ended there.

The author was forced to leave the farmhouse. He met another woman,
his future wife, at a dance. The wife stayed at home taking care of their
children while they were small and then took a job at a construction
site. The passionate times at the beginning of their relationship gradually became more a matter of routine. The glory of their sex life varied
with changing moods: the children were sick; there were financial problems; and some illness of the spouses themselves – all of which interfered with emotional life. There were arguments too: the couple fought
and threatened each other with divorce and sulked. The man describes
how reconciliation usually was sealed by exultant love making.

In middle age, a change occurred in the sheltered life of the couple.
The wife made a visit to her foreman in the evening. The husband's life
fell apart because he thought he had lost his beloved. The wife continued to visit the foreman every Thursday evening, always returning
home before midnight, and each time, as a result of the emotional
turmoil, they ended up making love. The situation upset the husband
so much that he found it difficult to eat or work. He made mistakes in
the bookkeeping tasks involved in his warehouse job, because his
thoughts were constantly occupied with his life at home. He swore he
would get a divorce once the children were grown. The wife, for her
part, swore that the object of her parallel relationship was unable to
perform sexual intercourse. The husband wondered if the passionate
disposition of his wife was a result of these meetings, or the conflicting
emotions of the spouses. Then, the wife's male friend left town and the
family's life continued as before. The wife's relationship had caused a
rift in the couple's emotional life for years and the man claims that
even now, decades later, they are not able to discuss the matter. Some
years later, the wife was diagnosed with severe vascular disease. The
husband took early retirement in order to become a round-the-clock
nurse. Every night the wife's pains interfered with his sleep as she
shifted around all night asking for assistance.

During all their years together the couple has practiced *coitus interruptus*. In the beginning, there were no birth control pills, and contraception was often not available at all in rural areas. Gradually the man
became so adept at stopping in the middle of the sexual act that both
spouses were fully satisfied, 'assuming my wife has not been lying to
me her whole life'. According to him, his wife did not want him to
wear condoms. In the past 20 years, love making between the spouses

has been sporadic. Now, both are afraid of the sexual act. Embracing and caressing imposes health risks on the wife and during the act itself the husband has to practise caution and restraint.

Another rift has occurred in this long marriage when the husband met a woman during a trip abroad. He fell passionately in love with at first sight. They met later at a dance and were happy 'among all the others in the full dance hall':

> The tender looks and embraces... . An old man, I felt a tremor again, and my legs felt weak when I was near her. My jogging trail goes by her home several kilometres away. We have made a schedule for my route. She will be at the window. For a moment we see each other again. Sometimes when it is dark she meets me on a side road, and after passionate kisses and hurried embraces we both need to rush off. Sometimes when it's already dark I arrange a visit into town in my car at the same time as she does. Those times, we spend a moment together on some side road. These brief moments are tender and dear. The curse of living in a small place torments us with the fear of being found out.

The lovers have decided to be so careful that their spouses will never find out about the relationship. 'We have been able to do that for twelve years. If it ever comes out it will cause pain for four people.' At the moment of writing his text, the author described himself as a physically active person who likes to exercise, ride a bike, go to the sauna and swim. He considers himself a romantic person and longs for love. He likes to look at nude pictures, including the kind that depict the sex act. He considers himself happy, loving two women. Although his fantasies and dreams are directed at the other woman, he looks forward to the few moments his wife wants and is able to make love. He thinks of himself as a *one-woman man* in the sense that he has not made love with anyone but his wife, with the exception of the 'close call' in his youth.

The man of the generation of sexual restraint in our example is resisting the temptation of starting an extramarital sexual relationship because in his life, self-control, fidelity and taking others into consideration are more important than fulfilling sexual desire. He is successful in following the ideal sexual script because he is strongly bound up with the restrained sexual morals of his time.

Of all the men from the generation of sexual restraint who were classified as monogamous, four are currently retired. Three are married and one lives without a steady relationship. By professional status, two are white-collar workers and two are manual workers. The number of children ranges from zero to three. All represent a traditional, religion-based and ascribed monogamy.

One story followed the monogamous marriage-script as a way of keeping the author's desire for young boys at bay. This married teacher (48M55) had some homosexual experiences as a young man and his first sexual intercourse took place in a Hamburg brothel. When he was 23, in the early 1960s, he made the decision to live in a faithful hetero-sexual marriage. He has kept his promise, although he wishes he could have intercourse more often with his wife. This father of two children has worked all his life as a teacher of technical subjects, surrounded by boys toward whom he felt sexual attraction. He tells us that he never acted on this illegal desire. 'The sexual pleasure and charge I feel toward boys shaped my behaviour and emotions in a way that made me want to be close to them as people.' It should be stressed that this confession was written in 1992, before the increase in public awareness about paedophilia that followed the scandals in several European countries in the mid-1990s. This may have made it easier for the author to present his desire for boys as something under control and basically unproblematic, although the reader may disagree with his assessment.

Out of the four monogamous women of the generation of sexual restraint, two are married and two live widowed without a steady rela-tionship. Two are white-collar workers, one is a manual worker and the last is a housewife. The number of children ranges between two and five. Older monogamous women often married young, choosing their first sexual partner as their husband, to whom they have remained faithful. 'We were the first and the only for each other' writes a house-wife with five children who has been married for more than 50 years (117F72). She continues: 'To this day I have not found anyone I want to go to bed with except my own husband.'

One monogamous teacher (2N77) was often infatuated as a young woman, but she did not decide to marry until she was 30. She describes her husband as a good father to the couple's four children, a wonderful and sensitive husband. However, he did not often display affection and remained very attached to his mother. The woman writes: 'I was the only one he was stern to. And still he loved me.' The couple's fondness for each other grew with each passing year. The relationship was complex but basically happy and unconditional. She sees their every-day life as exciting, not grey. Nevertheless, the author wishes that they had discussed things more. Even sex began to flourish quite late in the relationship, after the woman's menopause, when the couple did not have to guard against pregnancy.

All authors of the generation of sexual restraint who represent the traditional relationship type of eternal love insist they made the right choice and are very happy. Notwithstanding temptations, they have lived a life in accordance with the script of the Christian ideal.

Choosing monogamy: a liberated woman

In the second main story of this chapter, a woman of the generation of sexual revolution had a long searching phase during which she had several lovers before settling down in a monogamous relationship. The expression 'a one-man woman' is explicitly contained in her story, in the same way as 'one-woman man' was in the writing of the man above.

Six of the 24 men in the generation of sexual revolution and five out of the 48 women described faithful monogamy. A translator (106F39) born in 1953 described her one great love that was preceded by active searching. The searching phase was followed by a marriage that was a conscious choice, and a life of happiness:

> I now live content as the mother of two boys, together with my husband who is both my best friend and lover. Together we try our best to find private moments for more intimate communication – moments that preserve the warmth between us and remind us that we are still man and woman, which is easy to 'forget' in the midst of long workdays, children's school and kindergarten, football practice and matches, dirty dishes and laundry.

This woman writes how she, after nine relationships that ended for various reasons, learned what kind of man she wanted and, first and foremost, what she did not want. The causes of the break-ups of even her longer relationships lay in questions of everyday co-operation and the gendered division of labour, not in sexual relations proper. In the searching phase the woman hoped to find a man with whom she could share her life and be happy. She remembers wanting to feel experienced and desired, while deep inside knowing she was a 'one-man woman'. The story contains the traces of childhood socialisation. Her mother passed down a clear script as a model for her daughter: 'It was normal to find a loved one, go out, and then get married – in a good, old-fashioned way.' At home this woman was also taught that women were at least equal to men.

The sexual relations of this woman of the generation of sexual revolution were often casual in the searching phase but not without feeling. She writes that she was very fond of her past partners and still thinks of some of them. She feels she has never been in a sexual relationship for just the 'lay', which is said to be what some of her acquaintances did to collect 'points'. While appreciating sexual liberation, this woman emphasizes the importance of the right to say 'no':

> I am a young person of the seventies, I turned twenty in 1973. The time period was greatly influenced by the sexual liberation of the sixties, and sexual modesty was considered really old-fashioned. Cohabiting and open relationships were new concepts and in fashion in Finland, often misconstrued to mean infidelity in both marriage and cohabiting relationships. But individuals had a hard time digesting it, and the result was jealousy, revenge and divorce. In spite of it all, most of my friends were really looking for a steady life partner – myself among them. Only a few would like to try out as many partners as possible.
>
> I would think that I belong to the first generation of women who really know how to say no. …. Listening to the women of previous generations, it often comes out that for most of their life they have sacrificed and suffered. They have not enjoyed their femininity or sexuality, and only few give the impression that they have really longed for their husband's arms. The reason might be either that pleasures were considered a sin and those who showed to the outside world that they were in love were considered foolish, or for various reasons they married a spouse they are no longer satisfied with. Maybe there was no-one better around, maybe they got pregnant and 'had to' marry, and so they have spent the years at the side of the wrong man. No wonder if many have become dissatisfied with their lives, bitter and envious, wishing to deny others their happiness, and trying to find solace in extramarital affairs. All because they did not dare – did not know how or did not have the courage – to decide about their own life. In their defence it should probably be said that because of a lack of birth control, the fear of pregnancy was always present in their lovemaking, which must have often ruined the pleasure. My generation, which began sexual relations when the birth control pill came on the market, has received a gift that older women could not even dream of.

She draws the following conclusions – typical to her generation – concerning education, work, salary and sexual relations:

... if a woman is well-educated, she usually gets a good, well-paid job, meaning she is her own mistress and can make her own choices in men as well as other things. She is not at anybody's mercy or and just fulfilling other people's wishes, living on other people's terms. ... In sexual relations, too, she has the courage to express her own desires and thus she gets as much pleasure as the man.

Let us return to the woman's sexual autobiography. In her mid-twenties, she travelled abroad to study languages. She got a room in a student dormitory, in the same hall where her future husband lived. She noticed how much they had in common and the interest was not one-sided. So they became a couple and still are.

In bed, even after thirteen years, we are a perfect pair, we have compatible dispositions in terms of passion and tenderness. The good result is probably due to practice; we have learned to know each other, each other's wishes and limitations. Even now when I think about my husband, I long to be in his arms, I know how good it feels. At this very point in our lives our only problem is that the opportunities for having sex are much fewer than the desire to do it. As I said at the beginning, there is not always enough time, or strength. Kids require their own time, so does work, and one has to maintain some kind of contact with relatives and friends, to avoid becoming completely crazy. Often at night when the kids have fallen asleep, we are totally wiped out ourselves and feel the pull of sleep. Perhaps in a way that is the reason we still long to be in each other's arms: we really have not had enough of each another yet.

Sometimes when circumstances allow it we like to watch a film together, maybe even an erotic one, which then stirs up our own feelings. We will start caressing each other already during the film, and the evening ends happily first in my, then his, orgasm; we know so well now how to do it right. Every time when he is just about to enter me, I feel so happy – with him.

I have always liked masculine men. There is something so attractive about them. Even now sometimes when I see another man with that special something, it may occur to me to wonder what kind of lover he would be, but I would certainly not put my own marriage on the line for the sake of an affair.

... Thinking about my life, I am happy that I was young in the seventies: the battle for sexual liberation had already been fought, but Aids wasn't a threat yet. I wonder sometimes how it would have affected my life and relationships with men, whether I would have had the courage to walk into so many arms.

The life course of this woman can be seen as a successful actualisation of the norms of the middle generation's sexual script. A fairly long searching phase with many relationships was followed by the discovery of the 'right one', and a happy sex and family life with him. The woman did not see monogamy as the only possible option, but has rather chosen it in a certain life phase as her sexual lifestyle.

Praising fidelity and equality

In addition to the story of the liberated woman above, among the generation of sexual revolution the faithful monogamy relationship type is represented by the stories of six men and four women. All of the men are married and have between one and four children. Three men are white-collar workers, two are workers and one is a stay-at-home father. Earlier we noted that it is usually part of the Finnish sexual script to experience sexual intercourse before marriage. Among the autobiographies of the men of the generation of sexual revolution there are also examples of not carrying out the sex act until the wedding night.

One traditional monogamy story of a middle generation man is written by a father of four (10M, no information on age), with a socially respected position, who like his wife has not had sexual relations with anyone else, either before marriage or later. The first sexual intercourse for both of them occurred on their wedding night ten years ago. The man feels that a working sex life at home is the best antidote to infidelity. The husband adores his wife's legs and 'dream-thighs'. He wants to please his wife and vice versa. The spouses tend to their relationships, for example, by dressing specially for lovemaking.

Another example of someone whose timing of starting sexual life deviates from the norm of starting sexual intercourse before getting married is a faithful, monogamous man (70M40) in a blue-collar job. He never touched a girl before he met his wife with whom he had his first sexual intercourse on their wedding night at the age of 23. Nowadays, the wife has lesbian relationships and the husband has found a friend at work – a 'little sister'. His primary sexual lifestyle was nevertheless classified as traditionally monogamous.

Contrary to the male examples above, the following three men had a fairly wild, experimental youth before moving on to choice-based

monogamy. They also have special sexual experiences and inclinations. A retired computer operator (173M46) was raped by his boss at
age 15. As a youth he had short relationships with girls, followed by
numerous partners, and in these relationships there was evidently not
much connection between sex and feelings of love. The man got
married at 31 after a three-year relationship. Today, love and sex are in
harmony in the marriage of this man whose hobbies include nudism.
'There is no need to think about having flings.' For health reasons the
couple cannot have intercourse, but the man writes that in spite of the
fact that he has not been able to have a 'normal sex life', he feels it is
full and versatile.

A male chauffeur (44M53) has been an exhibitionist, and has had
homosexual relationships and one-night stands. After getting married,
this father of two had been faithful for 25 years. His wife has had parallel relationships, and the husband has watched her having intercourse
with her lovers and encouraged his wife to maintain outside relationships. He is partially impotent and describes himself as 'deviant but
not dangerous'.

One man, a trade consultant (122M44) had all kinds of sexual affairs
as an exchange student in the USA and as a high-school student in
Finland, when in his summer job and in organisational activities. Her
recalls how he, as an exchange student, became involved in an
awkward situation when the daughter of the host family tried to persuade him to have sexual intercourse with him through all means
available. He was able to fend off the attempts of the girl who was on
medication. The man got married after graduating from university and
had two children. Once in a while he lived apart from his family in a
rural area where there were plenty of divorced, sexually willing
women, but this representative of traditional monogamy has not had
other sexual relations while married. The 20-year marriage has begun
to flourish especially after his recent heart surgery. 'Sex twice a week
keeps me happy.'

As we can see, not all examples conform to the standard vision of
calm monogamy. Most of these examples emphasize their happy
marital union to which their fidelity has contributed. Some did not
begin having sexual intercourse until their wedding night. Others had
a colourful youth. It is noteworthy that many monogamous men of
the generation of sexual revolution want to write about their experiences of rape, homosexual relations, exhibitionism and impotence. In
the stories of monogamous women of the middle generation, which

will be discussed next, the women speak of mental problems and of being a victim of incest.

The five middle-aged monogamous women are married, and have from two to four children. Their occupations are: an engineer, a translator, an artist, an entrepreneur and a family daycare worker. The artist (161F50) had many infatuations in her youth. She met a beautiful minister, whom she later married as a virgin. This devout mother of several children gives the impression of being impulsive, she takes psychopharmaceutical drugs and goes to therapy. Her minister husband wishes that she would behave with more restraint:

> I had a small crisis with my husband recently, and I don't know whether my subconscious is still processing it. I am not allowed to give kisses to men anymore. I have been in the habit of kissing a couple of my best friends on the cheek, and my husband has accepted it. 'As long as you don't kiss them on the mouth', he would say. Now for some reason he has begun to think that even a kiss on the cheek gives a sexual charge to a man, and he wants me to refrain from kissing other men. I see that behind this is his feeling of having an exclusive right to me, and in this sense I feel that he cares about me. As the result of an inner struggle, after thinking about whether I would be losing my right to myself, I said to him: 'I can stop the kissing.'
>
> In my husband, I face someone who is stronger. He is the patriarchal head of the family. Often I rebel, but deep inside I feel a satisfaction in being able to look up to him. He is safe, caring and tender. We have no secrets from each other. Sometimes it hurts, but we both feel it is so valuable that we do not want to give it up. Is this why I can lie on top of my husband, wide open, and feel a divine peace?

In addition to a loving commitment, the woman also has a love of freedom. She liked it when her husband finally said: 'I don't want to put reins on you.' Her story oscillates between descriptions of her submission to his jealousy and other demands, while stressing her own independence.

Women placed in the category of traditional monogamy have sometimes had infatuations outside of the marriage, but like the entrepreneur (161F50), they have dismissed them resolutely. This woman married into a poor household and gradually fell in love with her husband. The couple's sex life went well and they had three children. In middle age the woman fell intensely in love with an officer 'who messed up my patterns'. Nevertheless, she holds on bravely to marital fidelity: 'I am not going to go with him to bed and ruin this beautiful thing. My husband loves me both during the day and at night.'

In addition to flirtation and infatuations, the stories of the middle generation monogamous women reveal even physical parallel relationships. But since they remained very brief, we have placed the stories in the 'eternal love' category. A family daycare worker (95F43) became engaged after she found out that she was pregnant with her first born. The relationship between the spouses was at a breaking point at times, when she committed adultery. But the husband was understanding and the wife's brief escapades ceased. Nowadays she considers her husband, 'traipsing about in his worn underpants', one hundred per cent more erotic than the 'trapeze artists of Club Erotica'.

Sexual problems in childhood and youth do not necessarily translate into marital problems in adulthood. Even fighting can be part of a happy life with one's great love. A female engineer (59N40) who was the victim of incest and sexual abuse says: 'We enjoy being together, we have matured into a passionate love. My husband is an infinitely intelligent human being. We live a happy life, including our fights.'

To summarize, some monogamous women of the middle generation described – unlike the oldest generation – having had casual relations or intense infatuations during their marriage. Because of understanding husbands, these incidents did not lead to a deeper crisis. Without exception, the women emphasize the deep love they feel for their husband. Most of the women of the generation of sexual revolution represent the traditional monogamy type, where one holds onto one's spouse even though feelings and even acts of love are sometimes directed at other people.

Collecting experiences before settling down

Our third main story about monogamy is written by a woman (40F26) of the generation of gender equalisation. In this young generation, none of the 11 men, but nine out of the 48 women, talk about a one-and-only love. Four out of the nine faithful, monogamous women of the young generation have children. Of these women three are stay-at-home mothers and one is in a mental hospital. Three out of the five childless women are in a marital or consensual union and two are living apart together. Only five of the women in this group mentioned an occupation: a teacher, a receptionist, a typist, a barber/hairdresser and a student.

In the following story of monogamy, a long search leads to a happy marital relationship. It resembles the chosen monogamy of the woman of the middle generation related above, but this author writes much more extensively about her sexual relationships in childhood and youth. The author remembers having passionate moments with her girlfriends. 'We did not really think of ourselves as lesbian even though we would caress and even kiss each other. Surprisingly, boys too thought our interest in each other was only beautiful.' For this woman, the most titillating sexual experience was being with two boys at once. She has twice found herself in a situation where she is the only female of the evening in the company of daring men.

> Both times everything began under the guise of play and ended totally wonderfully. I believe that twice I have given two men an experience they will not forget quickly, and even if they did, I have something to look back on when I'm an old lady.

But after meeting her current husband she 'dumped adventures into the rubbish'. After just a few dates she knew the man was 'her other half'. The man did not immediately rush to 'eat out of her hand' as she was used to men doing, so she had to work to get him to believe that he really was interested in her.

> When I finally got him in bed and tried ... to dazzle him, I was told I was NICE!!! It was absolute torture to have to prove to him on all possible levels that I was the only one for him. This trial took half a year and during that time my moods fluctuated between jubilation and despair almost daily. When I had finally passed all his tests and he revealed that I had all along been the fulfilment of his dreams, I could have strangled him. I had been so scared that he would not recognize his other half but would keep looking.

The couple dated for many years, lived together and were married two years ago. They have a baby and 'there will probably be more in the future'. Their life is happy, 'the troubles are small and are mostly connected with use of money'. They talk things through. He is a regular 'household psychiatrist'.

> He is probably the first and last creature in the world, in addition to our children, whom I can honestly say I love totally. My husband is a skilful lover, he has wanted to learn everything about me and knows how to caress and make love to me in such a way that sometimes I feel like I could die. With him, everything is easy, exciting and fun. I think it is wonderful when he becomes wildly excited from just touching. For his sake I want to be beautiful, courageous and anything at all. ... My husband is the best thing I have ever encountered. He makes the everyday seem like a feast, in bed too.

According to this author, her attitude towards sexual matters has been mainly influenced by a colourful life, which is a result of a bottomless thirst for experiences and the search for everything possible. She hopes she can offer support and safety when her own children set off on their adventures. She explicitly rejects the morality of restraint and does not wish to adopt the role of a moral guardian.

Another woman, a housewife with two children (82F30), remembered being the victim of incest by a male relative as a child. This woman who describes herself as 'Emily of New Moon' had her first sexual intercourse with an older doctor who was a drunkard; the event has remained in her mind as some 'dry poking'. She got married at 23, to a religious man who, she describes as a 'natural lover'. Neither spouse has had parallel relations, but the woman is drawn to her supervisor at work. 'Perhaps we will meet as widows.' This example contains two themes already familiar from the stories of the generation of sexual revolution: recovering from difficult experiences as a child and feelings of attraction toward others than just one's husband.

Women of the youngest generation have often made strenuous efforts in order to lose their virginity well before getting married. This woman, a stay-at-home mother of four (120F30), had her first sexual intercourse with a skilful, older man. She describes how he kissed, licked and used his fingers to get her ready for him and made sure that she climaxed too. This way, she says she learned to enjoy the sexual act. During her marriage she has had intercourse only with her husband.

> Then I met my husband, a policeman several years my senior. There were plenty of doubters. People talked about the years that separated us, how they could divide us, create barriers. But we didn't care about that and found happiness. Now, ten years later, we can say that we have succeeded where so many fail these days. ... We

have equality in the household, there are no men's or women's jobs, everyone does what they can. That's also where a happy sex life begins. It can't exist if the other person is angry, disappointed, or unhappy. It starts from me standing by the stove mixing a sauce, and my husband coming up from behind me and kissing my neck, telling me how beautiful I am, standing there with a ladle in my hand. It's about telling the other person that you love him, that this person is the warmest, softest, sweetest, wildest, etc. Whatever good thing you can think of to say about the other helps create the foundation for a happy sex life. Friendliness is something that always comes back to you, and that only multiplies itself if you overuse it.

The couple uses sexual words to cherish each other:

Even though the person remains the same, his or her thoughts, feelings and actions change. Words, for example, and their meanings. In the beginning always when we made love, there were words of endearment such as 'pussy', 'birdie', 'troll', 'tool', 'pole', 'pleasure buttons'... . These days, we sometimes make love very slowly, tenderly, in candle light. Most of the time we hump, sometimes we even fuck. The first time my husband said: 'Let me fuck your pussy', it was like someone threw cold water in my face. It sounded really lewd and exciting. Now it feels totally natural to talk about pussy, cock... . Although only when it is just the two of us; when we talk with the kids, we use words like 'vee' and pee-pee...

Everyday routine has not invaded this couple's relationship:

There has always been a small child sleeping in our bedroom, and we have been exiled to one place and the other to have sex. We have screwed against the kitchen sink, on the dining table, on the living room sofa, in a chair, on the carpet. We have locked ourselves in the bathroom in the middle of the day, we have been down at the beach near our house in the middle of the night, on the jetty, in the sauna, or we have driven the car into the woods and pushed back the seat backs. Now when we finally have our own room, we are enjoying the bed....

I have been pregnant six times. One pregnancy ended in a miscarriage. One was an ectopic pregnancy. I have been so fertile that I got pregnant in spite of the contraception. That is why I chose to be sterilised. Since last autumn, we have only had sex for the sake of enjoyment.

The story of this woman who lives in the traditional, monogamous relationship, clearly shows how the young generation strives for pleasure also in a steady relationship. The sexual scripts have become more positive and emphasize pleasure, inventiveness and even sexual hedonism. The women in both the middle and young generation often emphasize the importance of gender equality and shared household tasks for the relationship as a whole and also for sexuality.

A married student with no children (42F23) had three sexual relationships before marriage. The first longer relationship is described as 'straight out of a daydream'. The partner 'got me to want him. With other people I haven't been able to reach such a wonderful state.' After that, she was engaged. The engagement was broken off when she became jealous of the man's outside relationships. Partner number three was a more experienced boy with whom the author began to have orgasms. Her main, strong emotional bond began when she was hitchhiking and was picked up by her present husband. He grew up in a permissive family, and the woman writes that she has consequently been freed of her earlier inhibitions and is able to enjoy sex.

The importance of fidelity is being emphasized in the generation of gender equalisation as well, even to a greater extent than in the generation of sexual revolution (Haavio-Mannila *et al.*, 1996). A childless hairdresser (96F20) who lives in a consensual union, began a frightening cycle when she was 13. 'A new guy every weekend, and the courage came from beer and liquor.' After the kissing phase, at the age of 15, she selected a partner for intercourse. As the sex act was painful and caused feelings of shame, she began to avoid close relationships. She fell in love with her future husband some years later. Now, when sex was accompanied by love, it became perfect. The woman sometimes dreams of an illicit relationship, but 'is not one of those people who deceive their partner'. Another woman, a typist living in a living-apart-together relationship with no children (43F26) wants to give her partner all of her love and passion and her whole heart, 'but only as long as she gets to be his only one'.

A woman who has been in a relationship with one man for seven years (69F22) seems a bit worried about having had no other sexual relationships:

I am not speaking with the voice of a lot of experience, because he was my first and only. ... I often feel like I am odd, because I don't crave a lot of experiences like other people of my age. But I don't want anyone else, and I guess you can't compare these things, although I suppose it is a kind of yardstick and says something about people's behaviour. People scrape up a lot of experiences, even though to me it is a question of quality, not quantity.

I'm in many ways privileged and lucky because I met the right and suitable person for me when I was only 15, and being able to avoid all kinds of experimenting.

This story shows how it has become part of the sexual script of the women of the generation of equalisation to acquire many different experiences. Someone who has only had one partner feels like an outsider.

The following story of a receptionist in a consensual union with no children (162F22) contains particulars that have to do with the sexual lifestyle of the youngest generation.

He was a nice good man, and he could not tolerate my loose ways. … He never pressured me to have intercourse with him, because he knew I was still a virgin. He was able to wait, but I was not. …Why could I not ask my boyfriend to help me out, when I wanted to lose my virginity?

On midsummer's night, this woman found herself in a tent in bloody sheets. Because she was intoxicated, she hardly remembers any of what happened. When her boyfriend heard about it, he left her immediately. That was the beginning of a phase of wild sexual life. 'One-night stands came and went, there was nothing beautiful to remember. … I felt more soiled than happy.' The author also experimented with different sexual techniques. On a trip she performed fellatio for the first time. After that she has avoided oral sex. By her 18th birthday she had not experienced pleasure during sex. She did not know much about her partners, perhaps their first and last names and sometimes their age.

But she writes that she then made another attempt with the object of her first love and realized she had missed him. The relationship took an unexpected turn:

I was happy again, I had a serious relationship, I was working, I was in love, and it was real love this time. The only thing that we both neglected to notice in the newness of our excitement was birth control. I realised I was pregnant. … But together we decided that I would have an abortion; it was not the right time to have children.

The author got engaged, but as the relationship continued, some sexual problems surfaced.

> ... (his) desire waned and mine, on the contrary, increased. We argued a lot about me initiating sex and wanting to make love when he didn't. He just was not into it at that moment. Sometimes months, often a couple weeks more than a month, would pass without lovemaking. I was really depressed and blamed myself for him not wanting me. I thought I was unattractive, even though he tried many times to tell me that his lack of desire had nothing to do with me, he could not help it that he didn't want to have sex, he didn't know the reason. I had learned to enjoy my sexuality and it had taken some time before I was able to show myself naked in front of my husband. ... We made love when he felt like it, perhaps every two or three weeks, until he reached orgasm, usually about five or ten minutes after he had entered me. We hardly did foreplay anymore, just kissed a little, and he usually put his finger inside me and after that he usually entered me. I didn't really get anything out of lovemaking, and often cried myself to sleep after sex. I secretly dreamed of something better, and masturbated myself to sleep at night and had amazing orgasms using my own hand. We were able to talk about our problem and I told him that I often masturbated before going to sleep and often during the day too, whenever the situation presented itself.
>
> I often wore garters and sexy nighties to get him excited, and was frequently disappointed to hear that he was tired or not in the mood. I suspected another woman, but I knew that there was no-one else, he was a one-woman man. I secretly read sex magazines and watched porn films. Sometimes I was able to get him to watch with me and sometimes we made love afterwards, but he seemed to not be interested in sex in any way, shape or form. I had wet dreams about other men, sometimes they were his friends, and in the morning I would wake up and wonder if it was true, but luckily it had just been a dream. I even thought about divorcing him, but I loved him way too much in spite of everything. I do have to admit that I would not have had the courage to do it. We were already living together and were otherwise happy. But every night I wondered if I dare propose we make love, if I dare initiate it; what if he feels awkward and embarrassed, having to say no once again.

The woman thinks she will continue her life as it is. She does not want to lose her security and the feelings of love, or be a one-night stand for other men just because she wants to make love more often than her husband. 'Perhaps we will get married in a couple of years and have children, perhaps our passion will increase as we get older. It's good to live in hope.' This woman clearly represents reflective monogamy.

Her story contains many turning points and causes for crisis in the sexual life course: the incompatibility of the partners' personalities and sexual desires, infidelity, abandonment, unexpected pregnancy and abortion. But where there is a foundation of feelings of security and true love, this couple which deviates from the norm in sexual roles (the woman is active, the man is passive) still no doubt belongs in the one great love type: the woman has chosen her sexual life course.

From traditional to chosen monogamy

The tellers of the monogamy narratives are average citizens with regard to both gender and age. Their social status and education level is fairly modest, but these stories are also written by highly educated, independent women. Many monogamous people have children and they have a regular sex life and live in a happy couple relationship. However, some monogamy stories contain dramatic turning points such as incest, sexual violence, exhibitionism, homosexual experiences, unexpected pregnancies, abortions, infidelity, abandonment and mental problems. Today, sexual pleasure and orgasm are considered as important in the context of a steady, long-term, faithful relationship. It has become part of a generally accepted sexual script, according to which a marital union exists for other reasons besides just procreation.

Maintaining a monogamous relationship is not always easy. Many monogamous people's stories tell of conquering a temptation to have extramarital relations. Some have had temporary, spiritually meaningless infidelities that have been quickly forgiven by the spouse and others have had platonic love relationships. Some monogamous people have drawn strength from religion as they strive to be faithful.

There are clear differences between generations in terms of the difference between what is the script of one great love and the reality. Authors of the oldest generation often married their first sexual partner. Some monogamous persons of the generations of sexual revolution and equalisation had a wild and fairly long searching phase, after which they settled with 'the right one' following a period of reflection. Among the youngest generation, the ideal of monogamy appears to be even stronger than among the generation of sexual revolution. It means putting a stop to the adventures of the searching phase.

There were two main types of implemented, 'successful' monogamous lifestyles. We can called them *traditional monogamy* and *reflective or chosen monogamy*. The first type is based on tradition and often includes religious prescriptions. Monogamy is an evident, unquestioned ideal, that should be upheld even when the relationship is not completely satisfactory. There are also distinct boundaries between fidelity and infidelity: an emotionally intense relationship that does not include sexual intercourse may be permitted. This traditional type was here exemplified by the life story of the 64-year-old man at the beginning of this chapter. This type of monogamy is socially more common in rural areas and in the lower social strata. By contrast, the two main female life stories presented here are examples of monogamy as a chosen lifestyle, where it was preceded by many sexual adventures and lifestyle experiments.

Chosen or reflective monogamy is motivated by the high quality of the current relationship, which appears to be more important than the principle itself. We might ask ourselves how this type reacts if the relationship deteriorates. For instance, if violence or deceit occurs, would it lead to a divorce? A new infatuation experienced by one of the spouses would also put the current monogamous lifestyle into question. In chosen monogamy, it is not always clear where the boundaries of fidelity are, and even a platonic but very intense emotional outside relationship could pose a major threat to marriage. This second type of monogamy is perceived as a free choice. However, we should remember that monogamy is still culturally the most valued lifestyle. 'Choosing' heterosexual monogamy is socially much easier than it would be to choose, for instance, a bisexual ménage-à-trois.

5
Consecutive Relations

In consecutive relations, the second relationship type, serial loves follow another. They may take the form of falling in love, a dating relationship, cohabitation or marriage. The stories about consecutive relations were often characterized by unhappy love, abandonment, disappointments and breakups. Discriminant analysis confirms the picture: those who have consecutive relations have experienced numerous loves, cohabitations and marriages as well as divorces. Consecutive relations were more often found in women's autobiographies – nearly one-third of the female authors wrote about them. Only one out of six stories in the men's autobiographies belonged in this category. The number of consecutive relations increased from youth through middle age and on to old age, because as the years accumulate, there has been enough time to divorce and remarry.

The authors of love stories that centre on consecutive relations do not differ from the other authors in terms of age, employment status or having children. A significant number of the storytellers in this type have divorced and are cohabiting or have some kind of steady relationship without being married. This is partly because widowed and divorced people often cohabit or maintain a living-apart-together relationship, for example, for economic reasons (such as preventing their children of previous relationships from losing their inheritance). The regularity of intercourse and happiness of the couple relationship is in the average range. The consecutive lovers have obviously had more lifetime sexual partners and parallel relations than monogamists, but many fewer than those people belonging to the parallel relationship type.

A story of serial disappointments

In the autobiographies of the oldest generation, consecutive relations have often occurred because of special circumstances. The narrators had often been aiming at a traditional monogamous marriage, but unhappy love or outside influences ended the first relationship. These stories also pictured a love life that is exceptionally rich for the genera-tion of sexual restraint, exemplified by various descriptions of versatile sexual positions, oral sex and female masturbation.

Out of the 18 stories by men in the oldest generation, only one, the text of a retired white-collar worker (22M69), was primarily classified as having had consecutive relations as his sexual lifestyle. This writer had lived in a traditional, monogamous marital relationship for a long time. He describes his younger self as incapable and shy. At age 24 he fell in love and married. His wife did not love him, even though she was willing to marry him.

> Things went well in the sack and that was the only thing that my wife was satisfied with, although she did not usually have orgasm during usual intercourse, but needed clitoral stimulation.

In middle age, the man began to go to public dances organized around the country by restaurants and organizations. Women usually go to these dances in women's groups, while men go with other men or alone; spouses are usually not brought along. This man writes that his wife did not like dances and did not want to go along. At the dances, the man fell in love, but also this love was unhappy. Nevertheless, the man was faithful to his wife for 40 years, although he writes that he sometimes was very close to being unfaithful. As the couple got older, the man was exasperated as his wife also complained during inter-course – the only part of him she had been satisfied with earlier.

> I stopped getting hard-ons, or rather, I went soft in the middle of intercourse, when instead of words of love, the argument would just continue. I brought it up with her, but she said that men are emotion-ally uninvolved in sex. If the man is in good shape, the sex is going to work and what the woman says has nothing to do with it. Because I had become impotent, she moved me into the other bedroom.

As we see, this exchange presents quite a laughable twist of the norma-tive scripts: as men are often claimed to be more instrumental in their sexual relations than women, the wife supposedly used this as an argument against her husband – 'shut up, you are not supposed to have emotions during sex anyway'! Shortly afterwards a family from abroad stay with them for a couple of nights and he had sex with the wife of the guest family. According to the man, his own wife was so convinced of his impotence that she did not believe her own eyes. 'I was careless and the sheets were stained when my wife came home. ... [My wife's comment was that] you would think someone had had sex on your bed if I didn't know that you're impotent.'

After this incident, the man began to have temporary extramarital relations, including with some prostitutes in Warsaw.

The couple were divorced after 42 years of marriage. After that, the author has had numerous consecutive relations with women, which he has sought by different means, including newspaper classified advertisements. He continues to long for his second great love, who has rejected him.

> When I loved her, I often also imagined a night of love with her, how wonderful it would be. Because I couldn't have it, I also lost my desire for other women. When I realized my love for her had died, I felt joy in my freedom, not being shackled by love anymore. Still, when I heard two weeks ago that she had gone loganberry-picking with a married man I know, who smokes, is small, and a couple of years older than I, and that she had spent the night with him at the cabin of a mutual acquaintance of ours, I still felt bitter, which I also expressed to her. 'That is nobody else's business', was her comment.

At the time of writing, the man says his life is dominated by a woman who would like to keep him all to herself. But the man also knows other women who would like to get better acquainted and start a relationship with him. But he has a dream:

> I would like to place this advertisement in the local newspaper: 'An 85-year-old man got married and had children in America. Is that possible for a 70-year-old man in [a Finnish city]?' It is, if you find the right partner, and there is something of the great adventure about it. The future will perhaps show what a shy boy like me has the guts to do.

This man has children from his first marriage, but longs to have more children – one additional reason why he dreams of other, younger women.

Although classified as the consecutive type, this text contains ingredients of many kinds of love: as a young man, this man was a one-woman man who was not loved by his wife. Then, he fell in love with another woman, who would not have him. His middle age was marked by a sentimental, unreciprocated love. As an old man, he ended his devitalised marriage and became a searcher. In this man's rendering story of a long marriage, the feelings and desires of the spouses were in conflict from the very start which eventually led to impotence, divorce and the dream of a new youth, of becoming a father again.

Happy second chances

Out of the 20 stories by women of the generation of sexual restraint, nine describe consecutive sexual relations. The oldest of these was a widowed primary school teacher (164F80) who read her story onto a cassette tape. As a schoolgirl the woman had several infatuations and from her student days she remembers a long, steady relationship with a romantic, dark and fiery 'romance hero'. Later she got engaged and married during the Second World War.[1] The wedding description is minute and sheds light on the special ceremonies adopted in war time:

> Our wedding day was December 4, 1943. A little more lipstick and face powder, and the bride was ready, and the groom was invited to come in. He was a tall and slim sergeant in a neat military uniform, his best one ... . It is a strange place to be, the wedding event. You are standing there, next to each other, cosy and safe, and still you are very tense. A friend recited poems while the coffee was served. As bride and groom, we sat next to each other on a sofa in front of the teacher's desk in the classroom. ...
>
> After the poems, we finally dared to lightly kiss each other. That was not done in the countryside then. It also was not customary to have the bride sing at her own wedding, but I sang ... for the wedding guests ... . [My husband's] war comrade, a goldsmith, had come equipped with a camera, but Sauli had no flash, and we did not have electric lamps yet, so we were left without a wedding picture. The engagement picture is good – so who cares! Now it feels bad that we did not even dance a wedding waltz. We hadn't applied for permission from the police chief. ...
>
> We were all the more in love as a married couple in the short moments we had together, and we enjoyed each other now with no restrictions. There were five of us young people in the sleigh, when

[my husband] went back to the Front again … . The weather was mild, the snow was wet and the young mare was in the reins. We sang the wedding songs again … Everything that came close to a deep feeling, that helped us forget the war for a moment and to stay sane in the midst of it. Peace must come, someday we will live a normal everyday life … it can't go on like this forever? In that hopefulness we embraced the wedding guests, in that faith the most *beloved* sergeant in the Finnish army, left and headed east, saying: 'Life doesn't end here, we'll write!'

We filled a binder with letters as a married couple, and spent just two short holidays together. The last one was a busy, 30-day leave in May, after which you left for the final time, after which I saw you … to the train for the last time, and after it left I realized I was standing alone on the platform, surrounded by emptiness.

The young couple used no contraception, but there were no children. The husband died in 1944 and the young wife mourned him deeply: she decided to maintain the house together with her husband's sister.

In 1946, just before winter, this teacher moved back into the school and while buying furniture, she met her second husband, a widower. (There were at least two other widows in the village who, according to the author, had already tried their best to win him. One offered liquor, a sauna bath and food, while the other would have provided him with a more civilised social circle. There were fewer eligible men who had been to war and returned than there were uncommited women.) Her second, happy marriage lasted 27 years. The couple had three daughters. She tells us that her second husband gave off an erotic vibe that kept their relationship good through old age. The author considers herself lucky for having had three men enrich her life, and for having two honest husbands who were equipped with a sense of humour.

Another story that focused on consecutive relations among the oldest generation is by a widow (165F69), who worked as a painter, housekeeper and office worker in different phases of her life. She took part in the war, doing service near the Front, and dated several men in the army. Many men proposed marriage, but she did not marry until she was almost 30, which in those days was considered late. After the wedding the passion soon faded. The husband could not make her pregnant so they adopted a child. Later the husband wanted a divorce, saying: 'I don't know how to be married.'

I left as if from a strange place, to wander through the world as a poor girl. At that time, single women did not receive support from society, and economic difficulties thwarted my sexual appetite for years. I was used to having sex with my husband and sometimes I missed a real man so much that my head hurt, a man who would caress me and say tender words in my ear like my husband did when we were first dating.

This woman achieved sexual satisfaction through masturbation. Then she had intercourse with a man who turned out to be an alcoholic. She justifies this choice by appealing to sexuality as an animalistic drive, writing that she yielded to him 'when she was in her worst heart'. Later the real love story of her life began.

I was rescued on my way to work. I came to know the most wonderful person in the world, a widower. He had many problems due to his wife's pious coldness towards sexual advances as well as a great difference in age [he was much younger]. During the last ten years of their marriage, the wife did not tolerate any touching and he could not even imagine being unfaithful, even when the passion and the desire were obvious. ...

When we were married, my husband was already retired. Our age difference was almost 10 years. In spite of that, we felt like children playing with each other. We did not need to care about anything else but our own living environment and each other. In the evenings we used to play beautiful musical tapes and dance, and sit cuddling each other in front of the fireplace, especially on sauna nights. We sipped and savoured wine in the evenings. We also travelled abroad. My husband was usually quiet, but we were able to discuss anything. We understood each other well. He regretted not having met me earlier in life. He would have wanted to be my one and only. He was also a very jealous type. I came to notice that, and I gave no reason for suspicion. My husband used somewhat vulgar-sounding language about sex organs in everyday language, but in the context, and tone of voice he used, even they became poetic words and we gave genitals private nicknames. When I was lying on the bed naked (I still have a young girl's figure and breasts) my husband would touch and caress my bare skin, and kiss my nipples. 'Your breasts are like grapefruit halves, beautiful.' ... Everything was harmonious. So my husband said: 'I wish we could live many more years as healthy and as happily as we have always been. After getting to know you, I feel again the vigour of youth and happiness. Now I want to live a very long time.'

Two days after we had taken a sauna bath, I had to take my husband to the hospital, where he remained bedridden for almost half a year. The last three months I stayed day and night by him. It was a difficult time. Even there he sometimes caressed my body and wanted to feel me close to him. I cuddled him lovingly. Even two days before his passing away he wanted to feel me close: 'Put your head under my arm as we always did in the evening at home.' I knelt next to his bed and did as he asked. Then I took his 'little john' into my hand and pressed it tenderly. It was not passion anymore, but tenderness and love, which I hoped to pour into him. ... After he died, and I was alone with him, I kissed his lips which never again would whisper 'my dear wife.' I kissed his 'little john' that had given me so many moments of joy. ...

Now I live only for my memories. When and if I recover and end my mourning I will try to paint and write, as my husband wished. I am a loner and try to prevent myself from becoming totally isolated now, when there is perhaps nobody in my entire future whose shoulder I can safely lean on. I wish that people would not look down upon older people's love relationships, because in old age, love and friendship are really necessary. ... I would so gladly be the shoulder for another good man to lean on. I miss the quiet solace of the farmhouse, which I had to give up; now I live in a townhouse.

After a long searching phase and an unhappy first marriage this woman found an almost perfect marriage. Her memories beautifully reveal how happy sexual life can be in old age.

Solving bedroom tragedies

Just as in the oldest generation, members of the middle generation often describe the failure of the first long-term relationship as an unexpected, shocking and tragic event. But there is increasing evidence of a lifestyle built on serial relationships. Embarking on and leaving relationships is perceived as a necessary part in the search for a relationship that will be both sexually and spiritually satisfying. The beam has been lowered with regard to getting a divorce. In the generation of sexual revolution, psychotherapy also enters the scene to help solve several 'bedroom tragedies'. Sexual counselling is linked to the spread of the new ideal of articulating sexuality: the scripts now favour talking about sexuality, which is seen as one criterion of sexual satisfaction.

Being able to talk about sex is presented as a reason both to resolve and end a relationship.

Of the 24 middle generation men, four were classified as having consecutive relations. The story of an engineer with four children and a rubber boot fetish is extraordinary (113M54). According to this author, his first wife's family sent him to a mental hospital because of his deviant sexual tendency. Pressured by her parents, the wife filed for a divorce. The husband remarried but in his new wife's eyes, he soon became 'a bastard and a villain and a damned shithead'. He reports that he instilled nothing but feelings of disgust and contempt (although his wife evidently still made all the food for him).

> During a couple of weeks at home all I heard were a couple of words: 'It's time to eat' or 'Coffee's ready'. Communication had broken off completely and all feelings disappeared. Before winter last year my wife said she would leave me and that no-one would take me, that I would be alone and that she had heard a prediction that I would have a sudden, bloody end and she would be widowed. My wife's more than outrageous behaviour launched a deep depression in me. I also had many neurological symptoms. One morning, I lost my equilibrium completely when my wicked wife screamed: 'Coffee!' My equilibrium was totally gone for 15 minutes. I also experienced short spells of blackouts, like in epilepsy, but they could not be traced, even with careful examinations. The doctors thought divorce was the only option if I wanted to avoid more serious consequences.

Following the inevitable divorce, the husband experienced a deep depression, and when he was writing his text he had not had any sexual contact in six months. Then he began calling a chat line and paid escort service numbers from his trailer:

> I had reached a comfortable stage with my sexual fantasy and was able to openly talk about the little fooling around with rubber boots. About half of the girls disregarded the matter with sympathetic puzzlement, but the other half got very excited. After one girl heard about it, she met me again on the chat line and said she wanted to do it with me wearing rubber boots. One girl became so excited over my story that the conversation turned purely to sex. We turned each other on so much that judging from the sounds she

was making, she had several orgasms and I had a huge erection and was very close to coming.

Through an advertisement, the man somehow managed, one week before writing his sexual text – to get a Philippino woman to visit him at home. We are not told about whether he paid her to do so. In the man's view, he could not have imagined a more perfect partner to fulfil his sexual wishes. This story is an example of the life histories of men who are disappointed by Finnish women and choose foreign women – often from Asia or former socialist countries – as their partners. They consider them to be more compliant and devoted than Finnish women who are more equality oriented in their partnerships. Due to the breakup of the Soviet Union and the increasing globalisation of domestic work, prostitution and international marriages, Finnish men could easily enter such relationships, from the early 1990s and onwards. They are relationships built on women's economic inequality, which is not to say that they always exclude feelings of love, gratitude or devotion. However, in this text the author makes no effort to discuss the event from the immigrant woman's point of view.

A department head, a father of two and living in a cohabitation partnership (88M39) describes his consecutive relationships as something he and his friends saw as completely 'natural' – as being part of the script of young men of the generation of sexual revolution. These relationships did, however, end because of his premature ejaculation.

Our relationship consisted of night after night of repeated caressing, which ended in releasing. At first, I was satisfied, but gradually the pressures began to grow inside my head. ... The situation was confusing, because mentally I was brave and ready enough for lovemaking only after our caressing had been going on for a long time. But by then I would have already ejaculated. Hence things did not progress. After six months the relationship ended. ... I thought it was natural that at that age girlfriends changed frequently for no particular reason.

The same pattern began to repeat itself with others as well. I would always go out with a new girl ... My own shyness and doubts concerning premature ejaculation prevented me from acquiring actual experiences.

It was a difficult time. I did not talk to anyone about it but mulled over it on my own. My friends thought of me as a stud with women, since I changed women as often as a gypsy swapped horses. If only they had known the reason behind it! My own depression was increased by the tall stories my friends told of their own adventures.

The man was 23 when he met a woman, whom he describes as balanced but at the same time a 'regular student girl' with no surprises. They began going out, and the kisses and the caresses were enough for both of them. While the man completed his army service, the woman moved into his apartment. He stayed with her while he was on leave, but maintained 'a clean record'.

> We were living together, we were engaged, but we did not make love. ... We decided to get married. I liked her, it was not a great love story, but the most important thing was that she did not seem to mind my problem. If she had even noticed it, I had ejaculated a couple of times while we were caressing each other. I understood, however, that our decision would unavoidably lead to the start of a sexual life and the discovery of my secret.
>
> Soon after our wedding I understood that it could not wait any longer. One Saturday night I decided that it had to be dealt with. We drank some wine in the course of the evening and eventually went to bed. I began to caress her and took off her nightgown. At the same time I took off my own clothes. Shyly, she took hold of my stiff member and began to stroke it. With the wisdom of my previous experiences I knew that I would not be able to withstand the caresses for long without ejaculating. So I decided to enter her. I rose on top of her and put my penis inside her. I began to slowly move in and out right away and I could soon feel the familiar throbbing tremors in my loins. I continued going in and out while I was ejaculating and then continued for a little while longer. When my penis began to go limp, I rose off her and rolled onto my side of the bed. We held each other and fell asleep in each other's arms. In the morning we did not talk about it. The first time rapidly established a pattern that was repeated every Saturday. Wine, quick intercourse, silence.

The relationship continued like this for six years. The husband was neither happy nor unhappy, but somewhere in-between. He had pushed the problem aside and lived a seemingly regular life, a façade from which real feeling was missing. The husband began to visit cafés and restaurants and found a woman he became more and more fond of. After their clandestine meetings had been going on for a little less than two months, he told his wife the truth in the sauna.

She was very shocked. She had trusted me and my fidelity blindly and had had no inkling of what I had been doing. Even though I had been faithful to my wife with my new friend, that naturally changed everything. I told her that I was in love with my friend. Life became chaotic after this. We talked about it all the time, went over our own relationship and thought about what to do. Although I finally had the opportunity to talk about my problem, I did not do so. It would not have made things any better, because the problem was a mental one. After a few weeks of chaos I made my decision. On Christmas Day, I packed a bag and left. A jump into the unknown.

Here the story shifts emphasis: the role of the main villain had been attributed to premature ejaculation, but is now seen as 'a mental one', presumably related to lack of open communication more generally. When the man was with his new woman for the first time, the same thing happened that always did:

I came almost immediately and rolled over to my own side. I looked at her and saw her confused, sad face … . We talked about it for a long time and agreed that together we would try to find a solution.

The couple sought family therapy, which revealed that the wife's prior sexual life had not been completely satisfactory either. She did not reach orgasm with men. 'This was not very exceptional at the time', the man remarks. He writes how with the help of therapy both were freed of their sexual problems and healthy self-esteem brought about a confidence in relation to other people. In his story, the man strongly stresses how grateful he is to all those who work to help others solve their sexual problems.

Out of the 48 stories of women of the generation sexual restraint, 16 were classified as focusing on consecutive relations. Compared to the previous generation, women of this generation talk more about purely sexual experiments and needs. Love, sex and dependency are usually interconnected in their stories, but they are experienced as discrete life areas. The examples are rather unhappy and depressing, which is a common characteristic of the stories of consecutive loves of the women of this generation. Men of the middle generation write more about successful sexual emancipation.

The following example is a detailed but quite typical story of women of the generation of sexual revolution. This author (32F43) is a divorced and childless medical assistant, living in a steady relationship. In addition to marriage, she has had one brief and one lengthy cohabitation as well as several short-term relationships. At the moment of writing, the author has been together with her boyfriend for a little over one year. The woman writes that she rejected boys as a young woman. While at the university, she met some boys but because she felt fearful and inferior she could not make love with them. When she was nearly 20, she fell in love with a married classmate, whom she describes as gentle, charming, attentive, artistic – and an alcoholic. The woman calls him 'Cock Number One', because those born in 1945 are cocks in the Chinese horoscope; she came to know several cocks in matters of love.

> I was in love with him and trusted him, so lovemaking could happen – my first intercourse. However, I did not feel actual sensual pleasure, I did not have an orgasm, did not feel pain, but not disappointment either, because I had not expected anything. The disappointment came several months later when the feeling of attraction and love tinged with shame and despair received a blow.

'Cock Number One' became interested in other girls. The woman walked the streets contemplating suicide. She threw herself into one-night stands, which was easy in the student culture of the 1960s, but longed for her first lover. In the course of her summer job she met a nice boy who she dated for two years. Sexually, the relationship was at first warm and natural, but then the author lost interest in him. She writes that she became nervous and restless, experienced side effects from the birth control pills, her studies were not going well and she ended the relationship.

In the context of political activism she met 'Cock Number Two', who then became her husband.

> He was small, nice, intelligent, not handsome, kind of shy in the company of women. We shared political activism, cerebral hobbies and a similar social background. But I realized soon that I was not sufficiently in love with him, because I was sexually more interested in other men.

The author was faithful for a year and a half, until she fell in love with a co-worker, 'Cock Number Three'. He was a womanizer, and as was revealed later, married but led a bachelor's life, went out dancing and also had relationships at work. When his interest in her began to wane, she writes she was 'ready for psychiatric treatment' and got a divorce.

The author describes herself, between 25 and 30 year old, as having an almost compulsive attitude to sex. She constantly became infatuated with new men and felt she had to have sex with anyone for whom she felt sexual desire. She was often drunk and she never had an orgasm during intercourse. This confused, scattered phase following the divorce ended after a relationship she had at work with a foreign man. Again, in connection with her political activism she met another foreign man, 'Cock Number Four', who became her most long-lasting partner.

> We were together seven years. I did not fall in love with him, but I felt warmth, friendship and interest toward him. I like him still, even though our breakup was rather long and painful. Our sex life was initially fairly nice even, but I did not know how to tell him, like I had not told others, what would give me pleasure and excite me sexually, and we did not discuss emotional matters openly and confidentially. He had a habit of sulking and that affected me very oppressively ... . But I would have wanted a child, for the first time in my life, but nothing happened.

Toward the end of the cohabitation the author had two one-night stands. One was a reignited relationship to a scoundrel, the kind whom she had felt a 'near pathological attraction' towards when she was younger. Back then, she had become pregnant by this man, but had an abortion. Later she ended up longing for a child. The second one-night stand was with a foreign sailor, with whom intercourse did not work at all, because he was unaccustomed to using a condom. She was afraid of Aids and did not want to have unsafe sex.

The man she was cohabiting with did not care about these flings, but was jealous of an innocent casual acquaintance, which did not include sex or infatuation. Three months after the breakup, she met a man several years her junior. Then, at a seminar held at a motel, she met a man who was temporarily working in Finland.

> We danced, talked and met a few times after that in the restaurant, at the movies, dancing. He was nice, fat, gentle, attentive – and married. But he was not a Cock. I was not in love with him, was confused by his attentiveness, grateful even. I had not planned on starting a sexual relationship with him, but when we kissed for the first time after all those meetings, a pure sexual desire awakened in

me. Making love with him was something I had never experienced. He kissed and touched me all over, tenderly and passionately, and a kind of natural, physical connection, almost intoxicating, was born between us ... . We met abroad a couple of times, but I began to be bothered and to feel ashamed meeting him clandestinely in some hotel, and I no longer wanted to travel there. He called me almost daily for more than two years, so I think that our relationship was not completely meaningless. He also never lied about being married.

While travelling in the north on holiday the author met yet another man, who lived in a devitalised relationship. She became infatuated with him and suggested they make love. This kind of initiative was not completely unusual in this woman's life, she had done something similar perhaps five or six times. The relationship ended in an embarrassing way for the author – the man's partner found out about it and changed her attitude toward the man: she began to want to make love again and ceased her hostile attitude toward the man. When this two-woman man announced that he could have a relationship with both women, the author ended the relationship, very angry both at herself and the man.

Two months later the woman began a relationship with a married foreigner who was temporarily working where she was employed. 'Cock Number Five' had all the ingredients she had fallen for before, except that he lied and concealed his true motives. The man said that he and his wife had agreed to a divorce, but when, after a year long relationship, the woman demanded to know what to expect when he returned home, it came out that the man had written to his wife and suggested they try to make it work. The man did not enlighten the author of this until he and his wife had already reached an agreement. The relationship had never been sexually satisfying. The man did not touch her or express tenderness unless the author initiated it. Still, she was completely sexually dependent on him and was not interested in other men regardless of the fact that her lover occasionally spent several months at a time in his home country. After the man returned home to his wife, the author describes herself as being completely numb for several months – the woman felt that her 'sexual appetite and genitalia had been amputated'.

Applying both psychotherapeutic and feminist discourse, this woman recognizes a certain pattern in her life: a quick infatuation for a married man, preferably a foreigner, the intense disappointment that follows and a collapse of self-esteem. The disappointment is followed by a longer relationship with a good, reliable man who is in love with her, but toward whom she does not feel the necessary sexual desire. Commitment is difficult for her and she used to think that sexual freedom need not be damaging to her. She now believes that she was afraid that in a more long-term relationship, the fear, hate and envy she feels toward men would be revealed. She points out that her fantasies have included images of prostitutes, queens, nuns and governesses, but not regular mothers and wives. She finds it hard to picture satisfying sex as part of marriage and family life. On the contrary, she considers marriage an institution that degrades and enslaves women, excluding genuine love and togetherness.

In addition to consecutive loves, this story includes 'love for an imaginary person': the woman sees her relationships which contain feelings of hopeless or self-sacrificing love as sexually powerful illusions, whereas more realistic relationships hold no interest for her. She interprets her relationship to sexuality as related to the lousy marriage of her parents and the fact that as a child she was the victim of sexual abuse by an older male relative.

Most stories by women of the middle generation included feelings of love and attachment in the search for consecutive sexual partners. Some women also told of seeking temporary relationships in bars but expressing dissatisfaction with them.

Searching for the right one

The young women of the generation of gender equalisation remove themselves from the ideal of monogamy in their stories of consecutive relationships. They do not have a 'one and only' but find and choose 'the right one' several times. Ten of the 45 younger women wrote mainly about consecutive partnerships.

One academically educated woman (146F33) fell in love at 14 and dated the boy for one year. After that, she had a nine-year relationship that ended at her iniative. She had various relationships, including a quickie marriage to a man from another country, who left her. She married a second time, this time with a man who used cannabis and was completing a work sentence, and had a child with him. The man was jealous and violent. 'It pains me to think that I loved him so much, wanted him, was almost one with him.' After the divorce she has had 'safe sex adventures', for instance with foreign conference acquaintances.

Another woman in this group (116F31), a cultural secretary with no children, has found 'the right one' three times. After her husband died of leukemia eight years ago, she fell in love with a married driving instructor. 'I was in a fever, I wanted him intensely, I lay awake nights and lost weight.' After that, she had a six-month relationship with a 'hare' who proved to be an alcoholic. In this continuum of serial relationships, the relationship with an engaged co-worker is described as the best thing to ever happen to the author. With him she experienced romantic, not just sexual love and the emotion of 'being in love': 'He was always in my thoughts, though latently. I could not imagine everyday life with him.' The man kept his wedding to his fiancée a secret and the author was profoundly disappointed when she learned about it. Now, for six months, she has been in a relationship with a friend and lover whom she met through a newspaper advertisement. They have not yet had sexual relations, but she writes that her 'instincts tell [her] that this is a good man – if not necessarily *the* right one'.

The third young woman whose story belongs to the type of consecutive relations is an attorney (24F30), who has had numerous men, young and old, from youthful experiments and occasional lovers to relationships that lasted for years. The biggest blow came when the man she used to live with was unfaithful. She writes that she sought solace with others, and finally had sex with a man whom she now loves very much and does not want to lose. They are cohabiting and have tried to have a child, without success. The author would also like to have more frequent intercourse – she finds sex satisfying, whenever her partner agrees to it.

Out of the 11 men of the youngest generation, only two were classified as having followed the sexual lifestyle of consecutive relationships. One of them is an office manager without children, living in a consensual relationship (5M25). He was married at 20, in his own words, without knowing what love was. In his view, his wife clung to him because she was even less secure than he was, and he did not want to hurt her. When love disappeared and even sex no longer worked, this man who was initially faithful, began picking up older women through advertisements and at dance restaurants. Eventually, he obtained a divorce. He has been able to maintain friendships with the women with whom he has had sexual relationships:

We went out several times, to the movies, for a beer, and had sex a few times, when her child was spending the night at the father's place. It was a very stress-free and clear-cut arrangement, a kind of therapy for each of us. I liked it very much, even though according to certain old-fashioned moral views it was immoral – to have sex with no deeper meaning! Still, in spite or perhaps exactly because of that, it was sexually a very satisfying 'relationship'. We agreed that as long as we are not sleeping with anyone outside of the arrangement, and as long as it feels good, we will get together every now and then. That is what we did, until each one of us met someone new. We are still good friends, the way I am with pretty much all of my sexual partners. We call each other occasionally and have been to the movies afterwards.

At the moment, the man is living with a woman physician five years his senior, and thinks that 'sex is good'. He writes that, as a matter of fact, he only 'discovered' sex one-and-a-half years ago, saying, 'I'm only at the beginning of the road'.

Another man of the generation of gender equalisation (7M31) with consecutive relations is an engineer with no children. He has not been as lucky as the previous example, writing how, as he gets older, he longs for freedom and closeness in the midst of an 'emotional jungle of physical desires'. His six-year cohabiting relationship cooled off. His argument for ending it was that 'sex seemed like work'. This reflects the youngest generations' increased demands for not only an open and functioning, but rather a rich and thrilling, sex life. He discovered dance restaurants, where women appeared to want less and be more interesting. However, he emphasizes that his relationships have not occurred one right after the other, but that they have been six months or even a year apart. They have ended for various reasons, and at the time of writing the text the author was not seeing anyone. Both young men thus seem to value a comprehensive view of sexuality: many partners is not their criteria, but finding out about sex and also giving purely sexual relationships their due share of emotion.

Consecutive relations as a new everyday morality

The tendency to have consecutive relationships seems to have different meanings for different generations. The proportion of people who have had consecutive relations increases from the young generation to the old, because young people have not yet had as much time as the old to fall in love, marry and divorce. As people age, many change from a searcher to a consecutive (women) or parallel (men) love type. When we look at the relationship types in the youth of different generations

(Table 1.2), we can see that in the younger generation, consecutive relations at a young age are somewhat more common than in youth of the older generation, a large part of whom were searchers at this stage of life. Young people today have the courage to make a commitment at a young age, because they know they can leave the relationship easily. Earlier, divorce was less acceptable. Older writers felt the need to think longer before entering a permanent relationship.

Within the older generation of men, the only story in which consecutive relations were the main type was characterized by 'serial disappointments', while the stories of consecutive relations of the two older women were characterized as 'happy second chances'. In the man's story, a long and miserable marriage began when the couple was very young and ended in divorce as the narrator becomes a searcher and dreams of becoming a father at 70. Each of the two women first had a long searching phase that ended in marriage. When the first husband had died, a life change took place when, at a fairly ripe age, they found 'the man of their life' with whom sex was good and brought much pleasure.

The purest example of consecutive relations seems to be the text of the woman of the middle generation who gets infatuated and disappointed with the 'Cocks' and who, according to her own story, continually jumps back and forth between the scoundrel and the good man. The story is an excellent example of how sexual infatuation can lead to frustration and a longing for a stable life, which then gradually becomes boring, and the cycle continues with excitement and security, alternating at the extremes. Most people are content with a stable, average partner.

The consecutive type women of the generation of gender equalisation have had many short and long-term relationships with men. They came on the heels of one another and sometimes the breakups were deeply painful. At the time of writing their stories some of these women had a steady partner, while others have temporary relationships. Young male writers seem to ponder questions of sexual morality more seriously than men of the preceding generation, who saw sexual freedom as something absolute and relatively simply defined. The younger men have frequently had relatively casual relationships, although they seem to have been serious when entering a relationship and in striving to find a steady partner. For both men and women of the youngest generation, consecutive relations appear as part of the new everyday morality: the dominant sexual script still stipulates one great love, but in practice people know that they are more than likely to search and find the right ones several times.

6
Searching

Searchers are infatuated or fall in love again and again. A searching lifestyle is typical of young people and often ends when they enter a stable relationship. Some stop searching after not finding a partner (and become embittered), and some continue to search for a partner through mid life and old age.

One-fifth of all sexual autobiographies fall primarily into the searching category. One-third of the young generation's stories primarily describe searching, one-eighth of the generation of sexual revolution do so, as does one in ten autobiographies of the generation of restraint. Forty per cent of the the oldest generation and less than one-third of the narrators in the middle and youngest generations were classified primarily as searchers in their youth. The older generation began sexual intercourse later than the younger ones, meaning their searching period was longer.

Only one out of ten in the generation of sexual revolution and 3 per cent of those in the generation of sexual restraint focused on searching when writing about mid life or older age. In the older generation only one in twenty was classified as a searcher in the present life phase. The narrators of the searcher type were on average 35 years old, when the average age in other groups was around 45. The majority of searchers were students; fewer than average were working for pay. The following examples describe three different forms of searching. First, we will look at searching in the youth phase of the life course – a search that ends when entering a steady relationship. Second, we will examine unsuccessful searching, or giving up the search. Finally, we will look at how searching may continue into middle and old age. The brief searching periods in-between committed relationships are not discussed here.

Searching in youth

In Finnish history, there appears to have been two exceptionally unrestrained periods of searching in youth: (1) wartime sexual freedom; and (2) the freedom in sexual culture that came with the 1960s that continued and became stronger in a certain segment of the young generation.

For some men of the oldest generation, the lifestyle of casual sexual relations in youth was sometimes connected to an exceptional situation that did not involve trying to find a steady partner. A man who has retired from his work as a technical drafter (171M71) was in his youth classified as a searcher and later as a parallel type. He describes how in his youth he was able to have intercourse fairly easily because he learned to pick the 'right women'. Most of the time they were 'war widows' who were older than he, or divorcees. During two-week leaves from the Front, one had, according to him, to 'right away find a woman who would put out easily'. The author had decided he would not get married or father children during the war. He could not imagine remaining unwounded, when 'the likelihood of it not happening seemed more and more improbable'.

As a result of wartime evacuations, some men of the generation of sexual restraint were able to have many short-term sexual relationships. The contraceptive method of choice was *coitus interruptus*. A teacher wrote:

> I was good for just about anything or anyone. [In a short time] I had slept with eleven women. Six of them were local, five from my home municipality. With two, it happened just once, with one it was just a night [he had several acts of intercourse during that one night]. (110M70)

Experienced women who knew what to do were in the mind of this man 'the sweetest'. The man had a relationship with a female neighbour, an evacuee with several children, that lasted throughout the autumn. This man brags about having slept with both the widow and all of her three daughters. The mother gets the highest praise: 'I have to say that she had the best wares.' A former driver (155M76) had an active sex life in his youth. An older widow was able to lure him to her bed already at age 13, and at 14, a maid in his grandmother's family was his everyday girlfriend. During military service he had casual sexual relations and contracted syphillis. This man writes that he during his searching phase and after marrying, that he had 'practised fornication' with nearly 50 women.

When soldiers returned to civilian life, there was a possibility for women of the oldest generation to date without it necessarily resulting in a permanent partnership. The following working-class woman was a searcher in youth and later had parallel relations.

> I went to work as maid for a big warlord at a nearby garrison. A romantic phase began, because the war was over and soldiers were returning to civilian life. For a time, they were housed at our garrison. So many infatuations, falling in love, parting and finally mopping up the tears, but no sex. The boys were still nice then and did not insist on going to bed on the first date. After the soldier boys were gone, there was a tall mailman (picked up by a war widow), a sturdy bricklayer, a nimble forester. (101F66)

The nature of searching changed in the middle generation. This time the cultural climate of social experimental change bred promiscuity and manifold sexual relations. In the same way as those of oldest generation had, most youth-time searchers of the middle generation later moved on to another type of love and sexual life. Only one man and two women were classified as searchers both in youth as well as in middle age.

Promiscuous searching is represented by a married, childless organisation secretary of the generation of sexual revolution (144F35). She describes herself as small, bohemian, multiartistic and younger-looking than she really is. There are hints that she has suffered from anorexia. She did not value money or material things, but was well educated and had a comfortable occupation. She has been able to travel a lot. Her basic partnership type would seem to be searching. Though her first experiences were adventures for the sake of adventure, as she became older she began to wish for continuity in her sexual and professional life. Nowadays she is a 'one-man woman', even though her husband comes from a culture that denies women sexual freedom. The author has had numerous boyfriends, and she presents herself as a woman who cannot talk to women and was not interested in 'women's things'; a 'tomboy' who did not even own a dress. Before, she preferred foreign men and had plenty of sexual partners. She found them to be good in bed. Having sex with them 'was like creating art, colours, reaching a space where you had the kind of ecstasy of well-being you could not even achieve with drugs'.

The woman recounts vividly her experiences prior to settling down:

When I was in England, in London, Stratford, Oxford ... . I toured around seeing cultural sights, wandering in pubs and discos. I met some nice boys. Once, in a pub in London I met Chris, who had moved there from Cyprus. He and I went around the city and once we drove his car to a hill where at night you could see all the lights of London. He started caressing me and gradually we began fucking. He did it slow and fast, and for the first time I felt wonderful while fucking. It's impossible to describe the feeling, but later I understood that was my first orgasm. It was a heavenly feeling. If there is anything that made me a woman, it was Chris. Unknowingly. Although, conversely: I could blame him for doing everything so well that I got so much pleasure out of it. I got greedy. I wanted to have orgasms and everything nice and I wanted to give men all kinds of good things.

The English boys taught me how to be 'good' to a man, and I continued to learn in Italy where I travelled after my high school graduation and my job. I had a very wild youth sexually, I screwed and let myself be screwed. I learned quickly what to do to make the man enjoy it too. I was like a little porn star. I didn't even particularly care about applying to university, for instance, because I was not admitted the first time. Instead, I worked and occasionally travelled. I went on Interrail, spent time on a Kibbutz in Israel ... or just toured abroad for the hell of it. There was money because I worked in my home town from time to time, and if I ran out of money, I got some from my father. My father probably didn't always like me slumming about abroad, but on the other hand, he was liberal for his age, knew languages and was unusually modern. He liked it that my practical English, Swedish and German developed, and that I learned French and Italian.

In terms of sex, I have wondered later how I managed to be spared from venereal disease, since I by no means always used a condom even in temporary relations. I was on the pill, but changed it to an IUD because the pill interfered with my menstrual cycle, a change which actually may have been a result of anorexia.

Five years whizzed by, just traversing the world, working occasionally. I returned to my home town and with my father's help bought a small flat. I met a young man and we moved in together. He was lazy and basically drank all the money he made. I threw him out and replaced him with the kitten I had dreamed of having since I was a child. I began to worry about being way past 20 and not having an occupation. I applied to a commercial college and was admitted. I completed a two-year business college degree and lived a secluded life. I felt my classmates were too fancy and I was too bohemian, though I got respect for being the only one in the class with her own apartment and who had travelled so much.

Christmas and summer holidays I spent abroad, studying practical German among other things. I met a foreign man, and we were together for a couple of years, but our marriage foundered because we were lazy about looking into the possibility of getting him a residence and work permit in Finland.

Finally I left that behind, changed boyfriends and got a job in youth services and started working [in my current job]. Men just kind of fell out of the picture. Except J. [her married lover who remains a friend to this day] who visited me regularly. ... Also my foreign friends visited me often.

I have had a lot of sexual experiences and sometimes I would amuse myself by making a list of all the men I had fucked. I was unable to have a steady relationship and I eliminated things like marriage. Sometimes I thought about what's wrong with me: I was old, and other people had husbands and children, while I was a lone wolf living with her cat. I didn't care for bars, because the ones in my home town were boring. I frequently visited Denmark where I had an Iranian friend. Together we had fun in rock discos in Copenhagen and Elsinore. Somehow I was planning a future with him, looked into job prospects in Denmark, but on the other hand, I was afraid of him: [he] was very absolute and uncompromising. On the other hand, he was sweet and nice and a wonderful sexual partner, but sometimes he would grab me by my hair, and I will not allow a man to batter a woman. I also didn't like it that he kept switching jobs and could not settle down. I might still be with him, maybe even living in Denmark, if I hadn't met a man who became my current husband.

When this woman was young, she had 'eliminated' the possibility of marriage, because she had assumed she was a type who would never marry. She wanted to be 'wild and free'. Four years ago she met a foreign man who kept writing, calling and courting her persistently. Three years ago they were married in his home town. According to the author, the couple has everything except a sex life. She thinks that 'he is lousy in bed, repressed and stupid'. At the start of the marriage the narrator had intercourse with a married friend and a couple of artist acquaintances. She never told her husband about this and was not found out, even though the husband's friends warned him about her sexual behaviour. The woman expresses the wish to be buried in the same grave with her husband – die together with him – but before that she would like 'to fuck J., P., B., M. and many others'. She was tested for Aids and was found to be HIV negative. Even though her husband claims she is a nymphomaniac and monitors her other relationships, she thinks that what she has experienced with him is the best life has given her.

A process manager of the middle generation (172M46) had so many frequently changing girlfriends that his friends said: 'Pussy's gone to your head.' The man fell in love, got engaged, joined the army and quarrelled so badly with his bride – who had betrayed him – that they broke off the engagement, because he felt so jealous and abandoned. His problem was that when he was in a relationship with one girl, his thoughts would always be with another. One of his numerous girlfriends became pregnant and he got engaged to her. When the child's mother pressured him to marry her, he refused, preferring to pay child support. He continued to have a large number of temporary relationships, problems with alcohol and even considered suicide. He was married in his mid-twenties after a long searching phase.

Many searchers from the young generation also had had numerous sexual relationships. Love was not a prerequisite for intercourse and a sexual relationship was not expected to lead to marriage. 'Screwing' became more mundane. One female student without a regular relationship (16M25) thinks 'it is not a more extraordinary act than going to the toilet, for example'. This author believes kissing is a more delicate issue than intercourse. One searcher, a student (57F25) presents her sexuality as a biological need. When her previous relationships ended she was in trouble because she could not satisfy her desires. She picked up one-night stands in bars:

> Being accustomed to regular sex, my body would complain of the lonely nights. When I woke up, I was horny for fucking. I was horny at work. The same thing when I was going to sleep. I had to learn a skill I had always considered enormously suspect – scoring one-night sex at a bar.

This woman reported that she had began her sexual life late – she used to be overweight and a 'bookworm'. At some point she began to have temporary relationships, including partner swapping at her folk high school. Now, she has had a steady partner for two years, but living with him, she misses the excitement and mystery of the time when they first met.

Some young women of the searching type had dozens of sexual partners. However, the story of an editor of a local newspaper (151F25) is an extreme example:

> I kept a journal of my weekend adventures, and once I made a list of how many men I'd had sex with. At 19 I got to about 50 – I had more than enough one-night stands. A typical example was J. whom I met at a Peer Gynt concert. ... I was like a rabbit under a snake's spell, I forgot everything and followed him to the house of some of his friends. There was a mattress on the floor. And so we fucked. He was wonderful. ... Wow, it was raunchy. He bit me on the cheek and shoulder. It felt like something.

When the editor was younger, she thought of herself as having two different selves. The good self did her homework and gained top marks, and the bad personality took over at weekends and she turned into 'Cindy' who wore high heels, a miniskirt and lots of jewellery. She occasionally worked as a professional prostitute in the course of ten years, thinking of herself as a nymphomaniac and enjoying the adoration of ugly, fat men. Deep down, she writes, she is a romantic and she believes one should only have sex with people one loves. In the midst of other 'business' she was searching for 'the right one'. She contracted gonorrhea and had two abortions. About four years ago she got married. 'We had both done our experimenting and we found each other good.' Now the problem is the incompatibility of their desires: she would like to have sex every other night, whereas he would be satisfied with once a week.

A wild sexual life is occasionally directly presented (and justified) as a result of social conditioning. One younger generation searcher living in a steady relationship, who also had some parallel relations (78F30), reported she adopted the art students' interpersonal sexual script of constantly switching partners:

> In that circle of art students it was quite common to change partners. If you wanted to possess another person, you were untalented and bourgeois. I learned the correct way. Men came and went. In [a suburb of Helsinki], there were the nosiest old ladies. The window curtains swung back and forth in the apartment buildings when I

sped into the yard on the back of a motorcycle, red wine chapped lips grinning.

The life of this woman was made up of endless searching, experimenting, abandoning, reusing. She picked up people and was picked up herself.

Let us move on to the male searchers of the young generation. One of those men (158M33) acquired experiences as a history student and his then girlfriend permitted him to go to bed with other women. Then, 'fatherhood exploded unpleasantly in [his] face'. He did not want to share his life with the woman and is currently only paying child support. Later, he fell in love deeply with a married woman with whom he had a year-long 'complete relationship'. When she abandoned him, he began to have relationships with other women. As a kind of revenge, he tried to make the partner bond with him, but to remain detached himself; at times, he had up to three partners simultaneously. When he finally married, he was able to remain faithful for six years and the couple had two children. Then – unexpectedly for him – his wife began a parallel relationship. Now he finds it difficult to trust his wife.

Hope abandoned

The sexual autobiographies also contained examples of 'unsuccessful' searching. Some eventually gave up, while others continued, searching into mid life and older age. Two autobiographies by women of the oldest generation, who were classified primarily as searchers, had given up searching. Both appeared to be rather embittered, hated men and even some women.

The first of the two is a library employee (28F57) with no children and no regular sexual relationship. She writes that she would not object to sex, 'but these are such sex-crazed times.' She does not admit to longing for a life partner, unlike most other authors. The other unsuccessful searcher of the oldest generation (26F55) has worked as a wine cashier, an office worker and a tour guide. She says she matured late sexually and did not have intercourse before 30 years of age. It happened with an acquaintance who was significantly older, whom she had up to that point been fond of 'in the regular way'. This woman disapproved of what she perceived to be the habit of doctors to encourage their patients to have sex. According to her, a doctor had told her: 'A proper woman carries condoms, because one never knows when she will meet a man she wants to go to bed with.' The author saw a doctor at age 33 because of a discharge and was prescribed birth control pills. They took care of her gynaecological problem:

> ... and it goes without saying that I lessened my requirements with regard to 'single-use' men. But I would not have just any man even then. In my opinion, the objective of prescribing birth control pills is to encourage women to have sex with men.
>
> I did my best; I went out a lot both at home and abroad. I spent way too much money on drinking in bars. I did not want to use the last resort, I mean personals ads, but what could I do! I replied to a few, to individual men and to ads for pen pals. I was prepared to be treated atrociously. It did not happen right away, but it did later. ... This method helped me find a few men.

As a middle-aged woman she met a younger man with whom she had a relationship for a year. She became pregnant and had an abortion against the man's wishes. According to her, he would gladly have taken care of the child. The man later died because of excessive alcohol use. This woman complains about men. She considers the present single phase of her life the best so far, when 'it is no longer necessary to push one's wares on the job or on a man'. She says she hates men and the sex propaganda which have tried to foist relationships on her even in mature age.

Her story reveals the amount of social pressure that is directed at women who of their own volition or for external reasons do not conform to the expectations related to the sexual life course. Living without sex is still a great challenge to the conceptions of a 'normal life story'.

Continued searching

Finally, we will take a look at people who continued their search at the time of writing the autobiographies. Most of them were young, but there were also some who were middle-aged, or even older. In our material, the prolonged search of older men was often connected with homosexuality.

One 57-year-old man living on a disability pension (133M57) had resorted to prostitutes as a young man and had sex with them in parks and outdoors. He writes about having had sexual problems, including premature ejaculation, and he also had homosexual inclinations. In the course of various therapies he fantasised about relationships with the nurses. He got engaged, but the engagement broke off. Right now he has no love or sex life with the exception of a few temporary relations and masturbation.

Another man of the older generation, whose primary classification is a searcher, is a 55-year-old long-term unemployed worker (159M55). He is divorced and has two adult children. When he was young, he had many kinds of sexual experiences and while married, he had parallel relations, for example in Russia. He now lives in a remote area as a recluse and is a writer. He has a female telephone friend and a male friend with whom he is planning some kind of relationship.

> What is special in my life? To sometimes call my female friend, a woman fourteen years younger than me, once, twice, or three times? To talk to her on the telephone for a moment ... . Then to write her twice a week, a total of about 15–20 pages ... . To receive letters from her?
>
> ... there is also a male friend who is part of my daily life. A 50-year-old alcoholic, unemployed, divorced man, who has become a compulsory nuisance, burden and source of trouble. ... There is no sexual charge between this man and me, I just try to tolerate him because in a way our backgrounds are so similar. ... I call him 'My Love'? Should I legalise my relationship with him when it is legally possible? My girlfriend, however, said don't do it yet, she is there too ...
>
> ... what if I started making overtures toward this male friend, only in the sense that I would then get rid of him? But there are two risk factors. I might be labelled a homosexual here in the country village? Because he is sadistically sharp-witted and -tongued in his mild drunkenness ... Second, I assume our relationship might even become deeper?

Only one of our middle generation men was a searcher in both youth and middle age. This homosexual sadomasochist (54M36) was married for four years. After the divorce he had numerous temporary relations with men and a longer one, but as he himself expresses it, he still continues his search.

> I did not want a divorce. It was a tough experience which took a long time to process. Formally the reason was my wife's infidelity, but the actual reasons went deeper. We never discussed them, because the topic was too sensitive. I was bitter because we had discussed my homosexuality before getting married.

After the divorce I was basically free to pursue my desires, but for some reason I was not ready for it. At 28, I was still confused about my sexuality, which did not seem to fit into any mould. But I was convinced now that a relationship with a woman had been a mistake and its chances of success minimal. My homosexual side was so strong. But at the same time I had doubts as to whether a normal, homosexual relationship would satisfy me.

I met J. in 1988. Before that I'd had many temporary relationships with men. I responded to his advertisement. ... I was unsure about the whole relationship in the beginning. I was ... looking for a sado-masochistic relationship. ... Jorma was a regular homosexual man and the world of S/M was foreign to him. I was in a situation where I sorely missed a more long-term relationship that would also function well sexually.

... Our relationship was good for a long time. We lived together at weekends. We discussed various things, even S/M. He wanted to understand it, but on an emotional level he did not respond. At one point I asked him to include some sadomasochism in our sex life. He seemed to feel awkward but went along with it. This made our sex more lively, but it didn't help really.

Around this time I began seriously to look into S/M literature. I read authors like Marquis de Sade, John Preston and Yukio Mishima. Porn shops in Helsinki had magazines with S/M topics. New studies on the subject were published in the United States, providing support for what I was feeling.

... Perhaps the road would have been easier had I given myself to S/M with more courage. The fact is, my searching has often gone halfway. ... It seems difficult to find sadomasochists who have accepted themselves. ... I want to live as the person I was created to be and express myself according to my abilities. I am 36 years old, but it probably is not too late yet. The search continues.

After this middle generation man we will look at women of the young generation, whose continuing search is illuminated by the story of a 33-year-old professional (149F33). She is living a physically latent phase in her sexual life. In her marriage she experienced a blind, young, passionate and self-sacrificing love, and the spouses had an active sexual life. Later, her extramarital flings at first improved the quality of married sex, but in the end toppled the marriage. A new, secret, unexpected and passionate love made the narrator realize how much her active married sex life was lacking. However, she thought the new relationship of three years operated only on the man's terms, so she ended it. Now she has one-night stands with married and younger men. She, like many others, expresses her longing for a balanced, continuous and safe relationship. A continuing search is exhausting, but the author believes she is mentally ready for a new relationship.

Another woman of the young generation who continues to search (80F23) also is not currently in a steady relationship. She works as an office assistant. She writes about having lusted for a regular man to the point where she could no longer take it, got drunk and picked up any man. The unsatisfactory nights were followed by regret and apathy. She had short relationships abroad and with co-workers. She underlines that the men came to her (in other words, she did not actively seek them out). These relationships did not involve real passion. Now she has decided that there will be 'no more sex without dating'.

Stories about a prolonged searching lifestyle among young men often included violence or commercial sex. Among them was the text of a single man who has worked in various occupations (35M34). He writes that he has long been trying to meet a girl in vain. He feels that women have treated him 'badly' while he has defended long-term relationships and having children. He thinks that girls react negatively to someone like him who is 'collecting experiences'. During ladies' nights at dances no-one has asked him to dance, and when he himself has done the asking, he has been refused. He has found reasonably priced women on the Reberbahn in Hamburg. This man frequents nudist beaches and takes an active interest in pornography.

Another young man with no family who continues to search (1M29) thinks of himself as a quiet, meek type who used to wish in school that the pretty girls in his class would come and sit on either side of him. He has been in love twice and strongly infatuated many times. When he was rebuffed, he sank into a deep depression and received therapy. He appears to have developed into a sexual harasser, who has been in the habit of dancing with women at dance restaurants in order to frighten them and maul them drunkenly. He writes that he has been fined and has received a suspended prison sentence for attempted rape. This man also suffers from severe impotence which has not been helped by therapy.

Like the previous case, this author seems unable to communicate and to suffer from a lack of emotional skills. They do not fit into the modern dominant sexual script where consideration for the partner, along with an emphasis on thrilling sexuality, have increasingly become the requirements for men. Women are harassed by some of these marginal searchers.

Stage of the life course or lifestyle?

Searching appears to take two quite different forms: as an increasingly common and expected stage of the sexual life course; and as a specific lifestyle. Searching in youth includes, on one hand, casual relationships where the intention is to acquire different sexual experiences, and on the other hand, the particular purpose of finding a steady partner. The search in Finnish culture seems to have been especially active and uninhibited in two historical phases: after the Second World War, and in the youth of the middle generation during the sexual revolution. The final part of this chapter is dedicated to the searching of the middle aged and the old who had either given up or continued their searching. Several unsuccessful searchers had become frustrated and embittered.

Casual search-related relationships in youth occurred in each generation. Some authors of the generation of sexual restraint changed partners frequently. During wartime military leave and directly following the war, a period of apparent unbridled sexual life flourished. The sexual license created by war and revolution has also been noted in connection with the French and Russian revolutions, for example. In Soviet Russia the 1920s and 1930s young urbanites were in fact in many ways more radical than the preceding or subsequent generations (Kon 1995). Most of the Finnish wartime searchers, however, were content with a settled lifestyle and many older women married their first sexual partner. In the younger years of the middle generation, sexual liberation became an issue of significance and value. According to one author, 'sexual modesty was old-fashioned in the seventies'. Hence, sexual experiences were sought because 'you didn't get gold stars among your friends for sexual modesty.' Some people of the middle generation had countless sexual partners before settling down in a marital or cohabitation union. Many of them later had parallel relations.

It seems to be part of the sexual script of the young generation that before settling down – which most aim to do – there is experimenting, adventures, relationships and cohabitation with several people simultaneously or consecutively. The 'odd ones' are now those who marry their first partner, as was typical among the generation of sexual restraint, where the lengthy searching phase that was characteristic of that generation was followed by marriage. Searchers of the young generation described their varied experiences of love and sexuality in erotic terms. According to the authors, casual relationships and wild sex sometimes had to do with their own sexuality being particularly potent (several women called themselves nymphomaniacs), or they said that the style of sexual life in their student community, in their travels or at parties had been 'wild and free'. Some authors interpreted multiple relationships in youth as something positive through which they came to understand how different people are. To them, broad experiences in youth were more an advantage than a disadvantage. But some young people, who were still searching, mentioned mental problems and violent behaviour towards women. Such problems may have prevented them from finding a partner.

After searching in youth, other styles of love and sexual relations have usually entered the picture. As was mentioned above, the youth of the generation of sexual restraint contained a long searching phase, and the final sexual lifestyle was formed only later. For the middle and young generation, it was much more possible to choose among several sexual lifestyles in youth than it was for the older generation.

7
Devitalised Union

In the following, we will discuss the fourth partnership type – the devitalised union. It consists of two subtypes both of which were originally based on passion and love. In the first subtype, love has faded but the sexual relationship exists and can even be satisfactory. In the second subtype, the sexual aspect of the relationship is not satisfactory but a close emotional relationship binds the partners together. The core of this relationship type is that the partners remain together, even though the marriage may be just a façade, either emotionally or sexually, or both.

In the sexual stories, the chain of events in the process towards devitalisation of the relationship is often as follows: the author falls in love, gets married and realises he or she has made a mistake, but does not get a divorce. New relationships may come and go or the author has one true love outside the marriage. In most cases, there was a beginning phase during which fidelity was considered important. Extramarital affairs become common among men after the age of 50 and slightly earlier for women. Some of the texts show that devitalised unions are revitalised with the help of parallel relationships, but most of the time that is not the case. If an extramarital relationship is discovered, the repercussions range from quiet acceptance to divorce. A woman living in a devitalised union often focuses on the children, while a man will seek parallel relationships. The reasons for staying together may be property, income, money, pressure from the immediate environment, or simply lethargy, an unwillingness to change and inertia.

The texts that describe a devitalised union make up one-tenth of all our love stories and they are equally distributed among the stories of men and women. Devitalised unions are discussed fairly evenly in the stories of different generations and in the fragments from various phases of the life course, although they are obviously less common in the stories of young people's relationships.

People who live in devitalised unions greatly resemble those living in parallel unions in terms of their demographic and social characteristics (in Table 1.1 they are combined with them). Their gender and age are nearly identical. Writers characterized as belonging to the devitalised relationship type have had less partners and parallel relations than authors belonging to the parallel relationship type and their couple relationship is less happy. Compared with people of the monogamous type, those characterized as living in a devitalised union are more middle class, more likely to work for pay, more likely to live in a city and to have children. They rarely have intercourse and are unhappy and unfaithful in their couple relationship.

'Like a block of wood': men's complaints

In the oldest generation, four of the 18 men's stories and one of the 20 women's stories were classified mainly as stories of a devitalised union. These narratives do not make wonderful reading. One of the overwhelming topics is that the wife's sexual desires are not equal to those of the husband (see also Chapter 9). From men's perspective, intercourse has been too scarce. In only one story has the situation improved with age. The emotional union of the spouses may still be intact, like in the following, typical male story (12M65) about a sexually devitalised union. This bank employee, a father of three children, loves his wife who is his first great love. He describes his wife as lacking interest in sex and for this reason the husband has had relationships on the side. But the emotional bond of the spouses has not completely broken down. In this way, the man represents the subtype of devitalised unions in which sexual life has withered, but other, positive emotional bonds remain and there is something besides indifference and hate that unites the couple.

> In the beginning of our marriage our sexual life was at its most active. My wife was willing and I really had nothing to complain about, but she thought my insatiability was sometimes a nuisance. She was meticulous in caring for our firethorn and always kept our home immaculate. It was clear that she was occasionally exhausted in the evening and just wanted to sleep when I wanted intercourse.
>
> I was insatiable. I wanted to make love with her at all hours, often several times a day. Romance was not always part of these activities,

it was more a question of satisfying a sexual urge. She was willing and perhaps she did not find it that unpleasant.

One of the high points of the man's love life occurred when the wife and her uncle went to a funeral out of town. On the way home they stopped in a restaurant to eat and the uncle treated her to a couple of glasses of Cognac. Unaccustomed to strong liquor, the alcohol went to her head and she was pleasantly tipsy when she got home.

> I think I was in bed reading when she, having already stripped all her clothes off in the hallway, appeared at my side and peeled the blanket off me and told me to take off my pyjama pants. I did as I was told and when I was done, she got astride me, fitted her vagina on the 'saddle horn' and the old horsewoman that she was, began a slow trot, rhythmically easing into it. I could hardly believe it, I thought I was having a marvellous dream.

In general, the man found his wife's passivity in lovemaking surprising. According to his version, the wife was very determined in other matters and would not let others guide her actions. Her passivity, which at times could even feel like submissiveness, did not, however, diminish the man's desire to make love to her, perhaps on the contrary. Part of the time, the man lived in another town and had a casual relationship, for which he felt severe guilt. The wife never knew about the man's occasional extramarital relations, but his relationship with an under age babysitter caused a major crisis. The 'adventure' with the 15-year-old babysitter while sexual but, in the mind of the writer, serious and, therefore, it should not be considered as actual infidelity or adultery. After this, the wife has become more and more reluctant to have sex. She finds it disgusting to read details of lovemaking and sexual techniques and she will switch channel immediately when there is a pornographic movie on television.

As the time of writing his biography, 19 years have elapsed since the occasion when his wife took the author by surprise. After that, he has only had sexual relations with her a few times. According to the husband's story, after the birth of three children, a couple of miscarriages, and the mentally and physically upheaval involved, the wife began to wish that her husband's sexual interest would subside. The physical changes connected with her menopause evidently provided her with the first acceptable reason to refuse intercourse. For her, it was apparently a relief and ending their sexual life did not seem problematic for her, because, according to the story of the husband, she did not experience an actual need for lovemaking.

The narrator interprets his wife's negative outlook toward sexual intercourse to be the result of the strict upbringing she had received in her religious and 'narrow-minded' home. She felt that sex and everything related to it was filthy and sinful and only loose women who were living a life of vice did so for fun. The husband believes that this viewpoint has been the reason that the wife almost never initiated lovemaking. According to him, she never made a sound during intercourse, did not sigh, not to mention exclaiming – that kind of behaviour was perceived by her as part of a sinful life and only to belong to women who cannot control their own conduct. The husband's affair with the 15-year-old babysitter reveals the unequal power relations between the genders. The older man made sexual advances to a young girl (we are not told what she thought about this event), excusing his morally dubious behaviour with his wife's lack of sexual interest.

Another example of a devitalised union is the story of a worker (99M62) who got married at a young age, because 'marriage was the price a man had to pay for sex back then'. (He also presumes that sex was the price paid by a woman for marriage.) With hindsight, he thinks the marriage settled into a rather routine-like state. The couple had children. The man contemplates the essence of sex:

> My own marriage was conflict ridden. It was like two cultures colliding. ... Despite the conflicts I consider my sexual life to have been normal, until my wife went through a premature menopause.
>
> And then ... there began to develop a real family tragedy. The lack of privacy in the apartment building increased the tension and so did the presence of the children. ... My wife and I achieved some kind of understanding [after an episode of infidelity on the husband's part] and we continued our life together. What's best is that I did not become an alcoholic. Our sexual life continued as well. ... it was not so much for the sake of making love, but perhaps to fulfill a biological need.
>
> This wonderful time continued a few years, until religion came back [the wife had earlier been deeply devoted to religion but abandoned her ardent attitude for a while] into the picture. This peculiar spiritual bacterium, which circulates among Finns in the name of various sects, this time it infected my wife. Our 'athletic fests' turned into 'company softball games' that took place once a week and not always even that frequently.

Nearing 60, my needs only kept growing. And it wasn't tempered by my diabetes which was diagnosed unexpectedly. One day I realised my desire was at a peak, but I had no erection. It was as if lightning had struck someone doomed to the electric chair.... When I described the situation to a doctor, I was told, laconically, that the symptom was among those associated with diabetes.

These days, the man lays in a water bed with his 'droopy dick that doesn't even bother to rise to the occasion from its bat hang for pissing'. He makes up for the missing erection by fantasising:

It's more peaceful, almost like a vacation, when my wife helps me, whenever she can spare the time from her hours of devotion and wants to have a moment of sin. The best times I have in my dreams, where I have the most exquisite sex with various women.

A typical narrative told from a woman's perspective is that of a widow with several children (50F81). She became infatuated with a man at work – a poor and handsome boy – and married him. Then the 'flame of love flickered' and the man insulted her by saying: 'You're like a block of wood.' When she was older, sex became more and more abhorrent to her. At just under 60 years of age, the husband became impotent for a while and they began sleeping apart. One time he tried to get into her bed and although she did not resist, she snapped: 'So it's starting again?' 'No, it's not', said the husband and he did not try again. When he died aged 63, the author found a sperm-hardened towel in the attic. 'This kind of marriage may look fine on the outside', she says.

A devitalised union can also be revitalised. An engineer of the generation of sexual restraint (137M70) living in a devitalised union, married while in his thirties. His wife would not agree to have sex for two years. The man was forced to masturbate, or, as he puts it, to 'take the semen cells artificially'. Later, the couple had four children. Today the wife agrees to have sex up to three times a week and he writes that he is living the happiest days of his life.

Women's revenge and resignation

Nine stories of the 48 women of the generation of sexual revolution were primarily classified to the type of devitalised unions. All authors

are white-collar professionals: teachers, care professionals or adminis-
trative workers. Four writers are in a marriage or cohabitation relationship, three have a steady relationship and two have no permanent
sexual relationship at that time.

One of the typical stories for this group is written by a married
teacher with two children (114F39). She tells of actively searching for a
husband when she was young, afraid that she would end up alone. She
had sexual experiments that led to an unwanted pregnancy and an
abortion. In her next relationship the condom failed, she became pregnant and married her partner. Soon enough, married life deteriorated.
The author had a relationship with her boss, who would have liked to
get divorced and move in together with her. However, the writer ended
the relationship. When the author was 36, she began to be interested
in sex again. Once again, we see the impact of sexual therapy on this
generation: she visited a marriage counsellor with her husband and
purchased a vibrator. The ideal of sexual openness and of special efforts
to keep the relationship alive, also enters these memoirs: in the
author's own words, the spouses had not 'tended' to their relationship
enough before; the man had sought solace in alcohol and she had been
whiny. 'Now we can talk about things', she writes.

Another middle-aged woman in a devitalised union is a married
business owner with two children (51F46). She married young against
her parents' wishes. 'The result was a life-long tragedy.' This author
describes several extramarital relations, treating her husband badly,
while enjoying the benefits of the liberated spirit of the times:

> I was free because I was no longer under my mother's tyranny.
> Without feeling any kind of guilt, I, always the guilty one, saw it as
> my natural right to seek revenge for a lost youth. The next five years
> were a veritable real-life hospital soap opera. In addition to my studies
> … . I had begun to work as a secretary at a hospital. I was intelligent
> and bright. I also had an external radiance that attracted men. In
> those times, in the early seventies, sex seemed like a light-hearted
> parlour game that required no emotional bonds. I realised I liked the
> game. I was good at it. In the waiting room of his office, my impotent
> dentist groaned on top of me and ejaculated quickly and laughing
> quietly said that I was a dream woman, a provocative combination of
> harlot and madonna. Many others agreed.
>
> All the men with whom I made love joyfully without really expe-
> riencing anything myself were people I had known for some time:
> friends, colleagues, mostly doctors, since it was a hospital soap

opera I was living out. Most of these relationships were very casual, incidental. ... Even though I myself was clearly a betrayer and an adulterer, I never felt like one. I was free, after all, I had my justifications. Instead I wondered a bit anxiously at the men who were all obviously betraying their wives. Perhaps somewhere on the outer reaches of morality there still lived the biblical teaching that the marriage bed shall not be contaminated. Even when men took me home while their wife was away, they preferred to make love somewhere besides the bed. That sometimes made me feel humiliated ... . According to my calculations, I slept with 13 men, but with only one did I feel genuine pleasure and satisfaction.

I was 25 when I fell in love again, back into the trap. In the grips of a compulsion for repetition that I was unaware of at the time I fell in love with an older physician. He was kind of like a troll but charming and well-liked, but in a close relationship he proved emotionally immature. And he was a lousy lover.

When in the course of four years I finally began to see that my love was hopeless, I realised I had to do something about my life. I was still married to my husband, who was fanatically immersed in his work. I lived a double life and he noticed nothing as long as he got his nightly rubber teat. I mourned for myself, the artist girl who had longed for love. I mourned my husband, the diligent, mundane man. We had never found a common language. I wanted to get divorced, but did not have the courage. I did not have healthy self-esteem or iniative to give up my safe pseudo-marriage – after all, I had lived with my husband half of my life. That's why I gave up my work and my men. I never told my husband about my experiences. Even though I did not feel I had done wrong, in my heart I asked for forgiveness.

The husband never said anything. The woman has wondered why he never wake up to the situation and expressed jealousy. During the past two years, she has had two young lovers.

In the stories of these three women of the middle generation, infidelity occurred in their devitalised union, but the marriage was never dissolved. The first story is about the infidelity of the husband and the other two are about the extramarital affairs of the women themselves. The first woman has stayed in her devitalised marital union because she continues to feel important to her spouse. The teacher remained because she received professional help and the business owner thinks she stayed having strength gained from the sexual pleasure she experienced with a young lover.

Out of the 45 stories told by women of the youngest generation, two were primarily classified as devitalised marital unions. A day-care worker (31F27) writes that her sexual life may look to be in order from the outside. Still, in her mind, some things could be different:

> My sex life could be more interesting than it is. Even though the pressures about enjoying the 'forbidden fruit' have disappeared with marriage, there are new interfering factors. The baby wakes up easily and this makes it difficult to have physical contact with my husband. ... I am often too tired and have no desire to have sex. To my disappointment I have noticed that my husband does not touch me except when he is trying to whip up my sexual appetite. I have even tried to talk to him about this. He says he loves me more than I even know, but why can't he show it? I'm not a mind reader.

According to the author, sexual matters are difficult for her husband. Sexuality was not openly discussed in his home. His mother thought that miscarriages and other 'female' matters should not be mentioned in the boy's presence. The author herself is more open and thinks that she has helped guide her husband and his mother in 'her' direction. She thinks that her husband assumes that the right time to have sex is exactly when he wants it. If she initiates it, the husband usually accuses her of pressuring him. 'I must be a bad lover, but I don't usually get a chance to show my skills when I want to. It's hard to pretend!' In this case the life situation of a young family with children makes sexual activity difficult. But the sense of the marriage being devitalised is primarily the result of the trauma experienced when the author has been rebuffed, when she wanted to feel attractive to her partner.

Two of the 11 stories of young men are classified in the devitalised union type. One of these writers (13M25) fell in love with a girl who sought his company at a camp site. The girl had recently become deeply religious and believed that there should not be sex without marriage. The man agreed to marry her, because he was aching to get into bed with her. Each spouse has had mental health problems. At the time of writing the story, the wife had just entered a mental hospital:

> After being rebuffed for many years, it is no longer so easy to see what is right and what is not. ... I know, I will someday experience the joys of a balanced sexual life. Maybe it will even happen with my wife, or maybe someone else. I promised to go into couples

therapy with her. Maybe it will help. Maybe not. It's still so fresh that it's impossible for me to say. But I have come to understand that the worst is behind me. My wife's situation, of course, is not easy. During her treatment, she is forced to encounter emotions she has never encountered before. It may also be that she will not agree to therapy. I don't even know that. If she is serious about changing the direction of her life, I will be there to support her.

This story, once again, reveals sexual incompatibility between spouses, at least as perceived by one of the partners in the union.

The stigma of a devitalised union

The contents of the stories and the demographic characteristics of the authors of the stories of devitalised relationships are very similar to those belonging to the parallel relationship type. The majority of these authors have had parallel relations, but not all. Those who live in devitalised unions differ from monogamous people primarily in that their union is not a happy one.

In all generations, after the first passionate phase is over, the relationship may be seen as devitalised because it has begun to seem mundane. However, in our examples, the problem is a more serious one than merely a perpetual need for continued romantic exaltedness. There are two types of devitalised unions: those unions where love and passion have died; and those where sexual relations are not satisfying for both partners. A pure type could be a marriage of convenience with neither love nor sex. The reasons people stay on in devitalised unions are often external, such as children or money, or pure inertia. A devitalised marital relationship breeds social shame. Few couples would readily admit that their sexual life is nonexistent and/or that they have become emotionally distant. In these stories one can recognize a kind of resignation and a reliance on various mechanisms that help authors cope with the grey every day of the marriage.

The stories of all generations contained examples of differences between the spouses' sexual desires. Men in the oldest generation complained about their wives' unwillingness to have sex. One older woman presented a woman's perspective about intercourse becoming more and more repulsive. Part of the women of this generation experienced everything 'sexual' as sinful or repellent. A pleasurable caress such as a tender embrace was instead called something other than 'sexual' (cf. Ronkainen *et al.* 1994). It was also important for this generation to preserve an impeccable social façade. Middle-aged and younger women living in a devitalised union, on the other hand, described how they have suffered from the sexual passivity and indifference of their husbands. They have sought relations with other men, as well as professional help. This clearly shows cultural transference toward naming and bringing forth women's desire (Heidendry 1997). At the same time, women are also feeling the pressure to perform. One of the women quoted above described her 'soap-opera' of sexual liasons, while she also reported having actually enjoyed only one of them. Women also feel compelled to have orgasms. The issue of women faking orgasms comes into play, as in a story by a woman who complained that she did not 'always have the energy to pretend'. In these stories, it is sometimes the case that the husband insults his wife by saying that he does not want to feel pressured into having sex.

Young and middle-aged women are increasingly defining sex on the basis of their own desires. Where older women felt that intercourse and sex were the same, repulsive thing, younger women demand caresses, discussion and tenderness of their men, because to them it is inherent to good sex. The nature and gender dynamics of devitalised unions have thus changed radically over the three generations. The basic problem remains, however, that the sexual needs and wishes of the sexes do not always meet. Sexual problems may reflect the impoverished state of the entire relationship. Before, it was uncommon to seek help or to resolve this situation, though the relationship sometimes improved with time. After the sexual revolution, sexual techniques and therapy have been used to revitalise relationships.

Among the youngest generation, it is no longer obligatory to get married to facilitate intercourse and sexual technique itself is rarely the key problem in the relationship. Instead, there is an increasing expectation that the relationship provides a lasting and powerful experience.

8
Parallel Relationships

The fifth type of sexual relationship is the love story that centres on parallel relations. These describe love and sexuality that are directed at two or more people simultaneously. The relationships may complement or compete with each other. The authors of these stories are sexually active. They enjoy sex and love and feel young, although that is not necessarily the case that they are young any longer. In these stories, the reader is imbued with an enjoyment of life, an openness to different kinds of relationships and sexual experiences. In some stories of parallel relations, the style of sexual life resembles 'donjuanism' in its quest for more and more sexual partners, but many narrators sustain long relationships with their new partners.

A parallel relationship is defined here through the concept of a steady couple relationship. A couple relationship may be a consensual or marital union or a living-apart-together (LAT) relationship. When someone simultaneously has a sexual relationship outside of the steady couple relationship, this is called a parallel relationship. Parallel relations were common, according to the survey and the autobiographies, especially among men. Finns have had parallel relations more commonly than those western Europeans and Americans on whom comparable data is available (Laumann *et al.* 1994; Leridon *et al.* 1998, 190, Lewin *et al.* 1997). But Finns have had proportionally less parallel relations than the residents of St Petersburg and Estonia (Haavio-Mannila and Rotkirch 1997, 152–3; Haavio-Mannila *et al.* 2001; Haavio-Mannila and Kontula 2001). According to the 1992 survey, of Finnish men and women who had ever been in a couple relationship, 52 per cent and 29 per cent respectively had simultaneously engaged in another sexual relationship. In Sweden, 38 per cent of men and 23 per cent of women reported having had parallel relations (Lewin *et al.* 1997, 78).

Parallel relations were the major sexual relationship type in one out of four stories. They are featured particularly in the stories of men of the generations of sexual revolution and sexual restraint. When relationship types are examined in different life stages, it becomes apparent that a parallel relation figures most prominently in middle age. Most men having had parallel relations are at present married or cohabiting, while only two of five women were doing so. These men have regular intercourse and live in a happy couple relationship as often as other men, whereas women do it less often. Many women of this type have divorced. This indicates that there is more stress involved in the infidelity of women than to that of men. The number of lifetime sexual partners is clearly higher among unfaithful people than among the others. Almost every second woman with parallel relationships or living in a devitalised union also described having had sexual feelings for or experiences with other women (Table 1.1).

Casual and workplace relationships

As in the previous chapters, we will take a separate look at stories focusing on parallel relations in the three generations – of sexual restraint, sexual revolution and gender equalisation. We begin with the men of the oldest generation. Of the 18 male authors in the ageing generation, 11 wrote something about parallel relations. In the case of seven men's stories, parallel relations were designated as the main relationship type.

First, we will look at the story of a married teacher and father of two (19M59). While married, he had had ten parallel relationships and a total of 15 sexual partners during his lifetime. The opportunities to have extramarital relations have been excellent because his organisational activities often provide him with travels to other towns. In addition to casual relations he has had many steady parallel relationships, mostly with unattached women. Maintaining many relationships for years has been possible because none of the women lived in the same place. The text focuses on the problem of the 'second woman', and the author justifies his behaviour towards his lover repeatedly.

> She ... was sitting near the door at a summer celebration of some educational institutions ... . I asked her to tango. Her body was – and is – supple. But still, our dancing wasn't very well matched. Probably for that reason too, she announced she would walk back to her apartment. Walk, I said, it would only be half the distance if we

went together. Let's go then, she said, and looked into my eyes and smiled. She was probably enjoying the surprised look that her easy compliance must have brought to my face.

Following a brief correspondence and some reprimands on the woman's part, directed at the deceitful married man in her life, the couple met at a weekend event. When the man entered the hotel room, the woman welcomed him dressed in a flowered robe, wearing only black lace panties underneath.

It will be nine years from that day next July. It's a little over a month from our last meeting. The next one we are planning is in about one month ... . I have often said to her, both lightly and a bit more seriously as well: you should get yourself a man. Her reply has long been the same – I have one, right here and right now. I don't need more than one. She has promised to let me know right away if she changes her mind about that. We live 400 kilometres from each other. In the end, that might be what keeps the relationship alive. At least it protects us from outsiders. We have nothing to do with each other when there are mutual acquaintances present at some event. But we will still arrange to spend the night together.

This habitually unfaithful teacher also started an affair with a married woman whose husband has long been impotent. This extramarital relationship has so far lasted several years, but the man meets his mistress less often now because 'the lady is already 55'. The man claims not to have quarrelled with his wife in a long time. He has dreamt of being able to go back with her to what they had 30 years ago but knows this dream is unrealistic. He thinks parallel relations have increased his energy and motivation at work, allowed him to sleep more soundly and peacefully, given him a good appetite, as well as the knowledge that he is not a 'useless person'.

The following story is told by a tour guide, the father of three (34M61), who has a good sexual relationship with his broad-minded wife. The man tells that he became a Don Juan or Casanova whenever the time was opportune. He has had 20 parallel relations and 30 sexual partners in his life. The author describes how as a 'scrawny little boy' he liked to play with girls, specialising in licking their genitals. In his text, he offers up a picture of himself as a skilful lover, and says that his wife too has had extramarital affairs. As a tour guide on trips abroad, the man has had many relationships with travellers in his group as well as with foreign women:

> ... I liked serving people and met all kinds. I also heard many different stories. And I became a kind of male Leelia [the love advice columnist for a certain women's magazine] for them. It started about 16 years ago and continues still ...

He maps out the relationships that were made possible by his line of work:

> [On] the first trips I stayed clean. But as they say, tour guides and models need strong morals. I didn't have them for long. The first time I slipped, it happened with a lady close to 30 years younger than I. We danced after a few drinks. Then she said she needed to stop by her room and asked me to go with her. We already had our arms around each other in the hallway. And after we got into her room, things took their course. It turned into a relationship that lasted a couple of years, and then eventually ended. She came on many of my trips. And when I left without her, she always cautioned me to behave. Sometimes I did, sometimes I didn't. I started having one-night stands every now and then ... . The ages of my partners varied a lot. The same goes for their occupations. The youngest tourist was a 19-year-old lady whose grandfather I could have been. ... The oldest was already close to 80, though she took a nitro first, just in case. By occupation, they were anywhere from a deaconess to a dairy maid.

According to the man, being a tour guide requires treating everyone in an evenhanded manner – although it is not possible to pay the same amount of attention to everyone. The author gradually gave up affairs with tourists, when he became an object of derision and created bad blood.

> In the beginning I went to restaurants a lot with my own group. But that often caused friction. I mean in the sense that I always tried to ask the unaccompanied women to dance. Regardless of whether they were young or old, ugly or beautiful. So that got me comments about how I was dancing oh so fine with *some* people. And was forgetting the others. I began to get tired of it, but I wasn't a dancing machine. So gradually I stopped going out with the tourists. I will

organize their evening, and make sure that everything is fine, and wish them a lovely evening. ... My colleagues gave me a new name: Wolf-Sam, and the more nasty-minded ones: Backwoods-Casanova, but what did I care.

One incident still makes me laugh ... . One female tourist was absolutely set on going out with me to Hotel L ... . When we got to the table, the waiter came to take our order. And it happened to be a guy I knew. He said in broken Finnish: 'Hello hello, you here. A new woman again, you great Casanova, every time a new woman.' It was enough for that woman. She took off like a bullet. After that she didn't say hello when I greeted her.

This Backwoods-Casanova tries to present a positive self-esteem in sexual matters. At least according to his story, his wife knew and tolerated her husband's extramarital affairs. If true, this kind of open marriage is an exception.[1]

Marriages seem to remain more successfully balanced when both spouses have parallel relations. Mutual parallel relations in the oldest generation are rare, because women of that generation have been faithful. But trips to southern Europe have given Finnish women the opportunity to have casual relations, although they are not always able to hide them from their husbands. A married father of two and small business owner (171M71) writes:

My wife is 67 years old, but she is still really lively and it seems, has also become sexually liberated. Her self-esteem has improved, as I have always encouraged, and many of our friends admire her many talents ... . I just overheard my wife's friend complaining to her: 'who were you to decide [on their trip abroad] that this man in the middle was yours'. The friend threatened to tell me, but my wife said she would deny everything ... . I didn't ask her about it and she did not attempt to explain. I don't know if my wife has had a sexual relationship. I felt no jealousy because I know that temporary relationships like that will not really affect our marriage.

The wife of the tour guide quoted above (34M61) had, according to the husband's story, also had parallel relations, though not nearly as many as her husband.

[My wife] hasn't stood by and watched my dalliances with her finger in her mouth, and I have told her that if she wants a taste of another man, it won't be the end of the world. Because I was the first one for her and, of course because she too has the right to have experiences of her own. And I've even almost seen it a couple of times. Also, when she has gone on trips to the south with her girl-friend, I've happened to see condoms in her make-up bag. And that's good in terms of being safe.

Attitudes toward temporary, spousal infidelity are today the same among Finnish men and women. According to the survey study approximately one in four people accepts temporary infidelity. In the light of these findings, at least some men of the generation of sexual restraint have not particularly disapproved of their wives' occasional travel affairs, because of the belief that they will not lead to anything permanent. Some have seen the wife's parallel relations as justification for their own infidelities. This is a result of the weakening of the sexual scripts that uphold moral double standards in the Nordic countries. In other cultures, for example in Russia (Haavio-Mannila and Rotkirch 2000) and the USA (Laumann *et al.* 1994), men are much more accept-ing of the husband's infidelities than those of the wife.

Among women of the generation of sexual restraint, six of the 20 texts contain a story about a parallel relationship. In four, parallel relations are the main relationship type. The following married clean-ing woman with no children (25F57), whose husband has also had extramarital relationships, describes her numerous parallel relations in colourful terms. Her text is an important exception to the picture of especially women's 'restraint' in this generation. She herself aptly calls this lifestyle a 'double life'.

My searching and wandering on the path of a double life certainly did not end when I got married. Already in the first years of mar-riage I fell in love with a young boy who, at some point, even became my bed partner. This boy was really a child, and sexually inexperienced, but it was good for us while it lasted. He moved a lot because of his job, and as young people naturally do, married a young girl. I was left in a sexual vacuum, since my husband had taken a job on a boat for more than six months. I was already 40 at that time and had settled seriously to work on land. My double life demanded some searching again, and it wasn't difficult because I lived in such a big city that there were enough people to 'feed honey' and give some back to me. I learned to dance then too and got my driver's license, so I was able to move about outside of my immediate surroundings. I did not want to use my home for this fake life, so I went a little farther away. I drove, because I have never used alcohol beyond the occasional courtesy drink, and never wanted drunkenness to be my companion. I thought I chose my temporary companions pretty carefully, and naturally they were married men – I didn't want young boys running about talking 'past their mouths'. That one kid had already bragged in his home area that he had been with me intimately and word had it that it had even been quite good. My God, all the talk that went around.

This woman talks about seven different parallel relationships. In her lifecourse, she has had 15 sexual partners. In several of the relationships she fell in love seriously. Collaboration at her workplace with a man with whom she was powerfully infatuated, led to a sexual relationship:

I found the man of my dreams finally, when a fresh-baked math teacher came to my work place one autumn. Our eyes met right away, but at least not our heads. He already had a wife, but that didn't slow us down. From that day, my heart sang for him only. Well, a little for my husband as well, of course. No, when I really think about it, only for Blue Eyes. We began a shameless flirtation, naturally in secret and being careful. We talked enthusiastically when the situation arose, but for three years we did not touch each another, I swear. I stopped going to dances and sitting in bars with a glass of orange juice, and saw and heard only him.

At this juncture the author also contemplates, in an unusually frank way, the social tensions in a relationship between a cleaning person and an educated man:

Measured on a value scale of wage classes there was a ten-class difference between us, but I guess it didn't matter when it was about a person's inner being, and why not some of the outer too. He was just a bit shorter than I, but he thought I was handsome and had provocative breasts. He was one of those people who will never become an adult, and will yearn for his mother's plump bosom for the rest of his life. My husband has never in his life noticed that I have breasts at all, who cares about such useless pendulums. After three years of testing, Blue Eyes and I happened to be in the same storage area at the same time and that's when he grabbed me in his arms and kissed me. That was a decisive moment in my life, as he said it was in his. ... Between us, there were two marriages, 20 years and an academic degree – which I didn't have – and about 40 kilos of loose fat, which I did have.

Hesitation aside, an ardent sexual relationship followed the passionate falling in love:

It started slipping when we no longer saw anything but each other, being in the same building all day. We began to meet in the weirdest places and at weird times ... we fit each other like cast and mould. We were able to use a small one-room apartment where we could enjoy each other in peace. We were gambling so much that we could never appear together anywhere because our relationship would have been pegged right away, since people knew we saw each other during the day at work, too. He was the person who was made for me sexually.

Our joy together lasted exactly 13 years, until my husband became so ill he had to retire, and hanging about outside the house ended there and then. Blue Eyes and I discounted the possibility of divorce, because his wife became seriously ill as well. We decided to leave things to the hands of fate, which can sometimes be really strange. Of the two of us, only he is a widow. His wife died on the same day that my husband and I left that city for a house far away in the country.

Today this sexually intense woman lives in a small place with her sick, alcoholic husband. She has found a young man, even in this remote area. This time, a severely disabled man:

... My nerves collapsed again, or rather, I was what they call fatigued, and I went to a hospital to rest for a week. My husband started yet another (for a change, his last) bout of drinking and I just didn't have the energy to watch him falling about, after a strenuous summer of many visitors. In the hospital it happened again! There was a man of about 30 who was in a wheelchair, who had been in a car accident, become paralysed and lost his ability to speak. Naturally we became the best of friends and for the sake of decency I even tried to avoid him, but he knew in which room he could find this pile of meat. We spoilt each other with caresses in one week, and now at least my heart is crying again. That poor boy is sitting limp in his wheelchair, waiting for me to visit (the nurse called me). That's another heart broken for me, I don't know how many there are in all. He called me (in writing) his love and asked that I never leave him. It is sick, I know, but on the other hand so damn dramatic. His sexuality was intact after paralysis and we wanted each other very much. I told him I'm married, but he replied, ask the doctor what we are allowed to do. We were given permission to do anything we wanted, two lonely hearts, and we did too. We did it and I can't say more right now. My thoughts are at a certain hospital.

The woman emphasizes how important it is to hide the parallel relationship from her spouse. She herself has been able to live a double life for long stretches:

In my double life, I have always told my partner that I am married and when I can't meet him because my husband is at home on holiday. I never gave my telephone number to anyone so I didn't have to be afraid that my friend would get it in his head to call. A wise man will believe you when you tell him when he can't call.

The second example of parallel relations among women of the oldest generation does not include stories of long-term love relationships like the story above. A married working-class mother (101F66) who has experienced eight parallel relationships in her life writes the following about her adventures while travelling:

There was a group of us women on a two-to-three-day trip to abroad, when a dark and handsome man joined us in the lobby of the hotel. In the course of the day he appeared again and began to express a clear interest in me. Towards evening he asked me if he could spend the night in my room – it would beat the conditions of his site hut outside of town. He was one of our construction workers, working in T. while his family was in Finland. Because I had a room mate, we set up camp in the vestibule of our hotel room. This partner of mine, who had played football, was only seven years older than our daughter.

This woman was an experienced traveller who enjoyed sex without love. For her, casual relations had offered experiences she had not acquired or been able to acquire before marriage. In her own interpretation, the liberation she has experienced in middle age is connected to her adoption of the behavioural models and concepts supporting sexual freedom in the 1960s and 1970s. She identified with the generation of sexual revolution, regardless of the fact that she is older than the actual generation of sexual revolution.

One nurse (157F63 years) had many sexual relationships and partners as a young woman:

> I met a lesbian girl who wanted me and she taught me to rediscover my own hands, which had been so familiar to me when I was young. My tendency did not indicate a love for women, even though out of curiosity and kindness I let the girl try and seduce me. She was hurt and began to hate me.

This woman married at a young age. She was unfaithful and got a divorce. After that, there was a steady flow of men, she had abortions, as well as four children. She lived for several decades with her second husband and had parallel relations. Following the divorce, the ex-spouses are on good terms and live in the same building without sharing sexual relations.

Forming parallel relations was often the result of a lacking and devitalised marital relationship. Many older women who describe parallel relations are sexually very active. Their descriptions of extramarital relationships are colourful. It seems to have been relatively easy for Finnish women of the ageing generation to find sexual partners whenever they have actively sought them. Sexual relationships with younger men have given them profound pleasure. Parallel relationships have made some women more independent and changed them, even helping some women to detach themselves from a dissatisfying and cruel husband. The stories of the older women who discussed parallel relationships in their sexual texts have many similarities. Each woman had experienced problems with her husband and his many extramarital relationships. Three were still married, one had a steady sexual partner and two had no current sexual relationship, at the time of writing.

These women, exceptional for their generation, openly accept their sexuality and do not regret their extramarital affairs. They have represented an alternative to the sexual morality of restraint and the great impact on women of that generation as discussed in Chapter 2.

Detached passions, casual sex

Finding a partner for sexual experimentation and parallel relations has not been difficult for most men of the generation of sexual revolution.

Prior to the age of Aids, sexual freedom and the birth control pill created a wide sex market where it was not always necessary to have money or feelings of love. Both men and women were often expected to want sexual intercourse almost anytime and anywhere. Some have indeed truly enjoyed free sex at least at some point in their life. It seems that an occasional extra relationship has not been a problem, at least not for everyone. Some middle-aged male authors, though, say that they despise and hate giving in to casual relations and that they have tried to overcome them. There were no similar cases of remorse in the stories by men in the oldest generation. Thus this is a tendency that points to the equalisation of the genders, and in this case exceptionally an equalisation in favour of the traditional female script (in most cases, gender roles change so that women accept men's behaviours and attitudes).

The numerous casual relations of men of the middle generation were connected to the process that women underwent, starting in the 1960s, of disengaging themselves from traditional notions of sexual morality. Fifteen of the 24 men of the middle generation told of a parallel relationship that had occurred during a marital or consensual union or other steady relationship. For ten of them, parallel relations formed their main relationship type. As in the cases presented above, these men had often formed temporary relationships in bar-restaurants or while travelling. Various training seminars have also provided opportunities for sexual relations with others besides a spouse. An example of this is the story of a married process manager with one child (172M46):

> I went to week-long training seminars for my job in southern Finland. I have a relationship there with a woman. We make love on sofas in lobbies, in my room, wherever we can. She tells me I'm wonderful. She is a little older than I am, a mother of a 15-year-old girl. She tells me that she feels no pleasure in intercourse with her husband. But she does enjoy it with me. Being with my wife has not given me any pleasure in months. Now the two of us enjoy sex for a few days at a time. There's a lot of alcohol at the seminar and casual relationships are common. ... People come to short seminars to drink and get laid. Not everyone of course, but many do.

This man wonders why one woman is not enough for him, why he has needed several, although he feels he has been living a stable life in spite of his outside relationships. He thinks that sex with his wife is functional but a little repetitive.

According to both the survey and the autobiographies, men of the middle generation had twice as often been unfaithful than their wives. A chef who is a father and lives in a consensual union (65M44) writes: 'I have certainly had some outside relationships. And I believe that my wife too went to the other side of the fence. Assurances of fidelity were not part of our breakfast-table talk. We didn't demand to know what the other person was doing.' This marriage, however, ended in divorce. While men's casual parallel relationships do not usually break up the marriage, especially if the wife has remained ignorant of it, the situation is different when the parallel relationship is regular. In the following story of a married policeman with three children (163M50), a relationship that started in a bar and then continued for a long time, was nearly revealed to his wife:

We sometimes had get-togethers for work, and this was another one of them. After we had bathed in the sauna and sat socializing, we went off to check out the local bar scene. The music was playing and the liquor flowed ... . At the bar, I noticed I was sitting with a nurse who was obviously older than me and who I knew had just got divorced. I asked her to dance and was greedily pressing her against me. She wasn't very beautiful, my wife is more beautiful even, but something in her made my desire rise and I began to pester her to make me a pot of coffee. After I kept at it for a while, she took the bait, and I left my group at the bar and took off with her. She made coffee and we drank it in perfect harmony sitting close to each other. After the coffee I resorted to more decisive moves and even put my hand to use under her skirt ... . That match took four hours. When I left, I took her phone number. I thought about it for a week before calling and thanking her for that evening. She was pleased to have been appreciated, and she invited me for a rematch.

So I had to go there again, and again and again. It became such a bad habit that now, eight years later, I still visit her two or three times a month. It's meant a lot of manoeuvring and a lot has happened. Once when this concubine of mine was at home with me, we had had some drinks and she was strutting about the rooms completely naked. My wife had had some changes at work and she showed up in the yard in her car in the middle of the day. Luckily there was a back door in the house and there was a forest nearby. I kicked her clothes under the bed and the lady whiled away her time in the woods until I was able to take the clothes to her. So it hasn't been boring. It looks like the current sexual balance [of fear] will continue for the time being.

Men's infidelity is often difficult for their wives. It robs them of self-esteem and might cause psychosomatic symptoms. Sometimes it has resulted in the wife seeking affairs of her own or filing for divorce. In their sexual stories, middle generation women do not mention quietly accepting their husbands' extramarital affairs. The issue for them might have been so painful or shameful that they do not even want to write about it. The stories of husbands and their mistresses reveal that many wives have closed their eyes to their husbands' parallel relationships, even when they have known about them. But apparently they were not able, or did not want, to bring this up explicitly in their own texts.

A remarkable 18 out of 47 women of the generation of sexual revolution talk about their own parallel relations. Parallel relations are the major relationship type for ten of those woman. In the story of a childless woman employed in marketing (20F47), living in a steady relationship, men follow one another and overlap, and there is no end in sight for her adventures. The woman consciously does not want to commit to one person permanently, even though she has had many offers of marriage. Her story is a unique depiction of the enjoyment she derives from her different relationships.

I was all over the place, at best I had three dates in one day (of course I didn't sleep with them, we were just 'going out'). I think this had to do with my parents who had just got divorced. ... I was young and beautiful. A blond, brown-eyed, curvy babe. And the men kept coming like flies. My English teacher at the time said: 'Don't ever get married, just make a thousand men happy.' I have followed that advice – I haven't been married and I've made many men very happy. Though I'll never reach that figure, because I only do wonderful men, but I'm on my way.

I went out dancing and to bars a lot. Occasionally I found someone to date, sometimes they were one-time deals, it depends. But I've met all my important men in a place other than a bar. For example, at work, at a language course, or a regular dance.

My first big love was someone well known – a handsome man about ten years older. He would have married me, but I already knew how to resist; he would have wanted me to be a housewife and I wanted to be independent!

In-between, I had an American, a wonderful man. Tall, brown eyes, a crew cut. He was tender, friendly, sincere, a gentleman. We were at an absolutely wonderful party at a yacht club (abroad). Everything was like in a film. I asked him to pinch me to see if it was all true. That's how fabulous it was. We both fell in love, and it was lovely. Our lovemaking was tender. Then came the day when we had to go our separate ways. I thought I would die of agony. I couldn't eat or drink, it felt like my heart would stop directly. We wrote to each other for many years and I still keep all his beautiful love letters. He gave me gifts of jewellery. And after many years I got a letter from him asking how I was, and telling me that he had gone to check out the places where we shared some of our life. And that he had thought about me (wonderful!!).

The woman is proud of having been able to console numerous deceived husbands:

Next, an abandoned man appeared in my life (Number 1), and there have been many in my path since. His wife had gone off with another. So I healed his wounds and tried to have a relationship at the same time. ... I have often observed that younger guys look for older company (they say they can't stand women, girls, their own age). I myself do not much care for very young or very old men. I'm most interested in someone about my own age. And this brings us to the fact that after 30–35, decent, available men do not exist (drunks/crazies – yes). So in order to get a bed buddy you have to get mixed up with married men.

This fragment shows how the sexual revolution gave women the freedom to have casual and parallel relationships, which the author seems to have greatly enjoyed. Sexually skilful, she has constantly sought and found new men and has had some old ones 'in reserve'.

The stories of women of the generation of sexual revolution focusing on parallel relations contained repeated references to oral sex which has given many of them particular pleasure. One white-collar employee, a mother of three without a steady sexual relationship (33F53) talks about how her lover got her excited by using his tongue, 'and I almost went completely crazy'. One married mother of three (51F46), also a white-collar employee, tells that her parallel relationships taught her that 'the mouth is an unusually sensitive and pleasure-producing part of the body for caressing genitals'. A working-class woman, living in a steady sexual relationship, also a mother of three (37F40), tells about how the man got her ready by 'talking dirty'. Oral sex, too, gave this woman a lot of pleasure:

> ... He kissed me 'there'. I remember how he first caressed my pussy. Then he spread my legs, kissed my belly, went down, circled his tongue around my vulva. I got tremendously wet, I was embarrassed, but at the same time it felt really good. Then, fierce lovemaking and explosive orgasms.

Not all women have gone along with oral sex when desired by the man. A typical example can be found in the story of a cafeteria worker and mother of two with no steady sexual relationship (85F53). When one man tried to persuade her to suck his penis, saying 'that will make it really big', she refused. However, this woman tells about wonderful extramarital sex that revitalised her marriage:

> I had to go on a camp in Lapland for my job. Somehow it happened that I woke up in the colonel's bed. The night had been amazing. He was about 53 years old, but an incredible lover. He was the first person in my life I 69'ed. He was a large, hairy, handsome man. I remember what his huge penis felt like in my mouth. I also went on top of him. It felt really good. I could decide on the pace myself. Slowly I allowed his huge penis to go inside me. I spread my labia really wide and then I could feel it – really deep inside me. We made love all night, until morning. We met again at the same camp a couple of years later and everything was just as amazing then too. He definitely had no problems with his sexual potency. My God what a man, if only I could be once more with him. Things always went much better in bed at home when I had been somewhere with someone else. I guess a bad conscience made me try my best.

Like women of the generation of sexual restraint, the following working class mother of three of the generation of sexual revolution, living in a steady relationship (37F40), has sometimes had a much younger lover, even an underage boy.

> I have also been to bed with the boys of my husband's brother. Originally it was my husband's own idea, but at some point it went out of his control. Especially one of the boys. And he still has not forgotten me, even though it has already been five years since the

first time, he was 15 then. Do not judge me, I haven't done anything against his will. He himself wanted to have sex and only later
did I realize that I had fucked a minor. I have not wounded his soul.
He is a completely normal young person, who still wants me, he
admitted it this summer. Passionately even, even young girls aren't
better than me.

The author clearly fears the reader's judgement. She has felt herself to
be 'ripped up and dirty inside' as well as 'a bad mother'. In spite of
that, the feelings of pleasure are seen as justifying the sexual relationship with a minor in this story – because both parties wanted it and
because the sexual intercourse was pleasurable. This attitude encapsu-
lates the sexual morality of the 1960s (see Chapter 10). This generation
also required sexual fulfilment within marriage. This comes out in the
story of the following arts professional and mother of one who has no
steady sexual relationship at the moment (136F49):

I will not touch upon our marriage except from the sexual perspective. That part of our entire 14-year marriage was incredibly active
and good too, but ... I never had a real orgasm with L. Our daughter
was born after three years of marriage, a much-planned and antici-
pated child, and we were fond of each other but ... I began to cheat
on my husband. And then he did the same. Apparently both of us
began going through a delayed teenage period of upheaval and
searching. We took care of our child and work in an exemplary
fashion, and we still do, but the cheating ... . Already then I knew
for some underhanded reason to keep sexual matters in their own
slot, but my husband did not. He became pathologically jealous in
the course of the years, started using more and more alcohol, and
finally became frighteningly violent.

One of this woman's parallel relationships subsequently led to a good,
steady relationship, ending the marriage which had been exhausted by
jealousy.

Descriptions by unfaithful men of the generation of sexual revolution of their wives' parallel relationships (for example 71M54, 4M37)
are part misery, part lascivious voyeurism. Some men claim they did
not care about the wife's unfaithfulness. Most men, however, describe
feelings of intense jealousy. It has clearly been easier for the men
themselves to maintain a parallel relationship than to be in the role of
the 'cuckold'. Women's stories show how the wives' parallel sexual

relationships have at times triggered extreme reactions in their partner. One journalist, a mother of one, and now living in a steady sexual relationship (14F44), was caught having a casual fling with a foreigner, whereupon her husband attempted suicide. The cook quoted above (37F40) tells about her husband's fatal jealousy. Openness and honesty – here considered characteristics typical of women – led her to attempt suicide:

> My husband learned to be more and more faithful, but I started taking all kinds of seminars, and almost every time I had an affair with some man. The sex boosted my self-esteem and I thought it was nice to meet new men. We would exchange a few postcards afterwards but there were no long-term relationships, after all, many of the men had wives and a family at home, just like I did. Men just don't tell their wives about cheating. We had an honesty in these matters, too, even though it almost took the life out of me. I had been truthful about my fling during the week's seminar, and my husband insisted on asking the same questions over and over. I was taking various medications and fell into a stupor. Our oldest son had said to his father that mother is not sleeping right; half an hour later I would have been lost to this world and looking for a new state of being. My husband began to watch my comings and goings, to shackle me to the home more, and sometimes brought some young acquaintance to our bed and then they would both take turns fucking me during the night, not at the same time luckily.

In this example, both spouses had their own extramarital relationships. This example of tragically achieved symmetry is unusual among the texts.

Moral doubts

Four of the 11 men in the youngest generation report having been unfaithful to his steady partner, but parallel relations are the major relationship type for only one of them. Three of the four men reporting parallel relations wrote that the partner had unexpectedly become pregnant. None of them formed a steady relationship with the mother of the child. The only young man whose story was mainly classified into the parallel relations type, is an academically educated father of one who is in a steady relationship (84M31). He made love to many women around the same time that he also had a long time girlfriend. He had sexual relations in many countries. 'And this travelling would have probably continued into retirement age if we hadn't parted and if there hadn't been that accident and if I didn't have a son.' The man sees his son regularly but pays no child support because he has either been a student or unemployed the whole time. The child's mother is married to another man. By contrast, 16 of the 45 young female authors wrote about parallel sexual relationships. For eight of them, the parallel type is their main relationship type. These women usually describe highly autonomous and reflective sexual lifestyles. At the same time, their stories of parallel relationships often present strong moral reservations. They are perceived as pragmatic, destructive, dangerous, or at least psychopathological.

Many social factors have contributed to young women's unfaithfulness. Travelling has presented opportunities for external relations. Some think that their strong sexual urge has made them look for excitement and change. Steady relationships may have become devitalised or may have been lacking love and satisfying sex from the beginning. A large proportion of the parallel relationships of young women did not, according to their own stories, lead to the break up of the steady relationship, even though sometimes infidelity provided the stimulus for separation. One married woman with no children occupying a leading position within her profession (125F34) describes in her detailed story her many casual sexual relationships abroad. The first one did not lead to intercourse.

> My studies included a summer internship abroad. It was my first time away from home and my husband. I became intoxicated by the new surroundings and from being worshipped. I could choose anyone's company. I fell in love with a boy who was not allowed to fall in love with me. His country was closed and we were from different cultures and religions. I slept next to him one night, and we kissed and held hands. He was a swimmer in his country's promotional team and could not afford to ruin his reputation or his affairs. The other reason was that they were fed hormones and he wouldn't have been able to be with a woman during the training season. That night left beautiful memories.

Later, the woman had loveless sexual intercourse several times during her internship. The husband of this woman is extremely jealous of her other sexual partners. The woman also faced aggressive advances made by her boss, a well-known sexual harasser, which eventually led to rape.

My new boss had a great interest in women. He started pestering me right away. Other employees advised me to hold a binder or something in front of my breasts when delivering papers to him. That only helped a little while. He arranged it so that we had to travel together in his car, and the harassment and physical advances began at the knees and went up to my breasts. We were in the midst of negotiations and the other party left for a moment, and suddenly he grabbed me, there at someone else's negotiating table. I was frightened and began to cry. ... His male subordinates were watching how he continued to harass me from windows that were facing us. It became an excellent coffee-table story: how I had been hounded back into a corner. I talked to female co-workers who said it was usual, and I noticed some felt, even desirable. You get more power in a flock of hens if the boss notices you and gives you attention.

My work was interesting and gave me energy. My husband was away, and I saw him three times that entire year. I was lonely, and had sex only three times, just casually with people I worked with. My boss raised the intensity of his advances. We took a daily car trip of a couple of kilometres, and as he drove, he at first fondled my breasts, and later as the relationship progressed, his hand would go between my thighs. I never touched him. I thought, OK, if this is for the common good, go ahead. I became attached to him as I watched his work up close, I was ambitious and in a good position. I didn't talk to anyone about it, not even when he attacked me and took me by force on a train. That too had been orchestrated, he arranged it so that we were sitting in the same compartment. He held a pillow to my face and tore my pants. I tried to wash myself in the train's lavatory and cried.

This, from the author's side, unwanted parallel relationship continued for five years. The boss helped the author's husband find a job:

... And I kept my mouth shut. Or I opened it if he wanted me to. He enjoyed oral sex very much. He would call me up to give him a massage and often it ended in me satisfying him. I thought I could endure it, I lived in company housing after all, and both me and my husband's jobs depended on my being nice. Others tried the same trick to get me to bed and to do them service, my husband's drinking was already pretty widely known. Five years is a long time. Sometimes I imagined I loved him, and it made it easier. I became a cross and bitter bitch and I was very strict with my subordinates. It was my way to survive.

The relationship with the boss has now ended, but the author continues to work in the same place. The story is an example of a kind of 'paid' sexual relationship in the workplace, to which the woman cynically submitted:

> When I read about sexual harassment in the workplace, I'm pretty amused. There are people who ooh and ahh about it, while they themselves live in some kind of cream-puff reality. People who live in the middle of it can't raise a stink because of financial or other reasons. Where would that get you. Another job would be lost. Or a boss or cabinet minister.

This woman's marital relationship is completely devitalised. The spouses have not engaged in sexual intercourse in years. The woman remains in her bad marriage and uses parallel relations as a survival mechanism. Right now she has a love relationship with a young, married foreign man who lives far away and calls her once a week. The woman understands she has been used and oppressed all her life. At the moment of writing, the woman says she would no longer accept situations in her workplace that she does not even want to write about. She has 'learnt to love herself and to respect those above her less, with the exception of God'.

The next young woman, whose story was categorised mainly to the parallel relations type, is a student who is married to a jealous man (63F23). She calls her need for parallel relationships a 'perversion of betrayal':

> In early spring, a couple of months after the onset of the winter depression, I did go to bed with my husband, and a couple of weeks later, with my closest fellow student. I didn't enjoy either one very much physically and got a bad moral hangover from both. So bad, in fact, that I entered expensive, private psychiatric treatment to eliminate this deficiency – my cheating perversion. My husband nagged at me about how I could do that to him. I myself could not understand how I could have wanted and been capable of doing it, and the next morning and the next day I regretted it so much, and all I wanted was to live happily and in peace with my husband.

The physical pleasure of a parallel relationship made one woman employee, without children and currently without a steady sexual relationship (168F24), feel very erotic. Her previous steady relationship was not satisfying, and the parallel relationships revitalised it.

> ... I had some on the side and I enjoyed it. ... I was 18, got my driver's license, I had a lover who was 40, and I was happy for the first time in a long time even though life at home was literally fucked-up. Sleeping with someone else also started me on my fantasy games at home: when I offered my organ to my boyfriend I might close my eyes and picture my tender, grown lover loving me sweetly. I began to have orgasms again, and he was visibly pleased with his returned skill as The Great Lover.

This traffic officer also seduced her much older teacher:

> Looking back, the affair that came next was damned reprehensible; I am a teacher now myself, I have high morals with regard to my students, and I make an effort to think of them as sexless beings ... . I was a pretty, frustrated 18-year-old woman with big breasts and a narrow waist, and I seduced my teacher. I'm still ashamed of my lecherous and provocative behaviour toward this recently divorced 50-year-old man; in my attacks of guilt I have consoled myself with the fact that he was not totally blameless for the physical relationship that developed between us alongside the traditional teacher–student relationship.

The woman looks for causes for her behaviour – the teacher was a friend of her parents:

> I think that relationship was a form of rebellion and defiance toward my own parents who, at the time, did not give a shit about how I was. What made the rape of this teacher so dirty and reprehensible was that he was an old so-called family friend and that as a little girl I had played in the sandbox with his little daughters, and thinking about all these sordid little details totally excited me in a funny, sick way. ... I have to admit that my sexual excitement was increased by the knowledge that my parents would no doubt kill me if they knew I was having an affair with this man. It would be interesting to know what effect our reprehensible fooling around has had on this man's relationships with my parents.

The woman ended the affair when her schooling was over, partly because he became 'quite a nuisance' in the relationship between her and the boyfriend.

Young women describe the various reactions of their partners to their infidelities. One female student in a steady relationship with no children (63F23) feels that parallel relationships enhance her steady relationship, that other men give a lot of feedback both sexually and spiritually. It is typical of this generation to strive for openness in parallel relations, too. The husband of this woman, on the other hand, refrains from other relationships.

> Unfortunately my relationship with my steady partner had already then, about a year ago, become a codependent relationship ... . As a counterattack to my ideas of freedom he refuses to even think about another woman as a possible sex partner. So he is very dependent on me and is sometimes even too active in terms of sex. My flings are often with young boys for whom I have to do everything in the actual sex act, or at least make most of the moves.

Parallel relations led another white-collar woman, in a steady relationship, with children, (149F33) to divorce her husband with whom sex was unsatisfactory:

> I travelled on business a lot and met new people – new objects of erotic interest. My love for my husband began to dissipate, and a new, unexpected, passionate, secret love – or actually a sexual relationship and many temporary objects of erotic interest, made me see how much was actually missing in my active marital sex life. As a matter of fact, at first these flings improved the quality of our marital sex, but in the end they toppled the relationship. When the object of my love changed, also the object of my sexual desire changed. I can't have an ongoing erotic relationship merely for the sake of the erotic, without a deeper feeling. Not even the values that relate to preserving the family could make me continue a sexual relationship that I was bored with and that no longer included a sufficient feeling of love.

One mother of two, who works as an employee, living in a presently faithful consensual union, and suffers from depression from time to time (150F26), has received solace and satisfaction from a happily married man. The relationship is above all spiritual although the couple have had sexual intercourse several times.

Among the young generation, the dissolutions of relationships that result from parallel relations are not very problematic because there are usually no children and little property, and whatever there is, belongs to each individual instead of being something the couple acquired together. Partners may continue to have their own apartment and possessions even though the couple may stay primarily in one apartment. It is then easy to get rid of a bagful or two when the relationship no longer functions.

Unlike the stories of older and middle-aged women, the stories told by young women sometimes express the belief that the author cannot help her infidelity. It is described as a biological need, a perversion, or simply a 'tendency to be unfaithful'. A difference compared with earlier generations is also that young people at least strive for honesty with all partners involved. Young women are often very aware of the many-sided implications of their affairs with older men – they have 'the male in their head' (cf. Holland *et al.* 1998). A touching example was the story of an 18–year-old woman who expresses strong responsibility for an affair with a much older teacher and family friend.

The scripts of infidelity

The texts exemplify the existence of two simultaneous sexual scripts of parallel relations. According to the first script, parallel relations are not allowed in the vicinity or neighbourhood of the spouse. If they occur, they are seen as competing with the earlier, 'main' relationship. This script suggests that the spouse should initiate a divorce from the unfaithful partner who should marry his or her lover. According to the second script presented in the texts, it is legitimate to have casual parallel relationships when you are travelling or otherwise outside the neighbourhood into which the spouse has access. Even workplace romances may be permitted as long as they do not interfere with family life. The relationships outside the home area can be characterized as complementary to the earlier or main relationship. It is, therefore, not necessary to end the earlier relationship because of these flings. A one-night stand after a party with co-workers is supposed to be forgotten and in practice this kind of casual relationship does not 'normally' lead to divorce. The danger that a casual relationship would disrupt the steady relationship seems to be relatively slight according to the texts. But sometimes one finds 'soul mates' in these situations and a more or less permanent parallel relationship is established.

The meaning of parallel relations has undergone a transformation across the three generations, a topic which is further explored in Chapter 10. To end this chapter, we will examine the sexual lifestyle of the authors of the parallel relationship type according to generation and gender. In the texts many male authors among the *generation of sexual restraint* describe their parallel relations in more detail and with more enthusiasm than their marital relationship. Parallel relations have helped some writers to endure living in a devitalised marriage. They have brought something stimulating into the midst of the grey everyday and increased energy in work and spare-time activities. In these cases the parallel relationship is complementary to the marital relationship. Among the oldest generation, there has sometimes been a severe conflict between staying committed to the spouse versus leaving the spouse.

Parallel relations among women of the oldest generation have taken the form of either acquiring casual experiences while travelling or seeking sexual pleasure in an extramarital relationship that might have included love. In the parallel relations of this generation of women, the woman has occasionally been significantly older than her male partner. Women of the generation of sexual restraint usually report receiving great satisfaction from their extramarital affairs. They note realistically that they offer both advantages and disadvantages. There were no shocking tragedies in connection with the parallel relationships of women of the generation of restraint.

Some of the descriptions of casual parallel relations by men of the *generation of sexual revolution* were recorded without emotion or coldly, in a way, dispassionately. These men desire adventure and enjoyment and often separate love and sex. This may protect from the guilt feelings that men feel when being unfaithful, in spite of apparent sexual liberation. By 'cleansing' their sexual relationships of feeling they do not feel themselves to be as sinful as they would if they admitted having also fallen in love with their parallel partner. Plentiful use of alcohol, women's activeness, erotic sexual acts such as oral sex, imaginative positions, a very long-lasting coitus, or many consecutive acts of coitus come together in the parallel relationship stories of men of the middle generation. For many men of the middle generation it has been important to be sexually able and they have energetically worked to give the woman an orgasm. Some men have been able to maintain the 'balance of fear' in engaging in sex simultaneously with their wife and lover. The fear and excitement of being found out might provide content for their life and encourage them to continue the risky relationship in order to spice up their dull life.

The stories of the unfaithful wives of the middle generation include above all casual relationships that were not founded on strong feelings of love. Women of the generation of sexual revolution seem to have adopted ways of objectifying their sexual relationships as purely physical in the same way as men have always done. Some of the parallel relations of these women have provided particular pleasure because they have featured many different kinds of sexual techniques, such as oral sex. The casual relationships that occurred while travelling may have been revealed to the husband, but otherwise the women have gone to great lengths to conceal their parallel relationships.

The parallel relations of young men seem to have been rather casual and transitory. *The generation of gender equalisation* has changed partners quickly when relationships have experienced cracks. Fathering a child has not always meant moving in with its mother. Still, some young men experienced guilt feelings for abandoning their long time partner or the mother of their unborn child. Many parallel relationship stories of women of the generation of equalisation are dramatic and graphically detailed descriptions of everyday life. There are pleasurable but also many painful experiences. The stories do not contain as much erotic passion as the parallel relationships stories of the middle and ageing generations. The young people's descriptions include jealousy, pain and despair, which is related either light-heartedly or with aggression. A lighter manner of expression reflects the fact that many opportunities are still open in the life of the writer, so it is possible to get over the infidelity of one's own or that of one's regular partner by finding a new relationship.

Part III
Remembering Sexuality

9
Joy and Suffering

The final part of this book approaches *the impact of sexuality and the meanings attributed to it* in the autobiographies written by people of different generations and at different stages of the life course. This chapter presents some of the best and the worst experiences depicted in the autobiographies: sex as pleasure, and sex as pain and frustration.

In our culture, intense sexual passion is extremely highly valued. Ideally, it represents a realm of freedom, one where 'the laws and identities governing everyday life can be suspended and the self be organised in ways that include aspects and qualities otherwise exiled' (Simon and Gagnon 1999, 32). Approximately one-tenth of all men and women wrote something on a particularly satisfying or extraordinary experience. The best experiences have been grouped into three categories: (1) *physical passion and endurance*; (2) *extraordinary sex*; and (3) *holistic experiences*. All these memories described physical or psychological sensations that surpassed previous experiences. Such experiences can become turning points in life, prompting a re-evaluation of one's sexual and social life. For instance, a life phase may begin in which sexual experiences are very important. The emotions towards one's partner come to contain a new and deeper desire and fulfilment. At the same time, potentially subversive pleasure threatens many social conventions. Many of the experiences became memorable precisely because they represent social transgressions.

The worst sexual experiences were connected with sexual violence. Stories of rape and sexual abuse have already been discussed in preceding parts of this book. One in four of the women's and one in eight of the men's autobiographies described sexual abuse and incest in childhood and youth. One in eight women and two per cent of the men discussed sexual abuse and violence in adult age. Especially in writing about sexual relations within the family (other than between a husband and a wife), the sexual autobiographies featured descriptions of fear, anguish and disgust in more powerful terms than in just about any other context. Most complaints in our material were, however, related to milder forms in the continuum of sexual violence and aggression (Kelly 1988)[1]. Our analyses of different sexual lifestyles in Part II already highlighted the frustration and pain experienced by one or both partners in a sexually incompatible relationship. The end of the chapter thus focuses on the experiences of being either *pressured to have sex* or *sexually rejected* in a long-term relationship.

Physical passion and endurance

The first and largest group of memorable sexual pleasure included stories of overwhelming physical passion. Passion was often connected to physical perseverance – exceptionally numerous or long-lasting acts of intercourse – or other extreme physical sensations, such as trembling, swooning and having multiple orgasms. Physical passion was also often associated with a particular partner and the outlook or skills of this partner.

Both the middle generation and the youngest generation wrote about physical passion, while they were depicted less in the oldest generation. On the one hand, this reflects the stage of life at which the authors wrote their autobiographies. The discovery of intense physical sexual pleasure tends to occur either in youth and early adulthood, or in middle age, after the first longer relationship. Especially for the women of the generation of sexual revolution, sexual satisfaction continued and often intensified in middle age. On the other hand, overall sexual satisfaction has increased in the middle and younger generation, thus also increasing the number of people who have experienced passionate sex (Kontula and Haavio-Mannila 1995b, 106–7). Some of the middle generation women connected their extraordinary moments to the experience of orgasm. The first 'real' orgasm was often connected to an experience of total abandon, of letting go, finding a 'real man' or becoming a 'real woman'. The woman of the following quote fell in love nearing the age of 40. She writes how she now, for the first time, felt that she abandoned herself completely:

> With him I learned what sex was about at its best. It really starts between your ears. You need to let go completely, the courage to be your own, primitive self, to forget everything else and throw yourself

into enjoying it full blast. And I did just that, in every way! I jumped in with all the energy I had accumulated over dozens of years.

... We had a fabulous time together. To me, the best moments were over the weekends. For instance, it was wonderful to wake up from a catnap next to the person I loved, knowing that no-one would bother us, that there was no need to go anywhere, and that we could devote our attention completely to each other in peace and quiet. You can make love all night, if both of you want to. (49F48)

Another middle generation woman in a regular relationship felt her life changed altogether after she turned 30 and met a Cuban man while on holiday. They began a relationship after the man had courted her for a week. She records experiencing an 'earth shattering multiple orgasm' and felt she had been initiated as a 'woman with a capital W'.

When one night he just took my hand, and I was sold. The tension was so intense that I shook like a leaf, and I was melting wax. He just walked me away. But what a man! I've never before experienced anything like it. I don't know if I had experienced an orgasm before, but *NOW I DID!* No question about it!

He was in no hurry, and he kissed and touched me skilfully. He asked that I 'come first'; and I did, I came and came and came and came ... . A multiple orgasm that shook the heavens and made me half-unconscious. As if the orgasms of eight years had swelled out of me all at once. I was initiated as a woman with a capital W. (20F47)

The justification for socially unacceptable parallel relations is often found in enjoyment or a love determined by fate. One middle generation woman presents her married lover as the prince who woke her from a century-long 'sexual slumber'. The desire and hunger are described as irresistible – the extramarital affair is justified because the couple would die if they had to stay away from each other:

I have been blessed with a strong sexual appetite. I did not even understand that it was possible to feel like this. Antti woke me from my one-hundred-year slumber. I am very grateful to him for that .... We complement each other. We are not able to stay away from each other. We have tried it. It would take the life out of us.

When we see each other after being apart, the hunger is so over-whelming that I don't even know how to satisfy it. We dream of waking up in each other's arms in the morning, making coffee, reading the newspaper, being together. I don't know anything that would be more wonderful. We have woken up in each other's arms, but in a tent at a camping ground. And at my place a few times. I want to fix him all kinds of good things, I want to pamper him. (87F42)

Memories of deep and physical passion were also described inside a regular relationship. Many women of this generation emphasize the importance of trust and caring as a foundation for passion. The best moments of the following middle generation woman, now living in a consensual union, contained a burning passion that was founded on tenderness. Her ideal man should also be able to have long-lasting intercourse.

The best moments of loving and sexual closeness in adulthood have been like this for me: 'He holds my hand protectively when he enters me. Our skin senses the tenderness and intimacy behind the touches. His words are caressing and erotic. Almost without noticing, tenderness turns into smouldering passion and a hunger to be sated. I want more, more, more. Can this hunger be fulfilled? I want to go deeper and deeper. And then it happens: the pleasure erupts in a scream that I cannot stop.'

... The man must be trustworthy, protective, tender, empathetic and able to give caresses. In addition he has to last long in intercourse, or at least be able to do it several times in a row. It is also essential that I have known the man for some time. (107F42)

One middle generation woman had a particularly enjoyable relationship with a married man who was 20 years older. She remembers how he 'ignited her passion over and over again' and shared her sexual fantasies.

In your arms I have been able to cry in my grief, and in those same arms I have laughed about the small, happy incidents of everyday life. I have fretted over my hanging breasts, and that at 35 I no longer look like I'm 20; and right away you made me feel beautiful. There is not a part of me that you have not kissed and admired. With you I have gotten something rare: we share our secrets and sexual fantasies – we are able to talk about them and to create more.

... Again and again you ignite the flame of my physical passion that burns like a torch, and then gently place me back on earth in a state of perfect fulfilment. Physical attraction and an irresistible draw to sexual play are a natural part of your persona, your voice, and the way you move and handle me. (111F35)

Middle generation men also cherish memories of total abandon. We have seen how the women often remembered passion with metaphors from nature and fairytales (trembling as a leaf, melting as wax, being awakened by the prince) and stressed the importance of time and trust. Many men rather refer to the 'overcoming of inhibitions' and empha- size the positions and time involved in extraordinary sexual perfor- mances. One such man recollected making love at a co-worker's home. It became 'the experience of his life':

Now we made love without any inhibitions. It was a really ground- breaking experience for me. Under me, she screamed my name to the rhythm of my thrusts. It was almost frightening to realize how much pleasure I am able to give to a woman. I discovered entirely new areas of pleasure.

... What follows is the most eventful and roughest night of love- making in my life thus far. We used various positions. It was the first time I did it properly from behind. I had done it once with M. but she had been shy. V. is not shy, and my inhibitions also disappear.

Occasionally we have oral sex, uninhibitedly for the first time in my case. Before, with M. and A. we had just kind of fumbled around with it. After ejaculating my erection stays and stays. From time to time I ask V. if she's finished. Everything is so confused that I don't really know about V. She says she has already come at least three times. I'm a little surprised. (172M46)

Some men remembered sexually active, even dangerous women – 'dark witches'. One middle generation man was simultaneously involved with two women who were superior in his mind.

... The involvement with each one was made up almost exclusively of sex. One of them, who sent me a brief note in the summer, became ... the wife of a police chief, came every other Sunday to visit me in Helsinki, and alternatively to visit 'her aunt' in Turku. She was dark like a witch and sexually delectable and sucked like a calf's mouth.

She told me her previous lover had been a 30-year-old engineer, who died in bed of a ruptured vein in the brain while making love with her. I'm not surprised, but I'm a man from Häme [denotes slowness in Finnish national tales], slow to turn on, and I never burst into full flame, so I survived. (71M54)

The *physical outlook* of the sexual partner and *special genital sensations* are strongly emphasized in the stories of the generation of the sexual revolution. By contrast, the stories of the oldest and the youngest generation also include more romantic or holistic descriptions of sexual intercourse (see below). The emphasis on specific physical attributes is also more common among men, like in these reflections made by men from three generations:

> My wife is the only woman whose body I have absolutely worshipped … I would most rather make love with her outside, in nature, whenever the chance appeared. I felt a very special pleasure when I was able to take her in my arms and fuck her on the beach right after she came out of the lake, fresh and tight, water droplets shimmering on her lovely parts. I could never get enough of her. (12M65)
>
> The size of the penis does matter. A 'proper weapon' gives a man security and self-confidence. But it's probably more important which 'nut' he is trying to fit his 'bolt' to. So the size of the woman is important as well. But the biggest and most influential factors must be between the ears and in how those tools are used. (65M44)
>
> R. was L.'s [former consensual partner] opposite, blonde, beautiful in a different way, and her hips made an arc I could not imitate on paper … . S.'s potato nose, wonderfully cheerful voice, and slim waist, which melded into a tight butt, gave colour to my life for one year. (7M31)

Women of the middle generation more rarely discuss physical details, but there are exceptions:

> Some envious man with a small penis must have said at some point that the size of the penis is not important in making intercourse good, but he was only partly right. Though men have no cause for worry: penises of every size and shape have lifted women to the heavens since the beginning of time, it's just a question of technique.
>
> … But I could not help noticing that the *Depth* of a woman's orgasm is affected by the size of the male organ; an explosion that reach the stars is the more possible the more material is inside. (At least this is the case with me). (111F35)

Younger women pay more attention to the details and techniques of extraordinary sexual experiences than women of the middle generation. One young woman says she experienced the most stellar moment of her sexual life when she had her first orgasm.

> I remember it like yesterday when our lovemaking finally yielded results from my point of view. It was May 28, after our daytime sex began to feel so intolerably good that I thought I would die right there and then.
>
> I could no longer simply wait for the feeling I long for to appear, so I started to imagine all kinds of erotic things in my mind, and then I felt an indescribable feeling spread between my legs and in my gut, and for one sweet eternity I was dying. All I was, was a trembling body, I couldn't think about anything, my whole consciousness went into experiencing and prolonging that feeling.
>
> It has been almost four and a half years since that extraordinary moment. After we discovered the right position and I understood that you have to work for an orgasm, not so much physically as mentally, we have lived together in ever-greater fulfilment. After that unique experience I became Arka's slave, I would have licked his shoes for the sake of what he did to me. (151F25)

The focal point in the stories of younger people was, however, not so much sexual enjoyment or orgasms, but the discovery of a special, deeper physical pleasure. One young woman in a regular relationship felt she had lost touch with deeper sexual fulfilment. Nothing felt 'better than good' and she yearned for something unexpected. A turning point came in the form of a man she met who got her to multiple orgasm.

> Everything changed that time I had massaged his body with oil, delighting in his sensations. He lifted me onto the sofa, pulled off my panties and pressed his mouth on my vagina. He licked me and I could feel how much he was enjoying it, and that made me enjoy it all the more. Fantasies flooded my mind. The difficult part was choosing the most pleasing and erotic one. I knew everything was possible. My body trembled all over, spasm-like contractions became more and more intense inside my vagina, until finally I had a multiple orgasm.
>
> ... I have needed a man who really wants me to feel pleasure, a man who takes me all the way. I can't get anywhere if I have to

worry about when the man will stop right when I'm just getting started. When you have mutual trust, it's easy to just let go. (142F25)

Another woman wrote about sexual technique in very minute terms, but within a romantic and sensuous frame:

> I think I give a man the greatest pleasure by really enjoying what I do to him. I can communicate to him the desire I feel. I think it's wonderful to turn on another person, to enjoy what he enjoys. The feel of his penis is wonderful. I like sucking it. I love pressing my face in his pubic hair and smelling his scent.
>
> I love when he comes in my mouth. I like the feel and taste of his come. I like spreading it on my body. It doesn't bother me if it's on my face, hair, or clothes. I like squeezing his balls and touching the space between them and his anus. It's sweet to put my finger inside him and give him new sensations. I like being able to control his orgasm. And I love being able to give him pleasure that perhaps no one else has ever given him. (142F25)

Extraordinary sex

In addition to physical passion, memories of intense pleasure were connected with extraordinary experiences of sexual games, with encounters in special places and/or with socially forbidden sex. As one man of the middle generation summarizes:

> ... To me, more important than the position is the place where the act takes place. I am rather sceptical of the acrobatics and descriptions in books about sexual positions ... . First from the front, and then sometimes more 'like the animals' from behind! Those are my best and most favoured methods. Different places and milieus also have an impact on foreplay and the quality of the sex itself. On the table top in the middle of eating, in a stuck elevator, on the corner of the wash basin, in a row boat in the Sulkava rowing competition, in a telephone booth, in a small Fiat, on a motorcycle, in the woods, in the water on the beach, etc. (65M44)

Sometimes the extraordinary memories were connected to a special partner, with whom it was possible to fulfil a fantasy, or who even surpassed every fantasy. For the generation of sexual restraint, other positions besides those with the man on top could represent such extraordinary experiences. A married man of the generation of sexual restraint described his sexual life with his wife at length and in detail. He talked of the only and unexpected sexual adventure with his wife (Inkeri), one of the absolute high points of his love life. Once, she had been treated to a few glasses of cognac and took the sexual initiative. She even wanted to see them more clearly from a large mirror that the husband fetched.

> After she got back 'in the saddle' we could see in the mirror, down to the details, how little john went in between the labia. We switched positions and watched how it looked from the mirror. J. had never before and would never again show such active interest in lovemaking and intercourse techniques, or enjoyed it so plainly with both her sense of touch and sight. (12M65)

Making love in a crowded place provides a classic sense of danger. A man from the middle generation remembers such a 'quick fuck' with his girlfriend. When they got the urge to have sex, many of the woman's family members and relatives were present.

> ... She and I looked in each other's eyes. Within seconds, an erotic charge sprang between us and we made our way to her room. When we got there and into bed, we didn't even take our clothes off. I didn't even get a chance to take off Mirjami's panties, I just slipped in through the side of her panties and we made love with a frantic passion. That act did not last many seconds. When I got inside Mirjami, we both came right away at the same time. We laughed and felt happy. We felt each other. (172M46)

In the younger generations, the sexual games or encounters depicted are more elaborate and often include bondage or light S/M. The following younger generation woman wrote that her husband liked long, blonde hair, pearls and G-strings. She enjoyed playing erotic games with him. As additional spice, they used shared erotic images.

> When I want really to please him, I wear pearls around my neck, a G-string, and put on makeup and nail polish, and appear in the doorway of the bedroom, asking: 'Is this the right address for the erotic dinner?' Then I slowly step toward him. At first I let him admire with his gaze my jutting breasts and my bare, round thighs. I kiss his mouth, eyes, cheeks, neck, hair, and make my way down

leisurely, without forgetting an inch, bypass his penis and go down all the way to his toes. Then I come back up, take his penis in my mouth and tell him how beautiful and hard it is. I get up and ride him until we both come.

Sometimes, to spice it up, I tie his hands to the bed end. Occasionally the opposite happens. I get taken care of so thoroughly that it feels like my nails will come off. The best part of it is that you get to just be there ... . With the help of erotic images I can orgasm really quickly, and if I say them out loud, they give him a hard-on fast. Laughter, too, is a part of good sex. (120F30)

Another young woman had warm memories of a lover she had known for years before a mutual sexual experience. They made love for the first time one night on her initiative.

He was one of those rare men who asks what a woman likes, and he told me cautiously about his own preferences, which also included other men. I was charmed by his openness and honesty. And it also turned me on a little to think about him making love with another man.

I wondered what it was about me that turned him on; he let me know through words and actions. He wanted to feel another person close to him ...

One evening this man wanted to shave the woman's legs. This excited her tremendously.

For over an hour I watched how this young man first caressed (I was madly turned on throughout the entire proceedings) my legs and thighs with an electric shaver. After that he fetched shaving foam and a blade from the bathroom, and I wondered how well I really knew this man (will the knife slip in his hand, will I soon find it in my breast or between my legs?), and I let him, meanwhile enjoying it hugely and getting very turned on, shave my legs. It's pointless to mention that afterwards I leaped on top of him and rode myself to oblivion. (168F24)

The youngest generation places a high value on a sexual self-discovery. This often creates seemingly paradoxical situations, where a young person both values fidelity and honesty in a relationship while having many parallel sexual relations. This paradox is partly explained by the high value placed on extraordinary experiences, what one narrator aptly called something 'better than good'. One woman remembered her intense physical attraction to her former boyfriend. Precisely the forbidden nature of the encounter and the threat of losing self-control made the encounter so pleasurable. The woman had spent the night with her ex-partner who was now dating another woman. They lay in bed side by side. The closeness led to an ecstatic experience. She was trembling from excitement.

> Finally, after hesitating for a long time, I quietly asked him to kiss me, because I knew that he was expecting it before he would do anything else. He turned to me, kissed me very skilfully and at the same time slowly inched on top of me.
>
> It felt as if I would lose my mind right there and then, I sank into an ecstasy the likes of which I had never experienced with anyone. I shook uncontrollably. I couldn't even make a fist out of my hands. Without exaggerating, it felt like I was close to fainting or nirvana or something. It lasted for maybe half a minute, till I was in control again and I whispered hoarsely, break, I need a break …
>
> I lay there for a moment catching my breath, and all I could do was to whisper endlessly: 'oh god oh god oh god …'. Timo was ready to make love right away, but I was afraid. Even the thought of total loss of control both enthralled and frightened me. (89F20)

Although the allure of the forbidden fruit affected the experiences of all generations, it is an especially valued experience for the young, who have grown up in a liberal society with fewer sexual taboos.

Holistic experiences

Women especially from the younger generation described great sex as a holistic experience, where physical intercourse was not as important as sensations of pleasure and of total spiritual presence. In contrast to the stories said to be the typical story of sexual pleasure from time of the sexual revolution, these memories do not focus on techniques and orgasms, but emphasize a broad interpretation of sexuality. Partly, the vocabulary used to express holistic views appears to be influenced by new age religiosity or popular psychology: the texts praise the correct use of 'energies' and spiritual and bodily union. Losing self-control, transcending boundaries and achieving complete closeness with another human being are once more the goals, and here they can sometimes be achieved even without sexual intercourse. Women of the middle generation often described finding sexual pleasure through a more knowledgeable male partner. Similar stories are found among the holistic approach but the responsibility for achieving or controlling pleasure is more perceived as one's own. 'I invented sex myself', is the recurring if ironic statement of a young woman (150F26). Another writes that:

> I expected to enjoy [intercourse] more in the future and I expected the man to provide me with this pleasure. I think that expectation came from books, because nowhere in what I had read did they ever hint that a woman can influence her feelings herself while making love. I did not understand one could combine the pleasure from masturbation with what I experienced with a man. Only after many years did I understand that finally the pleasure is made by me and not by the man. (3F29)

The fixation on orgasm is definitely repudiated. Sexual equalisation includes the sense of sexual agency being relegated to both men and women.

> I think that one of the biggest reasons for sexual misuse is a misunderstanding of sexual energy. We think that it is a personal force we are permitted to try on others and that one can enjoy in a feeling of personal power. But sexual energy is in my view merely one feature, one side of being a human person, a gift we have received. ... I do not dream about more [sexual] activity but about learning to treasure warmth and closeness. I also dream about independence in the sense of learning to recognize my real needs in love and sexuality. (32N43)

Another woman describes how easy she could awaken her own and another persons sexual interest, but found it hard to stop these feelings 'in time'. She consciously avoided 'playing with fire' and wanted to control her feelings. She found for herself a satisfaction that was more spiritual.

> Sexual fulfilment for me is different these days than when I was younger. I used to think that orgasm equalled sexual fulfilment, but now my fulfilment is more spiritual. I enjoy the desire itself, and the excitement of flirting and the awakening of interest, and the intensifying of passion during lovemaking.

I don't strive for orgasm anymore, but I have one almost every time we make love. I don't expect the man to give me one, I know how to move myself to be fulfilled. A man *cannot* make me feel pleasure, relax, be uninhibited – only my own thoughts and I can make it happen. This realization helped me enjoy sex in accordance with my feelings, not by trying by force. Feelings are born of thoughts and you can influence them yourself. (3F29)

Another young woman of the generation of sexual equalisation considered her most mind-boggling experience of lovemaking to be one that included a lot of touching, kissing and long-lasting petting. It occurred with a partner who had considered the woman's pleasure most important.

My most mind-blowing sexual experience, which included all of these positive epithets, occurred a couple of years ago. I knew the man somewhat already.

The first sexual encounter already taught me more about the language of my own body than all the previous ones combined. He felt that it was everything that led to intercourse that was most important in sex, not intercourse itself. To him, it wasn't even necessary to have the physical act of intercourse; fulfilment and feeling good could happen on many levels – even on a spiritual one. He emphasized that touching and the way you caress the other person is more important. It was easy for me to agree with him.

He was unselfish. It was more important for him that I felt pleasure and felt liberated enough to reveal my desires. He definitely did not hurry. I never before in my life have been kissed for hours from head to foot, between each toe, as pleasurably. He taught me my body's sexual 'points' and how I can turn myself on at the same time as I'm doing it to him. With him I learned to enjoy oral sex, to use a condom with ease, to enjoy being touched, to relax … (149F33)

However, this woman found it difficult to benefit from these experiences with other men. She writes that she had orgasm only in 'one out of ten' sexual encounters with other men. A similar example is contained in the story of a young woman, who describes how she met a married man with whom she spent the weekend. Afterwards, she was feeling confused.

… Before the first 'union' he kept me on tenterhooks for more than ten hours with his foreplay (so that I would be certain that I wanted his Married Manhood with all my heart), and god, I have never been so pathologically grateful than that morning to finally feel a man inside me ...

Never before had a man made me feel so secure; after we made love, he tucked me in under the covers of our bed from head to foot, and kissing my hair, fed me breakfast – Jesus! I am not used to being over pampered or being so content in my life, so I guess it feels very intense when someone pays attention to me, or to making me feel good. (168F24)

There were also some men who were classified as having a holistic perception of sex: they emphasized sensuousness and feeling liberated during intercourse itself. One middle generation man who suffered from impotence stressed tenderness, warmth, closeness and touching in sexuality. He had greatly enjoyed being on nudist beaches where sexuality was not a major focus.

All sexual needs and emotions must be expressed as tenderly, beautifully, warmly and intimately as possible, so that they make you and the other person feel the best way possible ... . I have always derived a lot of enjoyment from being without clothes – nudity relaxes me and makes me feel at peace. (173M46)

One man of the younger generation emphasized a woman's sensual closeness.

... A woman's warmth, the smell of her skin, and the skin itself are really the best part of sex. (7M31)

Holistic experiences often contain strong aesthetic components. The following memory explicitly compares a particularly wonderful affair with the expected romantic script – it was 'just like in the movies'. At the same time, the narrator also creates a certain ironic distance to the movie script, as the event is said to have been from a B-movie.

Our loving was like from a B-movie love story. When we left to go to a restaurant that night, we realized we were driving in his little, red Porsche down waterfront streets, into the sunset; in all the restaurants we went to, the last available table was always the most intimate one, with candles and all ... . He made me feel like a

Woman and Beloved, and I loved myself just because I knew he loved me.

We spent over half of those Sundays in bed (or on the floor or in the kitchen or on the beach), but in spite of the fact that I was fulfilled many times those days, I simply could not get enough of him. Even as he lay beside me or under me, I missed him and his touch, I wanted him closer even although he was already in my arms and said the words that I had always wanted to hear – it was so fierce somehow, the way I felt. If he had asked me to crawl naked on all fours during rush hour down the street I lived on, I would have probably done it, just to hear his ringing laughter. I loved him so much that it was unprecedented, so much that I cried when he was away, and also when he was near, because it felt so good so powerful that it was painful. (168F24)

Holistic descriptions are situated somewhere between transcending and losing oneself. In them, sexuality is often presented as a very nearly religious experience.

Pressure and rejection

The remainder of this chapter is devoted to memories of sexual disappointment and suffering. We will concentrate on the milder forms of sexual violence and dissatisfaction. The autobiographies describe this in two main forms – as pressurised sex or simply bad sex, and as unfulfilling and trivial sex. Predominantly, men are the ones who pressurise and women the ones who resist, but there are not a few examples to the contrary. Although sexual violence and aggression are present, it is one thread in a complicated weave of power struggles, secrets, loneliness and communication problems.

As shown in the previous part, a difference in sexual appetite is today one of the most common sexual problems. This is not about occasional variation in the intensity of sexual desire, resulting for example from worry and fatigue, but a more permanent difference. Sometimes the effects of ageing, stress or illness in a partner who has lost a significant part or all of his or her sexual appetite causes the difference in desire. The survey revealed that depending on the generation, at least 15–55 per cent of the women had experienced lack of sexual appetite. The lack of desire was most common among older women and least common among young women. Among men, the respective figures were 5–20 per cent. These statistical differences are glaringly depicted in the autobiographies written by men of the middle generation, who recall deep humiliation and 'hellish' powerlessness because they are rejected in bed. Finnish men were also more likely to report that they would prefer to have sexual intercourse more frequently than is the case at present in their couple relationship. Forty per cent believed thus, as did 16 per cent of women. Relatively few felt they had intercourse too often. A majority of men required more frequent than weekly intercourse in order to be sexually fulfilled. For many women, one act of intercourse per week was enough to feel fulfilled. Some men and women wanted to have intercourse approximately daily to feel fulfilled.

The sexual script of the oldest generation did not favour diverse expressions of sexuality for either sex. Wives were also supposed to yield to the husband's advances.

> ... I fell in love with a poor, gorgeous boy. After a while sex entered the picture, although it did not taste like anything. I became pregnant and we married. ... In the movies the wives say 'I have a headache', but in reality that does not work. I gave birth to my first child at home. Some 3–4 nights after the delivery my husband demanded his rights. I was torn, sore and weak from the loss of blood, and I told him I was sick. My husband got angry and went out. When he returned he said in a really furious voice 'is missus sick', threw himself naked on the floor and masturbated there. After that I did not dare to reject him. (50F81)

Men often complained that their wives were not at all interested in sexuality. Women complained that men were unable to accept a woman making a sexual move, and that foreplay was out of the question – with a Finnish man, there was 'no talking and no kissing', as the saying goes. Some women also complained specifically of their husband's clumsiness and lack of skill in bed. A few women described arguments and crying as the husband avoided sex:

> Finally it became clear to me that he – a co-worker my own age and divorced – tried to avoid being alone with me, which I very much wanted. There were always other people around, and whenever we took a trip or went on an outing he brought his son along. When it was just the two of us, I would sometimes suggest going to bed. He became furious and explained that only the man could do the initiating. Little by little he began asking me for small favours, like a ride or

a meal for a friend of his. 'Then we can go to bed later, maybe', was how I was repaid. Physically there was nothing wrong with him. Apparently he just had less interest in sexual intimacy than I. (76F62)

How much did I have to cry and fight in order to become pregnant ... . After the pregnancy and birth our marital/sexual/life stopped almost completely. ... If I tried to talk somehow about it or 'tried something', my husband labelled me a whore. (39F45)

The sexual life of the following woman of the oldest generation, classified as a parallel relations type, relied entirely on imagination. Her husband did not touch her for over a year. The matter was being handled with the help of the mental health services.

I am married but for over a year my husband has not laid a finger on me, not a wet or a dry one. It looks like he has the 'granny disease' as well as the visible and invisible damage on his body and soul that result from excessive use of alcohol. We are currently weeding through these problems in therapy through our municipality's psychological services. We do still sleep in the same bed, but there is no touching at all between us.

The couple lived together in a house in a peaceful area, so there were no external factors preventing a sexual life.

I don't want to be the one to initiate it ... . On the other hand, my husband can't approach me until he already has an erection, because foreplay has hardly ever been a part of our sex life. When for some reason he doesn't get an erection, we will sleep tight, back-to-back, being careful not to touch each other.

Our life together does not include hugs or caresses, because my husband's motto is the definition of a Finnish man who does not talk or kiss, only fucks like mad. I guess the ammo is gone now. But for my part, I'm still living a sexually active period inside my own body and mind. (25F57)

A man of the oldest generation who lives in a devitalised relationship originally began eagerly dating his then girlfriend (his future wife) after a hiatus of a couple of years. A sexually lively relationship began at the same time. The man always had a bigger sexual appetite than the woman.

I understood myself that I could be rather troublesome to I., and I suggested that I take bromic acid to calm down even for a little while, but she rejected such thoughts right off the bat ... . She must have thought that in time I would calm down of my own accord, as long as I could satisfy my most acute needs, and when sexual adventures have lost their novelty.

This did not occur, not even after more than 20 years of married life. The husband says he pressured his wife to have intercourse.

Despite my burning desire I was never aggressive, and was usually gentle and tender. But I would pressure her mentally: if Inkeri did not put out, I would begin to sulk in a way that she could not take for long, and eventually she would give in. (12M65)

The wife had dreamed about a time when her husband's sexual interest would finally subside. The matter was resolved as a result of her own health problems (see Chapter 7).

In one of the excerpts above, the couple sought professional help for their sexual and marital problems. This is quite rare for the oldest generation. Rather, the story of a man who pressured his wife for an extended period is typical until the appearance of an external reason, namely the wife's illness, finally stopped the man from pressuring his wife to have intercourse. Only then was the wife able to refuse to have the intercourse that she found so repulsive. No other methods were used to try to resolve the problems of this relationship.

The stories of the middle generation are full of instances of rejection. In part, this has to do with the life phase – many writers were living in relationships that had become devitalised long ago, had divorced or were contemplating divorce. This is the very generation in which men have divorced and remarried significantly more than the generation before them or than the women of the same generation. The typical story of middle generation women is the discovery of their own sexuality in mid life, in a new relationship. In the first, long-lasting relationship, they often felt trapped:

His need for a woman was insatiable, I have to say, and day and night we were together. I thought it good, too. It upset my mental strength however, I could not take so much closeness. I fled the bed. I hurt the other person's feelings then. I did not understand: when I was fine he had enough. I was irritated by his fits of rage, when we were with some people or in normal situations at home or out. (36F52)

During my pregnancies I refused to have intercourse; it had performed its mission to put it biblically! Then I demanded condoms.
Thus I managed to have only three children. ... My husband was
increasingly jealous ... . In my life I had for instance never once
been able to spend one evening without asking anybody for permission. (33F53)

In contrast to the oldest generation, the generation of the sexual revolution was already able to utilize non-fiction literature and professional
help in tackling sexual problems. Thus, it is interesting that it is the
men and women of this generation who would seem to suffer most
from such immense incompatibility problems. Also, according to the
survey, middle generation men saw intercourse as much more pleasurable and wanted more of it in their couple relationships much more
frequently than their female contemporaries. This might reflect the
fact that the sexual revolution was quicker to liberate men's sexual
behaviour. Its emphasis on sexual techniques and orgasm was perceived as too narrow by many women. Statistically, women of the
middle generation adopted a more pluralistic and liberal sexual behaviour rather later than did men. Today, young Finnish women are much
happier both with their physical sex and their couple relationships
than are middle-aged and older women.

Among men, age does not significantly influence sexual satisfaction.
The following quote is from a man of the generation of sexual revolution living with parallel relations:

My sexual relationship with my wife is really miserable at the
moment. In my view, it is at the root of the most profound conflicts
in our marriage. My wife's sexual appetite and needs are
significantly smaller than mine. She is a wonderfully skilful lover,
but her desire to make love is usually limited to once a week or two
weeks. I myself would want to have sex about three times a day, so
the difference is remarkable.

Indeed, she has often commented that it's such a pain, and takes
so long and is disgustingly wet and unpleasant and sweaty. I, on the
contrary, find it wonderful. I have to greatly restrict how I move and
what sounds I make when we make love, because I'm afraid that my
wife would not like it. I can never make love freely and without
inhibitions the way I would want to. Sometimes I would want to
make love for hours on end, but with us that's out of the question.

The man had a mistress, but he still did not feel he was getting enough sex. He had at one point attempted to discuss the matter with his wife and borrowed sex guides from the library. According to him, it only ended in fighting. He was often sexually rejected and for that reason avoided closeness in general with his wife.

> We live in a house of our own and sleep in different rooms. I have decided that it's better that way. If I slept next to her, I would want her more and it would be difficult for me. I remember when we still slept in the same bed and I sometimes tried to approach her at night or in the morning. She became furious. I was not allowed to even touch her. Being sexually rejected is not pleasant. I was often very bitter about it. (58M44)

This quote from a middle generation man is another example of the complaints of a rejected man:

> That my wife did not want to make love with me as often as I did caused bad fights. Her flippant comment: 'Again?' or 'Not again?' or after the act, 'Finally it came' irritated me. More and more it annoyed me that when I wanted to be close, she just huffed and acted out. (122M44)

A third man of the middle generation who lives in a devitalised marriage describes himself as a 'beggar at his own door'. He felt compelled to flatter his wife in various ways to get her to bestow sexual favours upon him. The repeated rejections rendered him quite desperate.

> I am rolling around in anguish in my bed, or should I say, the double bed I share with my wife. The cause of my anguish is that my wife has once more for a long period rejected all my mental and physical advances. I feel a strong urge to make love with her, but I am afraid to initiate it because I fear being humiliated by being rejected once more.

One Saturday night the man tried to please his wife in every possible way and steered away from topics that might create discord. They decided to go to the market to buy the last strawberries of the summer. At the market square, they had a disagreement because the husband wanted to buy a whole box of strawberries, but the wife only wanted five litres of them in her new basket. As a result of this difference in views, she shot him an angry glance, tossed her head and stalked off.

> I look after her and know that I have failed once more at building good relations. Without a warning, I had hurt her by preventing her from fulfilling her wish – ripe, red strawberries on white paper in her new basket. I knew that the possibility of approaching my wife physically was very remote, now that other forms of togetherness had toppled with the strawberry stems. Life is that precarious! That precariousness is the building material of Hell. (169M50)

By contrast, in the youngest generation we find such situations, sometimes quite happily resolved. This young woman is in her second marriage and happy to have escaped the pressures of her previous relations:

> ... I have felt pressured by the feeling that every touch has to lead to the bed and to sex. In my earlier relations I experienced much of that and now I have occasionally wanted to enjoy touching and being close without sexual associations. ... Of course the desires do not always match and then we talk about it openly. I never try to invent false reasons but tell in a beautiful way if I do not feel like making love when my husband does. That does not prevent him from finding satisfaction himself and I can participate relaxed and without faking. I refuse totally only when I really cannot stand the thought of making love. (3F29)

Typical for the youngest generation are the high expectations of sex. One easily tries out various methods for improving a devitalised sex life. If the relationship does not improve, sexual differences may be the reason for considering divorce.

The following young woman who lives in a devitalised marriage has been married five years and has two children. She would like a more interesting sex life. She would also like her husband to caress her more often and to have leisurely talks and caresses with him after intercourse. The children make it difficult to concentrate on lovemaking.

> Even though the pressure to enjoy the 'forbidden fruit' has disappeared with marriage, it has been replaced by other, should I say interfering factors. The baby wakes up easily and makes physical contact with my husband difficult. You are constantly alert to when

the baby starts crying, and maybe wakes up its little brother. It's hard to concentrate. Often I'm also too tired, and don't really feel like having sex. (31F27)

We also find women who complain of being sexually rejected, just like the older men did. Another young woman living in a faithful marriage had tried various means to interest her spouse in sex. The husband had often rejected her come-ons, which had already made the wife consider divorce.

> I often wear garters or sexy nighties to turn him on, and I am frequently disappointed to hear that he is too tired or not in the mood. I even suspected another woman, but I knew there was no one else, he was a one-woman man. I read sex magazines secretly or watched sex movies, and sometimes I got Petri to watch with me and sometimes we would make love afterwards, but sex in any shape or form did not seem to interest him.
>
> I even contemplated divorcing him, but I loved him way too much in spite of everything. But I have to admit that I would not have had the guts to do anything like that. We were already living together and were otherwise happy. But every night I wondered whether I dare suggest lovemaking, if I dare make a move, what if he feels awkward, having to say no once more. (162F22)

This chapter has discussed the highs and lows of people's sexual memories. Passion and lonely humiliation are the eternal extremes, but we have seen how the ways of formulating sexual problems and dealing with them vary with gender and generation. The next chapter will look more closely at the changing importance ascribed to sexuality.

10
The Importance of Sex

This chapter presents the importance ascribed to sexuality in our life stories. We will approach it by grouping the autobiographical excerpts where the authors explicitly reflect on the meanings of sexuality in their life.[1] The authors present sexuality either as (a) *the basic structure of life*; (b) a way of *escaping the everyday*, either in positive terms – as a cure – or as a more threatening addiction; (c) as a form of *bodily and spiritual closeness*, or (d) as a *source of disappointment*.[2] We then conclude Part III by discussing the generational changes in attitudes to sexuality in the 20th century.

The importance ascribed to sexuality depends on at least two factors: the role and strength of personal desire, and the importance assigned to physical desire and sexuality in culture and society. Although interrelated, the factors do not coincide. The strength of desire is partly due to biological, physiological and/or psychological reasons – regardless of generation and gender – some people are more fascinated by sex than others. These biological givens are then intertwined and framed by the prevailing sexual scripts in society.

The leaflet for the sexual autobiography competition did not emphasize writing about the meanings of sexuality, but the authors were asked to assess how important the experiences and sensations that were related to sexuality had been in terms of their life as a whole. Three quarters of both men and women wrote something about the meaning sexuality had for them. Different age and social groups wrote about the topic with nearly the same frequencies. Of the relationship types, people with parallel relations wrote most about the meaning of sexuality in their lives, while the monogamous and consecutive relationship types wrote about it least.

The number of persons emphasizing the central importance of sex is probably over represented in our material. People who think of themselves as sexually active and adventurous were more compelled to participate by submitting their sexual autobiography to our competition.

Sexuality as the basic meaning of life

> ... In my life, sexuality has been one of the most powerful experiences. Perhaps it could even be said that I am oversexed, because just thinking about the topic got me in a state where I had to masturbate before I could even begin writing, and I did it by hand standing up in front of the mirror. Well, to get on with it ...
>
> Now when as an adult I can examine sexuality in my life, I find that it has meant almost everything to me in life. That may seem like an exaggeration, but that is how I experience it, regardless of how other people do. (25F57)

The first category sees sexuality as a basic structure in life: it is a *basic feature of life*, a *constant tension*, or simply *the most important thing in life*. Of the autobiographies that did discuss the role of sexuality in their lives, about three-quarters of the men and one-sixth of the women offered an interpretation in which sexuality is the 'central aspect of life' or a 'basic human need'. As we have seen, mainly women wrote about 'constant erotic and sexual tensions': one woman in five assigned this meaning to sexuality, and in relative terms, this experience was most common among young women. The number of those who stressed the 'importance of sexuality in life as a whole' is significantly reinforced among the younger generations of women – one of four young women held this view. Approximately one-tenth of men and women saw sexuality as a 'stormy passion', a 'glow' and a 'pleasure'.

People with parallel relations typically belonged to the category in which sexuality is a basic structure in life (this was also the case for the author of the excerpt above). They often characterised sexuality as a drive, a basic need, an erotic tension, a reproductive force and a passion. None of these writers mentioned sexuality as a source of social or personal problems. Instead, sexuality is seen as 'the salt of life' – an everyday and necessary ingredient. However, the importance of sexuality in this category is sometimes perceived as a threat – the authors describe themselves as 'oversexual' or as guided by the 'beast of lust'. For them, sexuality thus has an *intrinsic value*, it is seen as an essential part of life, a continuous source of enjoyment and pleasure. People who were searching for love and those with consecutive relations also often saw sexuality as a continuous tension and a basic need in life.

Perceiving of sexuality as a basic structure was common for men of the older and middle generations and for women of the youngest generation, although also some women from the oldest generation gave examples of such a view point. The following middle generation man was a very active sexual adventurer with parallel relations. According to him, he has had up to one thousand partners. He also defined himself as 'oversexed'. He had married, but felt that his wife was not sufficiently interested in sex. In his view, intercourse could help prevent depression, loneliness and sleeplessness.

> I recall that at one point studying meant a lot in my life, and later it was work, but that is no longer the case. They have been replaced by sex. Right now I feel that there is only one thing that takes priority, and that is my son and his life. I love him most in this world. Sex comes second.
>
> I really enjoy, enjoy, *enjoy* sex! There is nothing more wonderful than making love. Unbelievably wonderful! I want more sex, more diverse sex, more unconventional sex, sex with no conventionality at all, sex that is totally free of inhibitions, boundaries, limits, sex with no fear, tender sex, rough sex. Life is so short. Let us enjoy it! (58M44)

In the following excerpt, a woman depicts her desire as a 'beast of lust'. The author has had numerous parallel and consecutive sexual partners during her life (she was classified as a parallel relationship type).

> Only now have you shown me that perfect, mature sexuality is an uninhibited, physical passion combined with an open and spiritual connection of the souls … . Sexuality is present in every mundane task, every person you encounter, every living thing and every object, and in every word and in every deed. In life, sexuality is a force; it is not possible to get away from it, nor should one try. It is God's gift to us. (111F35)

As the above citation indicates, the satanic threat of the 'beast of lust' can also be a divine and productive tension that adds joy and harmony, 'God's gift'. One woman of the generation of sexual restraint emphasizes the happiness and harmony that sexuality brings.

> ... Sex has brought joy, play, ecstasy and happiness into my life, and
> has created new life and children. It has made the days more colour-
> ful and brought sizzling tensions. It has perhaps helped me main-
> tain an open and fresh outlook on life. (157F63)

Two women of the middle generation of the parallel relationship type
talk describe themselves as easily excited. One of them regularly 'made
men crazy' about herself and she reported having had intercourse with
over one hundred men. Her partners were usually younger than her.
The second woman also had a colourful life and dozens of younger
partners.

> You always think that the greatest moments of passion are behind
> you, but these stormy relationships seem to pop up every now and
> then – some man lights my fire like a match to gasoline. (33F53)
> I am still hoping for at least another twenty sex-filled years. It
> makes me feel good, I feel glowing and alive. Without sex I would
> be a woman on a deserted island without clothes, food, without
> life. (37F40)

At the time of writing his autobiography, the only parallel relationship
type man who specifically emphasized the significance of erotic tensions lived in a good marriage. Before, he had had several long-term
relationships and plenty of one-night stands, which he had found very
satisfying. He had done his best to be the 'orgasm cannon' he thought
women wanted him to be.

> Sex has been very important for me. It is part of the everyday as well
> as of more special times. It's everywhere, but you don't get anything
> out of it if you gorge on it. You have to use your head, if that's pos-
> sible in the first place in that state. I have not been disappointed in
> sex, it has been more than half of my life and has washed away the
> greyness of everyday life ... . Infidelities and plain sexual contact
> have been the salt of life. (65M44)

Another man of the parallel relation type from the generation of sexual
restraint presented a veritable song of praise to female genitalia – to
him, the most important thing in the world:

> To those sweet, pout lips that the ancient Chinese have already
> dubbed 'the harbour of heavenly bliss' – could one say it more

beautifully? I worship it … . And when you start at the navel and approach it, when you encounter the hair zone, I begin to feel a wildness, as if I were treading on holy ground.

… And inside the temple itself, things can be different. Where one is restrained and polite to the visitor, another draws you inside and caresses the visitor from the stem to the tip and vice versa. Not to say that everyone wouldn't take good care of the visitor. But with some it takes longer to make the acquaintance … . All in all, I think this world would be a puny place if that harbour were missing from it. (34M61)

At the beginning of her story, a young woman refers to the wide range of love. She also describes the bisexual threads in her life. In her story, the focus is on the force of sexuality itself:

Eros has no gender. I have been sexually attracted to many different kinds of people, and I have never denied these feelings or desires. I experience each person as a sexual being. I could never be asexual, I am both feminine and masculine in the sense that I am interested in and admire both women and men. Sexuality and the fact that there are two sexes create the foundation for me for all human relationships and for being a woman. Wherever I am, I'm strongly aware of the sexual vibrations between people and also try to awaken them myself. (3F29)

Also in the following excerpt, a young woman of the parallel relation type writes that in every encounter, people appeared to her as sexual beings. She was very aware of sexual vibrations and made efforts to awaken them. Her writing was a veritable paean to sexuality and eroticism.

I look the man in the eye, smile, look at his body and attire in a way that he will notice. I communicate to him that I *see* him, feel him and smell his man's scent. I feel like a female meeting her mate.

This author attentively admired and observed other women in her workplace. She would impulsively comment if another woman's outfit or hairdo pleased her.

I consider my sexual experiences the most significant experiences of my life so far. They have taught me the most about relationships.

> Sex and the relationships that are related to it bring out people's true, genuine characteristics and behaviour patterns, which are normally hidden by pretence and covering up. (3F29)

This woman felt that she had lost some of the physical intensity of her passion with age (at 29!). On a spiritual level she continued to want lust and passion. She wondered whether she should seduce a new lover more and more frequently in order to maintain the ardour and tension she wants. However, she did not consider this a mature choice.

Similarly, two other young women 'could not imagine life without sexuality' (although one of them could well imagine that her marriage would at some point not include sex and still be happy). At the time of writing, each had a regular relationship. One had had parallel relations, the other considered herself a 'nymphomaniac', and was classified as a searcher.

> Sex is such a natural part of life that I have never actually thought about its importance. Just like one rarely wonders whether eating is important. Or breathing. On the other hand it is true, that also eating has different impact in different life situations. There are periods when I hardly remember to eat; while sometimes I feel that I do not do much other than eat during my free time. … We have the same built-in drive to reproduce as other animals, and nature has assigned sex to serve this objective. That is why sex feels good. (150F26)
>
> It would be difficult if not downright impossible to write an autobiography without making some references to the sexual aspects of life. In my case living in general and sexual life seem so closely bound together that it is impossible to separate between them. (151F25)

We thus see how some of the younger women adopt and reproduce the biological and instinctual perception of sexuality that in the 20th century was ascribed to men. Sex is here understood as something natural, strong, important and fundamental – a 'fuel, a source of warmth' (3F29). It is perhaps no coincidence that all these three young women are lower middle class and all describe their mothers as very cold and silent in sexual matters. They were not told about menstruation before onset; one (151N25) remembers how her mother severely forbid her to touch her clitoris in the sauna; another summarizes the sexual education given by her mother: 'You'll have the time for these joys later!' (150N26) Their proud assertion of their sexual pleasure and autonomy has not happened automatically. One of these women

(3F29) thinks she has 'traits, that some see as masculine' because she enjoys being active and dominant in bed. She emphasizes that gender roles are not restricted to biological sex: 'I think mental strength and gender are variables and it is good if they vary between both partners in the relationship.' She also writes in detail of how she developed her strong self-confidence, and how this differs from what is conventionally expected of girls. As a teenager, she indulged in heavy petting with a somewhat older boy from another school:

> The next day in school the girls were horrified, what had I done and with whom! I laughed … . My self-confidence grew, I felt I could choose while the other girls just waited and sighed and did not dare to take the initiative. I felt that sexuality would always be an element of my personality, an inner glow that warms me everywhere and affects all my human relations throughout my entire life … . I began to feel the role ascribed to me by my girlfriends and on the other hand by the men (or was it what I thought men thought?) too narrow. I did not want just to wait for some man to express interested in me. Perversely, I wanted to slow down and play hard to get, if a man was interested in me.

Later, this woman felt trapped in a traditional and conventional marriage, which she soon left:

> Sex was no longer voluntary but an obligation, as we were married. It was not a question of whether I wanted or not, but a good and dutiful wife was obliged to keep her husband satisfied. But my husband could not guarantee me pleasure. … He was sexually more inhibited than I was and did not want to be naked even in front of me. I wanted sex during the day, he did not think it was decent. … He did not think I was sexually attractive, because I was intelligent and balanced. (3F29)

Many of the problems of older female generations – lack of sexual education and feelings of shame for being sexually active – are thus repeated in the life stories of young women. However, some of them consciously refuse to reproduce this sexual script. They praise their right to sexual pleasure by appealing to the rhetoric of sexuality as a 'naturally' central aspect of life.

Escaping the everyday

The second type of importance assigned to sexuality is extant in autobiographies where sexuality also is an important part of life, but is not totally dominant or constantly present. Here, sexuality may represent a *zone of freedom* from everyday routines and sometimes also from social conventions and compulsory heterosexuality (Kaskisaari 1998). The authors can 'visit' such a zone of freedom and return with more energy and strength. These are stories of *sex as a cure*, a way to *relax* and *be invigorated,* and as a *resource of* growth *and healing.* Slightly more than every tenth writer assigned a meaning to sexuality that involved a break or escape from the everyday: a resource for self-renewal, growth, increased energy and healing. This interpretation was particularly strong in the texts written by women of the middle generation, where one in four presented this view. It was mentioned across all sexual types.

The following middle generation women present typical definitions of sexuality as a positive zone of freedom:

> Occasionally in my dreams sexuality has been like a tidal wave: it covers everything, rips trees out by their roots and washes them away. But it leaves behind seeds of other trees that grow farther away. New beginnings. At other times, it's like small, refreshing droplets. For example when an otherwise unpleasant visit to the dentist can be made more agreeable by entertaining myself with the thought that the male dentist would lean toward me one centimetre closer than necessary. (14F44)
>
> When external worries weigh on us we have 'tenderness festivities': we touch and hug each other. Almost always it leads to having sex. I think that is the intention! I also feel I am a good lover to my husband, not just a good wife. My husband is a good lover and is a very considerate and tender man.
>
> ... My current sexual life has given me the feeling that it is good to be a woman. I enjoy that feeling. (15F48)

Several men of the middle generation, like these parallel types, saw sexuality as a solace and a cure or remedy for emotional problems:

> When I was depressed, for example during the first five years of marriage when I believed that I would never have my wife's love, it soothed me and released tension when we had delicious sex. The same too, when I felt overwhelming hurt when my great love, E., went with

others, I derived consolation from spending a quiet family evening, and also from being able to enjoy her sweet embrace in bed. (22M69)

You often read about wives complaining about their husbands' indifference and coldness. I marvel at who has a wife like that. Myself, I have longed for a tender kiss as well as hot kisses from my wife all my life.

People often say that extramarital affairs and more long-term relationships only leave a bad aftertaste. I don't know how I would have coped without them. At the worst times I thought of suicide and alcohol. Some married ladies with whom I have had close relations tell me they suffer from the same deprivation as I … . Ahh, spending the whole day in bed with a wonderful sex partner. That's a pleasure I dream about constantly. (68M50)

The following young women explicitly compare sexuality to a medical cure:

With us, sex has been a 'cure' for many ailments. Weeping, longing, grief, joy and happiness too. It helps us to keep going in life. Sex is the best thing you can give another person. It's the most beautiful way of showing that you love and care about the other person. (120F30)

It has become so 'bad' that this girl cannot really fall asleep I the evening without my calming 'needle'. I recommend it to everybody as a substitute to sleeping medicine. (8F48)

The break in routine can also question the stability of everyday life. It represents a risk of becoming too dependent on sex, or of living out wishes that do not fit into the self-perception of the narrator. For authors who do not consider themselves to be homosexual, same-sex relations often represent this kind of 'escape' and/or 'trap' (Kaskisaari 1998). Men in particular vividly describe homosexual feelings and experiences as 'zones of freedom' but also as 'otherness'. The search for a sexual identity is central to such stories and it specifically takes place through the denial of a homosexual identity. This man had memories of peer masturbation from his childhood. He pondered the significance of boyhood experiences for later homosexual feelings and experiences. Here labelling sexuality as a 'brain programme', which behaviour can only slightly alter, conveys the otherness:

I think that the reason I did not become gay was because we (friends) never touched each other with the intention of masturbating each other. I did not learn to orgasm from another person who was of the same sex. The sexual programme in my computer, that is to say, my brain, was programmed to a level that is fairly inclined toward the same sex, but also sufficiently toward the opposite sex. (48M55)

Young women, on the other hand, frequently discuss the ease of encountering a woman when compared to dating a man. For women, same-sex sexual relations are sometimes framed as 'just one form of love', whereas men are more likely to deny same-sex attraction (Kaskisaari 1998, 307). One woman (86F30) spent several months in Stockholm with some feminist friends who were lesbian. 'It was somehow natural that I started going out with one of them. She was a lot older than me but it didn't matter. Because of the distance, it ended eventually, around the same time that I became pregnant.' Later this woman had other relationships with women:

The next summer (1984) I had a very painful relationship with a woman who was mentally ill, she attempted suicide several times, and so on. She was also the girlfriend of one of my best friends and I realized only later that she came to me only to exploit me and to destroy my friendship with her partner. (86F30)

The woman abandoned her lover even though she threatened to commit suicide. She has discovered her bisexuality, but she writes how due to social conventions, she finds having relationships with men easier.

Sexuality as closeness

Third, the importance of sexuality was described through the physical and spiritual closeness it created. For less than one-fifth of both men and women sexuality meant particularly the love, togetherness, warmth and closeness shared with a partner – a physical pleasure not limited to erotic pleasure. Women of the middle and young generation were relatively more likely to offer this interpretation of sexuality. Also several people living in devitalised relationships and those searching for love wrote about it.

The following text of a middle generation woman of the consecutive type married when she was 20. The marriage was unhappy and ended in divorce. When writing her autobiography, she was in a relationship where she met her partner approximately once a month. These meetings gave her 'renewed energy' for her daily life.

The best that sexuality has given me is closeness, a total closeness in which the spirit and the body embrace one another. That I can caress every centimetre of my friend's skin and stroke each one of his thinning hairs. That we talk and laugh together, and my own strong feeling that we belong together even though life did not give us each other. (119F46)

One timid man who was classified as a searcher in youth and monogamous in middle age did not experience his first kiss until he was 24. A shy boy, he had replied to personal advertisements and occasionally visited nudist beaches. Ten years ago he met a girlfriend who was his senior. He saw her at weekends and considered their sexual life good.

Sexuality has brought joy and pleasure to my life. It has also provided the warmth of the opposite sex, both spiritually and physically. In a physical sense, it is the best thing when you feel a woman's naked body against your own – nothing beats the warmth it brings. The soft, warm skin is both exciting and soothing ... Getting the acceptance of women has improved my self-esteem and given me self-confidence. But sometimes timidity sneaks up on me, for example at dances, when I'm supposed to ask women to dance, and I am suddenly overwhelmed by a feeling of inadequacy. (62M39)

The following women write about how the meaning of sexuality changes with age. While sexual pleasure may increase, sexuality itself is no longer 'the upper-most thing':

The best thing about sexuality is closeness, the moments spent together with the loved one, taking the other person into account and receiving the same consideration from the loved one. In one way or another, sexuality enhances sexual identity; it increases the awareness of one's sex.

Sexual feelings could be compared to a hobby. Even the most favourite activity is not always attractive. At its best, lovemaking could be like a rain shower, just as spontaneous. Sometimes the rain shower will drench you at length, sometimes only for a moment. Sexuality is a necessary part of life. Life would probably be dull without it. (31F27)

Gradually, I have come to understand that precisely closeness was lacking from my earlier relationships. Now that mutual closeness and sharing a moment of silence is self-evident ... . The best thing sexuality has given me is my son. ... I don't think I am a very erotic animal, on the contrary: I am cool and evaluating. I don't see eroticism in different symbols: nuts and bolts, pins and holes, nor in balloons. (21F38)

The following young man feels that the most exciting phase of the consensual union he lives in has already passed, but treasures the sexual relations that remain.

Making love is one of the most important events in the relationship of a man and a woman, and may also be spiritually important. Because it makes a person feel significant and that way even gives a person more spiritual strength, positively influencing the durability of a couple relationship ... . The happiest moments for me, of course, are when I make love with my partner and everything works out well and we are both satisfied. (56M32)

Sexuality as disappointment or renunciation

Without a doubt I am by contemporary standards quite a deplorable woman. Sex has not been my biggest joy. When it should have been at its best, it was a luxury I did not have enough strength for. Managing everyday life demanded my physical and spiritual strength so completely, that I could not experience the passion of the 'feast'. It was just one of the endless responsibilities that belong to a woman's every day life. (2F77)

Finally, sexuality is in some autobiographies mainly described as a source of disappointment or renunciation. Very few of the men but almost one-fifth of the female autobiographers wrote mainly of problems and disappointments associated with sexuality. For the most part, the root of the problem was that their romantic or sexual dreams had not been realized. They had not found a satisfactory partner or had the courage to form relationships. We find two categories of people who expressed disappointment in sex. On the one hand, they were people who were still searching and who had not abandoned hope of a happy sexual relationship. On the other hand, there were those who had given up, who did not believe they would or wanted to find anybody, or did not think sexuality belonged to their lifestyle.

The following young generation woman did not have a steady partner yet. After moving to a quiet area she rarely encountered interesting men, but had not lost all hope:

Sex is still very important to me. I think about it almost daily. But my attitude is less overwhelming than before. Life without sex seems worth living too. Once in a while I feel bitter about having to live without sex, but usually I'm happy that I haven't committed myself to one man. This way, life is constantly full of possibilities. (132F34)

The loneliness experienced by the following men was felt much more bitterly. A man of the generation of sexual restraint who is living in a devitalised marriage had a habit of voyeurism in his youth. He married young because he thought marriage was 'the price that a man had to pay for sex'. His wife became menopausal early, at the age of 35, and the man himself had problems with erectile dysfunction. At age 60 his sexual urge was strong and he had many sexual fantasies, but his penis 'remained limp'. This author expressed irritation at the prevailing public image of a Finnish man. In his opinion, women bore a central responsibility when sex did not work. For him, this even provided an explanation for male violence and suicide.

My experience has been, and it is the same for many others, that there she lies expectantly, naked or with her shirt in her teeth, waiting for it to begin. Try engaging in foreplay or licking or what-ever … . No matter how I washed, many a woman who was under me was a block of wood, and to suggest a variation in the position was almost criminal.

I knew two couples fairly intimately whose lives ended in a pre-mature, violent death. In each case the wife humiliated the husband to the extreme, in rationing sex and in doing so also hurt him men-tally, deriding him in front of other people. (99M62)

The following young man was classified as being in love with a fantasy.[3] He had taken some initiatives but had been rebuffed. He felt oppressed and considered himself a failure as a man.

The truth is that I'm badly lost in this life of mine, and in this world. It's probably pointless to say that my sexual anguish is the biggest, single cause. I no longer know what I should do.

I have to ask myself if there is something wrong with me when women don't seem to like me … . What if it did work out, if there was no liquor-induced messing around, or the tough demands of satisfying the partner, or the strange emptiness and doubt in my head. (138M29)

Others were not searching but had more or less happily renounced sexuality in their lives. Several writers felt the importance of sexuality is overemphasized and/or that sexuality is of little importance in their own lives. These authors were usually women from the middle or older generations. They did not perceive sexuality to be part of their current life phase. In such declarations, sexuality is as a rule defined as intercourse with somebody – autoeroticism, sexuality as a constant tension, sexuality as closeness or other broader definitions of sexuality are excluded. The following woman of the generation of sexual restraint, who was classified as a searcher in youth, a parallel relationship type in middle age and living without sex in old age, experienced her first intercourse at age 30. She had sought men through advertisements, but had been deeply disappointed in her experiences. When she was approximately 40 years old, she dated a man for about one year, got pregnant and had an abortion, against the man's wishes. Since that time, men have not been part of this woman's life. She was happy because she no longer had to 'push herself' on men.

> I felt that it was not at all wise to inform my first sex partner what he had saved me from. Men are conceited enough as it is. People encourage you to be open, but it is often unwise. From other people I would want that they talk, write and sing less about sex. If someone is able to get along without it, let it be permitted! Also, I would hope that the word 'cunt' would not be used so much, but that is probably a utopian wish. (26F55)[4]

Another woman of the generation of restraint had waited for the appearance of a great love while living in a rural area as a young woman. When it did not happen, she became a recluse. The woman writes that her chance for a serious relationship with a rich man passed when she 'lost her nerve'. Gradually she became 'hostile' toward sex. She also felt she had been slighted in working life because of her sexually attractive co-workers. The bitter feelings of many sexual disappointments crystallize in the story of this woman.

> That sex has been given special status has been the cause of much suffering, hurt and trouble to humanity. Happiness is just hopeful anticipation ... . Some are unhappy because they do not have sex, others are unhappy because they have too much or it is not satisfying ... . A person who sees everything through sex does not

notice the other things in life. And it seems that too much sex is absolutely the most frustrating thing in life.

... The common belief in the all-validating power of sexual attractiveness has greatly hampered my prospects in working life. When it has been decided that a woman will be chosen for a particular position, all they take into account is looks, even when the person doing the hiring is a woman ... . On the other hand, since in most places one of the objectives is financial, it's clear that someone has to do the work too, and that the babes and the beauties really are not able to do anything but beautify and charm. (28F57)

A woman from the middle generation expresses a similar view. Interestingly, she feels she has to excuse and justify her reluctant attitude towards sex more than the older women did ('I know I am unfair'). This, as well as her psychological vocabulary, might be a result of the sexual therapy she has been attending:

I hope I would soon become so old that sex no longer interests me. ... I experience sex mostly as dependent on men's (!) greedy pleasure and aspirations to enjoyment, infantile primitivism and demands on women. I know I am unfair and unreasonable and I also know that this murderously rejecting attitude of mine is a consequence of earlier sexual abuse – or rather of the fact that I let my sexual urges use me instead of directing them with my reason and wishes. (32F43)

Generational changes in the meaning of sexuality

The role of sexuality in life was not always clearly tied to the generation or gender of the author. However, we have detected some major generational shifts in the meanings ascribed to sexuality. To end this part, we will summarize the generational changes in relation to findings above and to the question of infidelity and parallel relations, which were discussed in Chapter 8. We have seen how the most memorable sexual encounters centred on physical passion and endurance, special physical sensations, extraordinary sex, or holistic sex. This was observed in stories from all generations, although what was perceived as 'daring sex' varied. In the oldest generation, a monogamous man remembered his wife's sexual initiative and dominant sexual position as the highlight of his sexual life. In the youngest generation, transgressive sex was related to sexual role-play or sadomasochistic games.

Many autobiographies of the generation of sexual revolution focused on concrete physical sensations related to the positions employed or to the size and form of the genitalia. By contrast, some women of the youngest generation depicted sexuality as a holistic, not exclusively physical experience.

The category that emphasized the closeness created by sex was most pronounced in the young generation. Due to generational changes in sexual scripts as well as to the phase of life, disappointment in sexuality was rare in the youngest generation and most common among women of the oldest generation. Our excerpts show the broader context in which pressurised sex occurs. Pressurised sex is indeed often 'a general experience within one or a number of relationships' (Kelly 1988). We have termed this general experience of the partners in an unsatisfying relationship 'bad sex'. This term also includes the feelings of degradation and rejection experienced by the partner who pressures (or would like to pressure) to have sex. Such bad sex was described by authors of all generations, but its contents varied.

In the generation of sexual restraint, sexual incompatibility was often due to one spouse's firm beliefs about proper gender roles and sexual behaviour. Women's sexual activity was seen as an anomaly, just as men were not supposed to 'talk or kiss', that is, to show or discuss their feelings. The couples from the generation of sexual revolution were often caught in vicious circles of rejection and pressure. In this generation, sexual happiness had been a goal of the marital union, but it was often found only following a first longer, marriage or cohabitation. In the youngest generation, by contrast, sexual compatibility was a criterion from the very beginning of the relationship. When the first phase of physical passion was over, or hindered by everyday obstacles such as work or small children, the relationship as a whole was readily questioned. The requirement of a satisfying sexual life is increasing and is especially voiced by young women.

The meanings of sexuality depicted in our autobiographies constructed sexuality either as the basic structure of life; as an escape from the everyday; as a form of bodily and spiritual closeness; or as a source of disappointment. Relatively many men saw sexuality as a basic thing in life, although this was also true for women of the youngest generation. Sexuality could represent an escape from everyday routines in the form of a zone of freedom, a cure or an addiction. Especially women from the generation of sexual revolution described sex as zones of freedom. By contrast, men from this generation often described sex as a cure and solace.

Same-sex relations sometimes represented a threatening or an alluring zone of freedom. Men tended to relate their homosexual experiences as an additional threat to their (heterosexual) manhood. By contrast, women and especially young women did not write about same-sex relationships as being a special problem. It seems to be easier for women to transgress the boundaries between heterosexuality and homosexuality that exist in our culture (Kaskisaari 1998, 307). For the young women, the main criterion was whether the couple relationship functioned or not, almost regardless of the gender of the partner, although it is true that one young woman told how social conventions eventually made her settle for a heterosexual relationship.

The generational changes are summarized in Table 10.1. With regard to the role of sex in life, only the typically generational characteristics have been added to the table. In the oldest generation, sexuality can be described, in the words of one author (2F77), as a duty and a luxury. There are many memories of rich sexual experiences, but they are as a rule connected to exceptional circumstances – time or person. Also access to sexual education or pornography was random. This generation was brought up with the sexual script prescribing a dual morality, with a more permissive script for men and one of strict control for women's sexual behaviour, strongly connected with marital responsibilities and reproduction. Some of the women of this generation saw sexuality as the basic thing in life but it was much more common for them to perceive sexuality as mainly a disappointment. In this generation, parallel relations were mostly presented as a result of external circumstances, such as work-related travel (34M61) or the holiday travels of the women quoted in Chapter 8.

Table 10.1 Meanings of sexuality for different sexual generations.

Generation	Restraint	Sexual revolution	Gender equalisation
Sexuality is a	Duty and luxury	Source of pleasure	Tool of self-realisation
The role of sex in life for men	Basic thing in life	Cure Basic thing in life	Closeness Basic thing in life
The role of sex in life for women	Disappointment	Zone of freedom Closeness	Closeness Basic thing in life
Infidelity is justified by	Circumstances	Pleasure and passion	Psychological traits

The generation of sexual revolution adopted an emancipatory view of sexuality, as something to liberate and to enjoy. It describes sexuality as a private, potentially liberating source of pleasure. The new scripts of the 1960s understood sexuality to be legitimate if it was satisfying. It was a seemingly gender neutral script, where women and men were expected to enjoy the sexual revolution in the same way. Mutual orgasm came to symbolise the ideal sexual act. The tensions between liberalisation and gender equality were, however, present, especially in women's life stories. The 'successful' emancipation of women is reflected in how sexually active women from this generation often depicted sexuality as a 'zone of freedom'. In several stories from this middle generation, parallel relations were formally disapproved of. One woman (37F40) labelled it as her 'double life' and talked about 'succumbing' to extramarital relations. At the same time, parallel relations were positively depicted and justified by pleasure. When describing her relations with a much younger boy, this woman clearly feared the judgement of the reader. She described feeling 'broken and dirty inside' as well as being 'an unworthy mother'. Nevertheless, the sexual relationship with a minor is justified by the pleasure felt. The author thinks the affair is acceptable because in her view, both partners desired it and the experience of intercourse was very satisfying.

The generation of equalisation takes many of the liberties obtained by the previous generation for granted. This generation tends to see sexuality as one of the tools of self-realisation, for discovering one's own identity. Both women and men often approach sexuality in a broader context, as part of human relations, many-sided personal development. Mutual pleasure is still highly valued, but it tends to be approached as part of a larger quest for a 'good life'. The right to refuse sex is stressed, especially by women. Both men and women also value sexuality as a source of closeness. It is also seen as important to be honest to oneself and to one's partner and to be able to talk openly about sexual problems.

However, a lack of sexual education, ignorance and shame colour the childhood memories also of this generation. For instance, one woman born in 1969 was surprised when she discovered her growing pubic hair and was totally unprepared for menstruation at the age of 12 (168F24). Still, at least some young women developed an active and independent sexual life. More young women perceived sexuality to be the basic structure of life than in the previous two generations. Some young women see sex as an uncontrollable, natural desire much like the 'hydraulic' model of sexuality that has traditionally been adapted by men (Weeks 1985). At the same time Aids and the rules of political correctness in sexual relations have developed new anxieties and taboos. The script prescribes that certain social relations, such as those involving very young persons, the relationship between a teacher and a pupil, and so on, should remain outside the sexual realm. Generally, infidelity is also more disapproved of in this generation than in the previous one. In justifying infidelity, young people approach it as a psychological process; it is less a question of social order than of personal inclinations.

Unlike women of the older and middle generations, young women often see their tendency to be unfaithful as something outside their control. Parallel relations are thus seen as a problem, which can be solved either by ending the relationship or by a therapeutic self-acceptance. They can be understood as a kind of addiction, a 'perversion of betrayal' (63F23). Some young women, on the other hand, wrote of their partner's acceptance of their desire to be unfaithful and of the act itself, and the resultant competition for the woman's favour with other men. Parallel relationships are presented less as a question of social conventions and more as an individualistic way of claiming that 'I have the right to be this kind of person'. One woman (149F33) put the word 'infidelities' into quotation marks – she had parallel relations, but did not interpret them in the traditional framework of a sinful lie.

Conclusion: Changing Sexual Practices and Scripts

In the course of the 20th century, sexuality has been *secularised* (Weeks 1986; Heiskala 1999). Less governed by divine or governmental laws, adult sexuality has become more dependent of the individual's own choice of lifestyle. It has also gradually become detached from the institution of marriage. Four major trends in the development of sexual social life were apparent in the results of our study. They all reflect the general trend from traditionalism to liberalisation. The first is the *secularisation* of sex. Increasingly, sexuality is perceived as a personal choice detached from religious and other ideological values imposed from above. The second major trend is the *liberalisation* of attitudes and the emphasis on sexual rights and health of people who belong in differing categories of gender, sexual orientation, or inclination. The third change is the *growing diversity of domestic life forms*. The traditional connection between marriage, the family and sexuality has been severed. Fourth, sexuality has become more *hedonistic, pleasure-oriented and recreational,* as the role of reproduction in sexual life has diminished. (Weeks 1986, 92–6; Heiskala 1999; Lottes and Kontula 2000).

In this book we have described sexual practices and scripts on the basis of sexual autobiographies collected in Finland under the auspices of a competition. Survey data has been used as complementary material. As far as we know, this is the first time that it has been possible to use people's sexual autobiographies as research material. From the point of view of the study, it was encouraging that most people had the courage to write about intimate experiences using their own name. Compared with the survey material they did not deviate from the average population in terms of background or experiences.

Throughout, we have compared the sexual lives of men and women from a generational perspective. In our study of sexual social relations

194

and sexual scripts we have distinguished between three generations: the generations of *sexual restraint* (born between 1911 and 1936), *sexual revolution* (born between 1937 and 1956), and *gender equalisation* (born between 1957 and 1973). The stories of writers of different ages, who recalled their childhood, youth and relationships after youth, made it possible to examine changes in sexual issues from one generation to the next.

Five sexual relationship types were detected in the autobiographies. The categories are monogamy, consecutive relations, searching, devitalised unions and parallel relations. People who were classified as belonging to one of these groupings told of their tendencies to make certain choices in their sexual life or of repeatedly drifting into similar situations or circumstances.

An analysis of how sexuality is experienced concludes the book. The importance assigned to sexuality was found to fall into four types. Sexuality was experienced as the basic meaning of life, breaking loose from the every day, closeness, or disappointment. These types have evolved from one generation to the next. Where the oldest generation interpreted sexuality as duty or luxury, the middle generation saw it as an obligatory source of pleasure, and the youngest as a tool for self-realisation.

Sexual generations: the breakthrough of a new morality

The autobiographies revealed changes and continuities in the transmission of sexual information and in the first sexual experiences. The stories revealed that childhood was a sexually active period for many writers. Sexual games among children, including examining genitals, were rather common. Some authors told about having attempted 'real' intercourse already before school age. When these games remained a secret among children, they generally produced positive memories among the writers. But when parents had found out about them, their negative reactions had fostered oppressive memories that in some cases still bothered the writers as adults.

As a rule, parents did not offer much to their children in the way of models for couple relationships and sexual life. Living in close quarters, some children had noticed that their parents were up to something strange to them in bed. Surprisingly, many recalled that they had never seen their parents touch or kiss one another, even in the memories of the youngest generation. However, children of the youngest generation received more clues about their parents' sexual life through finding pornographic and contraceptive products in their bedrooms.

Some of the infatuations and feelings of love between children were expressing those feelings, and resulted in dating, but shyness and insecurity kept a great many from expressing these feelings. In dating, diverse forms of petting were often employed, including petting that resulted in orgasm, even when it was considered improper to have intercourse. The generation of sexual restraint at least tried to preserve virginity for the future spouse while for the younger generation, lack of experience constitutes a burden. For girls too, sexual experience has become sought after, regardless of dating status, although the loss of virginity still affects a young woman's social status more than it does the status of young men.

Women of the younger generation have increasingly taken the role of initiator in their first intercourse. Men usually wrote about the enjoyment they experienced in their first intercourse. Women, on the other hand, often wrote of their physical indifference and hardly mentioned whether they had experienced an orgasm or not. The quality of first experiences varied to a great extent between men and women, from blissful lovemaking to grave disappointment and painful intercourse. For a few women, first intercourse took the form of sexual abuse or rape.

When looking at which of the study's five relationship types people fell into as adults, it was observed that various childhood experiences had no obvious or logical connection to this. The only systematic result found was that negative reactions on the part of parents to children's sexual play caused anxiety in childhood and in many cases continued to be felt in adult age. In addition, men whose sexual life stories classified them as belonging to the parallel relations type were more likely than other people to describe sexual information they had received or observations they had made as children, including witnessing adult lovemaking and animal breeding. It also appears that people who focused on parallel relationships in their stories often had a sexual interest that began in childhood and was stronger than other people's.

The *sexual scripts* have changed significantly between different generations of autobiographical authors. For the oldest generation, the script that bound sexuality to marriage was dominant. The only exception was during wartime, which loosened the norms of a normal life. Those of the generation of sexual restraint began their first relationship/-marriage at a later age and generally stayed in it even when the relationship and sexual life were unsatisfying (devitalised). Sexuality, then, was strongly subordinate to the marriage relationship and not even love justified forming a sexual relationship. In the oldest generation, women in particular were taught and downright forced to adhere to the script of restraint. Girls' sexual experiences were interpreted as dangerous and could easily result in a bad reputation that could prevent a respectable marriage. Women were told emphatically that men were not to be trusted in any respect. Especially in the oldest generation, there were examples of how people adhered to the cultural scenarios of their generation against their wishes. Some older narrators have not allowed themselves to engage in physical sex with their beloved while married to somebody else. They explain their choice to stay faithful by referring to the sexual script, which condemns infidelity. They act altruistically and explicitly do not want to destroy the lives of the other people involved, namely their own life and that of the spouse of their new partner.

The middle generation learned to discuss sexuality in public as a result of the so-called sexual revolution. New meanings of sexuality have largely been communicated through public discussion and mass culture. After the 1960s, sexuality has moved from the private sphere to being a publicly discussed and shared topic (Kontula and Kosonen 1994). The norms concerning life phases have expanded the area that people are permitted to express sexually, and also what they should express. People are both more willing and more obliged than before to invest in attaining sexual satisfaction and, as we have observed, young women in particular present increasingly diverse conceptions of sexuality. Information concerning sexuality increased significantly and spread among people. Women's sexual rights became a topic for discussion. People who were young during the 1960s wrote of the books, manuals and pornographic magazines from which they had garnered information on sex. An accepted script now included sexual relationships that were based on love, or a regular relationship other than just marriage. There were women in this generation who spoke of needing a man and sex (including masturbation). Previously condemned forms of sexuality such as extramarital relations or relationships between partners with a significant age difference were now defended on the basis of the enjoyment they brought.

In the youngest generation, it became acceptable to sexually 'test' partner candidates, to search and to seek the pleasure derived from sexual experiences. Only parallel relationships were looked upon with some reserve. For the generation of young women, pornography was the most common information source. This information led to new interpretations of sex and it's meaning which gave greater emphasis to enjoyment. It also leads to the renewal of the gender specific scripts that determined sexual behaviour. In the youngest generation, the conflicts are perceived as taking place not so much between society and the individual as inside the individual.

Women of the generation of sexual restraint have frequently experienced sexuality as a source of closeness, but also as a duty or a source of problems. For women of the middle generation sexuality has become a sort of resource for other aspects of life. The youngest generation of women often experience sexuality as the continuous presence of eroticism and a basic part of life while men, regardless of generation, have viewed sexuality as a basic part of life. Young men additionally wrote more about the value of touching and closeness. Thus the conceptions and interpretations of men and women have become much closer.

A second, notable change in sexual scripts has to do with *sexual habits*. A new script in which varied methods of touching and intercourse have in some ways become the norm for good lovemaking has enhanced the one-dimensional man-on-top lovemaking. The generation of sexual revolution also experienced a revolution in sexual habits, which became more diverse, partly through the models supplied by pornography and popular science. The new script idealised long-lasting lovemaking, mutual initiation and enjoyment.

For the youngest generation, embarking on a sexual life has become completely separated from marriage, and diverse sexual habits and the right to mutual enjoyment are largely unquestioned. Lack of sexual satisfaction is by itself a sufficient condition for terminating a relationship. At the same time, sexual issues and related preferences have become subjects that are articulated in discussions with a partner. Sexual activities and satisfaction are also valued much more than previously. It is acceptable to have and to seek casual relations for both sexes, although women who did so often described themselves as unusual women, who live outside the good girl/whore dichotomy. Masturbation has also become a much more central part of sexual enjoyment. Eroticism is something to invest in. The partners' enjoyment continues to be an important criterion in legitimizing a sexual relationship, but finding and expressing oneself are also important factors. As one young woman puts it, unlike the preceding generation of women, the women of this generation also know how to say no to sex when they so wish.

In all generations, the highlights in the autobiographies were usually memories of extraordinary, unusual sexual experiences, which sometimes literally changed the lives of the authors. The most pleasurable sexual encounters involved ingredients of excess and transgression: physical passion or unusual physical endurance, special physical sensations, and special techniques and positions. They could also involve an especially intense combination of spiritual and physical closeness or aesthetic experiences in special surroundings. Although stories about exceeding the limits were found in all generations, what was perceived as 'daring sex' varied. In the oldest generation, the wives' sexual initiative could exemplify such an unusual experience. In the youngest generation, transgressive sex was related to sexual role-plays or to experiences of total fusion with the partner. Many autobiographies of the generation of sexual revolution focused on concrete physical sensations related to the positions employed or to the size and form of the genitalia. By contrast, some women of the youngest generation depicted sexuality as a holistic, not exclusively physical experience.

Descriptions of sexual pressure and bad sex in couple relationships were found in all generations, but their contents varied. In the generation of restraint, sexual incompatibility was often due to the gendered sexual scripts, in which women's sexual activity was seen as an anomaly, just as men were not supposed to 'neither talk nor kiss'. The memories from the generation of the sexual revolution often described couples caught in vicious circles of rejection and pressure. In this generation, sexual happiness was frequently found only after the first, longer marriage or cohabitation. By contrast, the youngest generation has sexual compatibility as a criterion from the very beginning of the relationship. When the first phase of physical passion is over or hindered by everyday obstacles such as work or small children, the relationship as a whole is readily questioned.

Generational change is perhaps most clearly seen with regard to parallel affairs. As they have become increasingly common, they are also justified in totally different ways. The oldest generation used to justify infidelity by circumstances and the middle generation with the pleasure the secret affairs created. The youngest generation both values fidelity in a couple relationship, and enjoys many parallel affairs. This seeming contradiction can be grasped by the emphasis on a self-fulfillment, great experiences and creating a good life that guides the youngest generation into both types of behaviour. Young people could put the term infidelity in quotation marks and were prone to seek individual and psychological explanations for parallel relations.

Old and new relationship types

While sexual life has become less inhibited and more versatile, and the physical sexual satisfaction for women has increased, new problems in sexual social relationships have also emerged. They have led to an increasing devitalisation of relationships, parallel relations, separations, and starting again with a new partner, that is, taking a second, or a third chance and so on. Since reproduction as a major function of sexual interaction has lost its centrality, the relational aspects of sexuality have gained importance. A salient version of male–female relationships puts romantic love or lustful fun as the basis for intimacy and marriage.

> The cultural *legerdemain* says that romance is the basis for long-term, indeed, lifetime commitment. This as a contradiction: romance is by definition transient, situational, and affective; lifetime commitment is permanent, institutional, and contractual. (Weigert 1991, 174)

It is often difficult to continue a relationship when the passionate phase of love has ended. Companionate love is less exciting than passionate love and limerence.

The increasing focus on relational and recreational sex, instead of reproductive sex, has made a lifetime sexual commitment less salient as a sexual lifestyle. Nevertheless, the majority of young people – even though they reject marriage and the family as a model for their own lives – seek emotional commitment (Beck and Beck-Gernsheim 1995, 16; Holland *et al.* 1998, 102). Nowadays it is relatively easy to change partners because the 'pure relationship', which is not constrained by external obligations (Giddens 1991; 1992), is an ideal, which legitimises the termination of an unsatisfactory relationship.

The narratives were classified into five types: *monogamy, consecutive relations, searching, devitalised union, and parallel relations* – both as whole stories and separately for three life stages: youth, mid life and old age. The information provided in the stories was also objectively coded into variables, for instance, numbers of partners, frequency of intercourse, and so on. A discriminant analysis of the data coded according to the list of variables was conducted in order to test the reliability and validity of the intuitive coding. The results supported each other. The partnership types differed from each other on three dimensions: the happiness, the sequentiality and the number of couple relationships.

Only one-sixth of the sexual life stories were primarily classified as one and only monogamous love during the lifetime. The stories of the oldest generation, more often than those of the middle and young generations, belonged to this relationship type. We distinguished between two types of monogamous lifestyles: traditional and reflective monogamy. For the first type, monogamy is the self-evident ideal prescribed by tradition and often also by religion, which should be upheld even when the relationship is not satisfying. The second type, reflective monogamy, is by contrast motivated by the high quality of the current relationship. The level of emotional and sexual satisfaction appears more central than the principle of fidelity of itself. The first type was more common in the oldest generation, the second in the younger generation.

One-quarter of the stories focused mainly on consecutive relationships and the same proportion focused on parallel relationships. These relationship types were most common in the autobiographies of the middle generation. This is related to the sexual revolution, which started to secularise, liberalise, and equalise the sexual life in their youth. After the sexual revolution, families have become more prone to a pattern of serial monogamy (cf. Weeks 1986, 95). An obvious sign of the spread of the consecutive relationship type is the growing divorce rate. One in two marriages ends in divorce in Finland.

Parallel relationships form a common partnership type in the middle generation for several reasons. People of the generation of sexual revolution have had many opportunities to encounter attractive partners because many of its members have been working for pay and living in urban areas. In its youth the middle generation was exposed to the idea that sexual pleasure is acceptable in itself, not only as a means for reproduction. The secularisation and liberalisation of sexual attitudes in this generation legitimised romances outside of the permanent relationship. Thus, members of the middle generation were not seriously inhibited in satisfying the sexual desire when they experienced a need to do so. This generation also had higher sexual self-esteem than the older generation – a personal feature necessary in conquering new partners.

Two different sexual scripts regarding extra sexual relationships were discovered. According to the first script, parallel relations are accepted as long as they take place outside the home area or the vicinity of the steady partner, for example, when travelling or at the work place. The relatively liberal attitude to these situational parallel relations may be due to their mostly casual and temporary nature. According to the second script, parallel relations are condemned in the proximity of the steady partner, especially if the extra relationship is permanent. Nevertheless, some autobiographers have been able to maintain a 'balance of terror' in having long-lasting sexual relations with several partners simultaneously.

Parallel relations were sometimes found to be complementary to a devitalised permanent relationship. Occasionally the authors were of the opinion that their relationship with the spouse had continued thanks to their outside relationship. Sometimes extramarital relationships competed with the marital relationship. This often created great tension and anxiety, and frequently led to a separation.

One-fifth of the sexual autobiographies were classified as searching for a partner. This story type was most common in the narratives of the young generation. In addition, many people of the other partnership types were classified as searchers in their youth. Their sexual lifestyle had changed in mid life or older age. There were very few 'full-time' searchers in the middle and older generations.

Living in a devitalised union was the main relationship type for one-tenth of the authors. When one looks at the relationship type separately in different life stages, it is possible to detect an interesting phenomenon. In the generation of sexual restraint, the proportion of devitalised unions remained the same in youth, mid life and older age.[1] Contrary to that, many authors of the generation of sexual revolution reported that while they lived in a devitalised relationship in youth, in mid life they either had consecutive (women) or parallel (men) relationships. Hence, the members of the middle generation did not stay in a devitalised union in the same way as the members of the older generation had done.

With the exception of some young women suffering from, in their own words, 'perversion of betrayal', most of the young authors had been faithful in their steady relationship as long as it had lasted. But in the autobiographies of the youngest generation of gender equalisation, there were also many stories of wild sexual experiments and adventures, light and elusive relationships, and changing partners. Young authors were quite romantic and most of them explicitly longed for a happy and permanent relationship. A new form of moral consciousness – acting decisively while experiencing contradictory emotions – was also discovered in the stories of the generation of gender equalisation (cf. Weigert, 1991, 180). There is creative tension in the sexual lifestyle of the young generation.

Continuing discrepancies between genders

In addition to comparing the three sexual generations, we have contrasted the sexual practices and scripts of men and women. We have tried to show how the configurations of the sexual system bear on the experience of being female and male and, conversely, how the definitions of gender resonate with and are reflected in sexuality (cf. Vance 1989, 9).

Men and women were fairly different in terms of the manner in which they spoke of sexual matters or in relaying different scripts to the next generation. By transferring the 'sex is enjoyable' script to boys through men's stories, older men interested boys in sexual matters. Girls, on the other hand, heard such stories only occasionally because women do not speak in a similar manner and also tried to stop men from talking about sex. Girls of the older generations often connected sexual matters mainly with a romantic script, which did not include an expectation of physical pleasure and enjoyment. In this respect, however, the youngest generation is becoming equalised. The youngest generation differed from other generations also in that the stories began to include accounts of sexual play between girls, as well as detailed descriptions of various masturbation techniques used by girls. Sexual matters became part of the girls' experience at this point. For its part, this has reinforced the script of 'a woman who enjoys her sexuality'.

The popularity of two of the five relationship styles – parallel and consecutive relations – was clearly associated with gender. The three other styles, monogamy, searching and living in a devitalised union, did not vary according to the gender of the author. The stories of men of the older and middle generations, more often than those of women, focused on parallel sexual relationships outside the permanent relationship, whereas the respective women's stories more often centred on consecutive relations. In comparison with the older and middle generations, in the youngest generation the gender roles in sexuality were fairly similar and equal. Young women had adopted many traditionally male sexual practices and attitudes, and young men reflected on their relationships almost as much as young women did.

The stories about sexual incompatibility, which were so common in our material, were associated with both emotional and sexual dissatisfaction. There were plenty of complaints regarding incompatibility of expectations concerning, for example, the frequency and duration of sexual intercourse. Not only men reported a higher interest in sex than their partners; several women wrote that they would like to have sex more often than their male partners were interested in. This is consistent with the findings of Davies *et al.* (1999, 563) who found that women emerged as the lower-desire member in half of their sexually discrepant samples.

Contemporary research often emphasizes the constantly changing forms of sexuality as a social practice (Connell 1997). In addition to the dramatic changes in gendered scripts and behaviour outlined above, our research also points to some trends with a relatively strong continuity. Thus the meanings ascribed to sexuality were found to be quite resistant to generational change, especially which regard to men's experiences of the role of sexuality in life. Even though gender differences in sexual interest have diminished, men tend to be more interested than women in the purely physical pleasures of sex. On the other hand, women tend to be more interested than males in love, nurturing relationships and lasting social bonds. However, many female authors are eloquent on the joys of physical sex. The polarisation of gender roles has certainly decreased, which does not mean that there would have been many narratives of totally abolished gender (cf. Plummer 1995, 158). There were many stories of heterosexual relationships in which 'the male is in the head' of both partners. (cf. Holland *et al.* 1998). Several women authors were conscious of and worried about adjusting their personal life to comply the, sometime, humiliating conditions set down by a man. Often they were not able to resist male power because they were afraid of losing that man.

In summary, sexuality is increasingly central in the life of people as a source of pleasure and enjoyment. We might even ask: when should we expect a counterreaction? Especially young women seem to function as agents of change. They have adopted sexual practices which earlier were particular to men. The normative expectations or scripts with regard to sexuality have changed in concordance with behaviour. New criteria, such as valuing holistic sex, not centred on genitalia and orgasm, have developed.

Lifelong monogamy has lost its status as the dominating sexual script. Most of the authors had at least at a certain stage of their life cycle as sexually active singles or in non-monogamous partnerships. However, monogamy prevailed as an ideal sexual lifestyle in the dreams expressed in most sexual autobiographies.

Serial monogamy has emerged as the normative form of sexual citizenship. This is a sexual lifestyle that used to be more often practised by women, while men practised parallel relations. In this respect, men's sexual lifestyles appear to become more similar to those of women. Or, is it rather that the dominant scripts are still more normative for women than for men? Does the script of serial monogamy apply more strictly to women, just as the script of monogamy used to do? The future will show whether men continue to have more parallel relations, or whether the gender gap in sexual lifestyles continues to close.

Notes

1 Research Material and Theoretical Perspectives

1. In all six surveys, the minimum age of the respondents was 18 years, but the maximum age varied: it was 54 in Finland 1971, 74 in Finland 1992 and in Sweden and St Petersburg 1996, and 81 in Finland in 1999. In each survey, there were 1000–2800 respondents; the total number of people participating was almost 12 000. The response rate was 41 per cent (Estonia), 47 per cent (Finland 1999), 60 per cent (Sweden and St Petersburg), 76 per cent (Finland 1992) and 91 per cent (Finland 1971).

   The 1971 and 1992 Finnish surveys and the 1996 St Petersburg and Swedish surveys were conducted through personal interviews and self-administered questionnaires. The interviewer presented the first part of the questionnaire orally and marked the answers on the questionnaire. The respondents themselves filled in the intimate part while the interviewer stood by. The second questionnaire was then placed in an envelope, which was closed and glued shut by the interviewee. Then both questionnaires were, in the presence of the respondent, put in another envelope, which in 1971 was sent via registered mail to the researchers, and in 1992 and 1996 to the interviewing organisation. The 1999 Finnish survey was conducted by mail and the 2000 Estonian survey by personally taking the questionnaire to the home of the respondent asking him or her to mail it to the research organisation. The different data collection techniques used in the two latest surveys partly explain their low response rates.

2. In the beginning of the 1960s women begun their first marital relationship at age 22 and the median time for the birth of the first child (by which time half of all couples had a child) was one year after the wedding (*Yearbook of Population Research* 1993, 135–7). In the 1970s, having a child was postponed: the first child was born a couple of years after the woman had entered her first marriage. In the 1990s women both got married and had their first child at the age of 28. The average age of mothers with first child born out of wedlock was one year less (*Official Statistics of Finland* (OFS) 1996: 16, 66). An increasing number of children born in the Nordic countries today are born to cohabiting couples (Ritamies and Miettinen 1996, 44–51).

3. If a couple continued their life together, the union would dissolve as a result of the death of the husband or wife after 45 years (median). The man would then be 72 years old and the woman 70 (OFS 1996, 16: 61). The life expectancy of men being 73, and of women 80 years, a man would live as a widower for an average of three years, and a woman as a widow for an average of ten years.

5 Consecutive Relations

1. Finland fought against the Soviet Union in two wars between 1939 and 1944.

205

8 Parallel Relationships

1. According to the survey, parallel relations are as a rule kept from the steady partner. Seventy per cent of the spouses of people who had had extramarital relationships during the present marital or consensual union did not know about them.

9 Joy and Suffering

1. According to Liz Kelly (1988), pressurised sex includes milder forms of sex against one's own wishes, such as altruistic sex (feeling sorry for the partner, or guilty about saying no) and compliant sex (when the consequences of not doing it are estimated as worse than the consequences of doing it). Pressure to have sex is situated in the middle of the continuum of sexual violence advanced by Kelly. She distinguishes it from verbal harassment, on the one hand, and coercive and forced sex, on the other.

10 The Importance of Sex

1. The importance ascribed to sexuality could also be analyzed from the standpoint of which scientific discourses the autobiographical texts employ (Foucault 1980, 17–35; Helén 1997, 25–9), which rhetorical genres are used – for instance, Kaskisaari (1995) distinguishes between romance, tragedy and irony in sexual autobiographies, or which metaphors the narrators use to describe sexuality and the relation between sexuality and love in the texts. We start from the classifications employed by lay people themselves and pay less attention to the textual strategies employed.
2. These categories are based on earlier typologies by Osmo Kontula (Kontula and Haavio-Mannila 1997, 53–82) and Marja Kaskisaari (1998). Kontula and Haavio-Mannila (1997) distinguish between seven different groups in which sexuality is an *intrinsic value* – a value in itself – or a *utilitarian value*, a means for something else (for example relaxation, proximity). All the intrinsic means here have been put into the first category, in which sexuality is seen as the basic structure of life. Kaskisaari (1999) analyzed and categorised the autobiographies that mentioned same-sex relations. She grouped them into (a) homosexuality as the main theme of the autobiography; (b) same-sex relations as a realm of freedom; (c) same-sex relations as otherness (often something to despise or reject), and (d) sexuality as the basic structure of life.
3. This rare type of relationship type was number six in the classifications presented in Chapter 1.
4. In Finnish, the word for women's genitalia is almost as commonly used as the word 'fuck' is used in contemporary spoken English.

Conclusion

1. In making this calculation, people of the searching type have been omitted.

References

Aapola, S. and I. Kangas, *Väistelyä ja vastarintaa. Tarinoita naisten selviytymisestä* (Evasion and Opposition. Stories on Coping among Women), Tampere: Gaudeamus, 1994.

Alberoni, F. *Rakastuminen* (Falling in Love), Keuruu: Otava, 1983.

Aromaa, K. and I. Cantell and R. Jaakkola, *Avoliitto. Tutkimuksia avoliiton yleisyydestä ja yleistymisestä Suomessa* (Cohabitation. Studies on the Prevalence and Growth of Cohabitation in Finland), Helsinki: Oikeuspoliittisen tutkimuslaitoksen julkaisuja 49, 1981.

Beck, U. and E. Beck-Gernsheim, *The Normal Chaos of Love*, Cambridge: Polity Press, 1995.

Bertaux, D. (1997) *Les récits de vie*, Paris: Éditions Nathan, 1997.

Bourdieu, P. 'L'illusion biographique' (Biographical Illusion), *Actes de la recherche en science sociales*, 62–63 (1986) 69–72.

Bozon, M. 'Les significations sociales des actes sexuelles'. *Actes de la recherche des sciences sociales*, 128 (1999) 3–23.

Bozon, M. and O. Kontula 'Sexual Initiation and Gender: A Cross-Cultural Analysis of Trends in the 20th Century', in M. Hubert, N. Bajos and T. Sandfort (eds) *Sexual Behaviour and HIV/AIDS in Europe. Comparisons of National Surveys*, London: UCL Press, 1998, 37–67.

Connell, R.W. 'Sexual Revolution', in L. Segal, (ed.) *New Sexual Agendas*, Basingstoke, Hampshire and London: Macmillan, 1997, 60–76.

Connell, R.W. and G.W. Dowsett, 'The Unclean Motion of the Generative Parts: Frameworks in Western Thought of Sexuality' in R. Parker, and P. Aggleton, (eds) *Culture, Society and Sexuality A Reader*, London and Philadelphia: UCL Press, 1999, 179–96.

Costlow, J.T., S. Sandler and J. Vowles, (eds) *Sexuality and the Body in Russian Culture*, Stanford: Stanford University Press, 1993, 1–39.

Cuber, J.F. and P.B. Harroff, *The Significant Americans. A Study of Sexual Behaviour Among the Affluent*, New York: Appleton-Century, 1965.

Davies, S.J. Katz and J.L. Jackson 'Sexual Desire Discrepancies: Effects on Sexual and Relationship Satisfaction in Heterosexual Dating Couples', *Archives of Sexual Behavior 28* (1999) 553–67.

Featherstone, M. 'Love and Eroticism: An Introduction' in M. Featherstone, (ed.) *Love and Eroticism*, London: Sage, 1999, 1–18.

Foucault, M. *The History of Sexuality I: An Introduction*, New York: Vintage Books, a Division of Random House, 1980.

Franceaur, R.T. *Becoming a Sexual Person*, 2nd edn, New York: Macmillan, 1990.

Giddens, A. *Modernity and Self-Identity. Self and Society in the Late Modern Age* , Cambridge: Polity Press, 1991.

Giddens, A. *The Transformation of Intimacy*, Stanford, California: Stanford University Press, 1992.

Gordon, T. *Single Women on their Margins*, New York: Macmillan, 1994.

Gordon, T. and E. Lahelma. 'School is Like an Ants' Nest. Spatiality and Embodiment in Schools', *Gender and Education 8* (1996) 301–10.

Greer, G. *The Whole Woman*, New York: A.A. Knopf, 1999.

Haavio-Mannila, E. *Suomalainen nainen ja mies* (Finnish Women and Men), Porvoo: WSOY, 1968.

Haavio-Mannila, E. and O. Kontula, *Seksin trendit* (Trends in Sexual Life), Helsinki: WSDY, 2001.

Haavio-Mannila, E., O. Kontula and E. Kuusi, *Trends in Sexual Life Measured by National Sex Surveys in Finland in 1971, 1992 and 1999, and a Comparison to Sex Survey in St. Petersburg in 1996,* Helsinki: The Population Research Institute, The Family Federation of Finland, The Population Research Institute, Working Papers E 10/2001.

Haavio-Mannila, E. and J.P. Roos 'Love, Generation and Gender'. Paper presented at the 2nd European Conference of Sociology, Budapest, 30 August 30–2 September 1995.

Haavio-Mannila, E. and J.P. Roos 'Love Stories in Sexual Autobiograhies', in R. Josselson and A. Lieblich, A. *Making Meaning of Narratives*, Thousand Oaks, California; London and New Delhi: Sage, 1999, 239–74.

Haavio-Mannila, E. and A. Rotkirch 'Generational and Gender Differences in Sexual Life in St. Petersburg and Urban Finland'. *Yearbook of Population Research in Finland* XXXIV, Helsinki: The Population Research Institute (1997) 133–60.

Haavio-Mannila, E. and A. Rotkirch 'Gender Liberalisation and Polarisation: Comparing Sexuality in St. Petersburg, Finland and Sweden', *The Finnish Review of East European Studies, 3–4* (2000) 4–25.

Haavio-Mannila, E., J.P. Roos and O. Kontula 'Repression, Revolution and Ambivalence: The Sexual Life of Three Generations', *Acta Sociologica* 39, (1996) 409–30.

Haavio-Mannila, E. and S. Purhonen 'Slimness and Self-rated Sexual Attractiveness: Comparison of Men and Women in Two Cultures' *The Journal of Sex Research,* 38, 2 (May 2001).

Hatfield, E. and R.L. Rapson 'Historical and Cross-Cultural Perspectives on Passionate Love and Sexual Desire', *Annual Review of Sex Research, 4* (1993) 67–98.

Hatfield, E. and R.L. Rapson *Love and Sex. Cross-Cultural Perspectives*, Boston, New York: Allyn and Bacon, 1996.

Heidendry, J. *What Wild Ecstasy. The Rise and Fall of the Sexual Revolution*, New York: Simon & Schuster, 1997.

Heinämaa, S. 'Simone de Beauvoir's Phenomenology of Sexual Difference', *Hypatia, 14* (1999) 114–32.

Heinämaa, S. *Ele, tyyli ja sukupuoli* (Gesture, Style and Gender), Helsinki: Gaudeamus, 1996.

Heiskala, R. 'Sukupuolijärjestelmän murros: Castellsin patriarkalismiteesi ja kulttuurinen muuntelu' (The Breakthrough of Gender System: The Thesis of Patriarchalism by Castells and Cultural Variation), *Sosiologia* 36 (1999) 122–310.

Helén, I. *Äidin elämän politiikka. Naissukupuolisuus, valta ja itsesuhde Suomessa 1800-luvulta 1960-luvulle* (Life Politics of the Mother. Female Gender, Power, and Relationship to the Self in Finland from the 19th Century to the 1960s), Tampere: Gaudeamus, 1997.

Helmius, G. *Mogen för sex? Det sexuellt restriktiviserande samhället och ungdomars heterosexuella glädje* (Mature for Sex? The Sexually Restrictive Society and Heterosexual Pleasure of Young People), Uppsala: University of Uppsala, 1990.

Hendrick, S.S. and C. Hendrick *Romantic Love*, Newbury Park, California: Sage, 1992.

Hoikkala, T. (ed.) *Miehenkuvia. Välähdyksiä nuorista miehistä Suomessa* (Images of Men. Glimps of Young Men in Finland), Helsinki: Gaudeamus, 1996.

Holland, J., C. Ramazanoglu, S. Sharpe and R. Thomson, *The Male in the Head – Young People, Heterosexuality and Power*, London: The Tufnell Press, 1998.

Häkkinen, A. *Rahasta–vaan ei rakkaudesta. Prostituutio Helsingissä 1867–1939* (For Money but not for Love. Prostitution in Helsinki 1867–1939), Helsinki: Otava, 1995.

Hänninen, J. 'Seksitarinan pornografinen käsikirjoitus: minä sain, olen siis mies' (The Pornographic Script of Sex Story: I Got, Thus I Am a Man), in J.P. Roos and E. Peltonen (eds) *Miehen elämää. Kirjoituksia miesten omaelämäkerroista* (On the Life of Men: Writings on Autobiographies of Men), Helsinki: Suomalaisen Kirjallisuuden Seura (1994) 106–39.

Jallinoja, R. 'Rakkauden kolmet kasvot' (Three Faces of Love), *Tiede ja Edistys*, 2 (1984), 105–15.

Jallinoja, R. *Moderni säädyllisyys. Aviosuhteen vapaudet ja sidokset* (Modern Decency: Freedom and Commitment in Marital Relationships), Helsinki: Gaudeamus, 1997.

Jalovaara, M. *Sosioekonomiset tekijät ja avioero Suomessa* (Socioeconomic Factors and Divorce in Finland), Master's thesis in Sociology, University of Helsinki, September 1996.

Janus, S.S. and C.L. Janus *The Janus Report on Sexual Behaviour*, New York, Chichester, Brisbane, Toronto, Singapore: John Wiley and Sons 1993.

Järvinen, M. *Prostitution i Helsingfors – en studie i kvinnokontroll* (Prostitution in Helsingfors – A Study on the Control of Women), Åbo: Åbo Akademis Förlag, 1990.

Kaskisaari, M. *Lesbokirja: Vieras, minä ja moderni* (Lesbo Book: Stranger, I and Modern), Tampere: Vastapaino, 1995.

Kaskisaari, M. 'Rakkauden täyttymys. Seksuaaliset erot ja romanttinen rakkaus' (Fulfilment of Love. Gender Differences and Romantic Love) in M. Hyvärinen, E. Peltonen and A. Vilkko (eds) *Liikkuvat erot. Sukupuoli elämäkertatutkimuksissa* (Moving Differences. Gender in Biographical Research), Tampere: Vastapaino, 1998, 273–310.

Kelly, L. *Surviving Sexual Violence*, Cambridge: Polity Press, 1988.

Kon, I. *The Sexual Revolution in Russia. From the Age of the Czars to Today*, New York: The Free Press, 1985.

Kontula, O. 'Eroticism and Health', *Publications of the National Board of Health, Finland, Series Statitistics and Reviews 6*, Helsinki: Valtion painatuskeskus, 1989.

Kontula, O. *Nuorten seksi* (Sexuality of Young People), Keuruu: Otava, 1987.

Kontula, O. and E. Haavio-Mannila *Matkalla intohimoon – Nuoruuden hurma ja kärsimys seksuaalielämäkertojen kuvaamana*. (On the Way to Passion – The Charm and Suffering in Youth as Described by Sexual Autobiographies), Helsinki: WSOY, 1995a.

Kontula, O. and E. Haavio-Mannila *Sexual Pleasures: Enhancement of Sex Life in Finland, 1971–1992*, Aldershot: Dartmouth, Hampshire 1995b.

Kontula, O. and E. Haavio-Mannila E. *Intohimon hetkiä – Seksuaalisen läheisyyden kaipuu ja täyttymys omaelämäkertojen kuvaamana* (Moments of Passion – Longing for and Reaching Sexual Closeness as Described in Sexual Autobiographies), Helsinki, Juva: WSOY, 1997.

Kontula, O. and K. Kosonen *Seksiä lehtien sivuilla* (Sex on the Pages of Journals), Helsinki: Valtion Painatuskeskus, 1994.

Kuivaniemi, M. *Väkivallasta vapaaksi. Naiset kertovat kokemuksistaan* (Free from Violence. Women Tell Their Experiences), Helsinki: Kirjayhtymä, 1996.

Laumann, E.O., J.H. Gagnon, R.T. Michael and S. Michaels *The Social Organization of Sexuality*, Chicago and London: The University of Chicago Press, 1994.

Lehtonen, J. 'Homottelu ja heteronormatiivinen kiusaaminen koulussa' (Naming People Homosexual and the Hetero-Normative Teasing at School) in J. Lehtonen (ed.) *Homo Fennicus – miesten homo-ja biseksuaalisuus muutoksessa* (Homo Fennicus – Homo- and Bisexuality of Men in Change), Helsinki: Sosiaali- ja Terveysministeriö, Naistutkimusraportteja 1/1999, 73–91.

Leridon, H., G. von Zessen and M. Hubert. 'The Europeans and their Sexual Partners', in M. Hubert, Bajos M. and T. Sandfort (eds) *Sexual Behaviour and HIV/AIDS in Europe. Comparisons of National Surveys*, London: UCL Press 1988, 165–96.

Lewin, B. *(ed.) Att se sexualiteten. Om sexuell socialisation, förhållningssätt och sexuella erfarenheter bland människor med medfödda funktionshinder* (To See Sexuality. On Sexual Socialization, Beliefs and Practices among Handicapped People), Uppsala: University of Uppsala, 1987.

Lewin, B. *(ed.) Sex i Sverige. Om sexuallivet i Sverige 1996* (On Sexual Life in Sweden 1996), Uppsala: Uppsala Universitets Förlag, 1997.

Lottes, I. and O. Kontula (eds) *New Views on Sexual Health – The Case of Finland*, Helsinki: Publications of the Population Research Institute, Series D 37/2000.

Lyttkens, L. *Den disciplinerade människan* (The Disciplined Human Being), Stockholm: Allmänna Förlaget, 1989.

Määttä, K. *Rakastumisen lumous* (The Spell of Falling in Love), Juva: WSOY, 1999.

Nieminen, A. 'Esiaviollisten raskauksien yleisyydestä Suomessa' (On the Generality of Premarital Pregnancies in Finland), *Sosiologia* 1 (1964) 14–18.

Official Statistics of Finland (OFS), 3, 9 and 16. Population 1995, Helsinki: Statistics Finland, 1996.

Peltonen, E. 'Perunkirjoitusta' (Estate Inventory) in J.P. Roos and A. Rotkirch (eds) *Vanhemmat ja lapset. Sukupolvien sosiologiaa* (Parents and Children. Sociology of Generations), Helsinki: Gaudeamus, 1998, 96–122.

Plummer, K. *Telling Sexual Stories*, London and New York: Routledge, 1995.

Ritamies, M. and A. Miettinen *Ensimmäiset parisuhteet* (First Couple Relationships), Helsinki: Väestöntutkimuslaitoksen julkaisusarja D 29, 1996.

Rodgers, R.H. and J.M. White 'Family Development Theory' in P.G. Boss, W.J. Doherty, R. LaRossa, W.R. Schumm and S.K. Steinmetz, (eds) *Source Book of Family Theories and Methods: A Contextual Approach*, New York: Plenum Press, 1993, 225–44.

Ronkainen, S., P. Pohjolainen and J.-E. Ruth *Erotiikka ja elämänkulku* (Erotics and Course of Life), Juva: WSOY, 1994.

Ronkainen, S. *Ajan ja paikan merkitsemät: subjektiviteetti, tieto ja toimijuus* (Marked by Time and Space: Subjectivity, Knowledge and Action), Helsinki: Gaudeamus, 1999.

Roos, J.P. *Suomalainen elämä* (The Finnish Life), Hämeenlinna: Suomalaisen Kirjallisuuden Seura, 1987.

Roos, J.P. 'Life-Style Studies in Sociology: From Typologies to Fields and Trajectories' in J.C. Somogyi and E.H. Koskinen (eds) *Nutritional Adaptation to New Life-Styles,* Basel: Bibliotheca Nutritio et Dieta 45, Karger (1990) 1–16.

Roos, J.P. 'The True Life Revisited Autobiography and Referentiality after the 'Posts' in L. Stanley (ed.) *Lives and Works Auto/Biographical Occasions, Special Double Issue of Auto/Biography*, 3 (1994) 1–16.

Rotkirch, A. *The Man Question: Loves and Lives in Late 20th Century Russia,* Helsinki: Department of Social Policy, University of Helsinki, 2000.

Saarikoski, H. *Mistä on huonot tytöt tehty?* (What Are Bad Girls Made of), Helsinki: Tammi, 2001.

Sarmela, M. *Reciprocity Systems of the Rural Society in the Finnish-Carelian Culture Area,* Helsinki: Folklore Fellows Communications 207. Suomalainen Tiedeakatemia, 1969.

Sievers, K., O. Koskelainen and K. Leppo *Suomalaisten sukupuolielämä* (The Sexual Life of Finns), Porvoo: WSOY, 1974.

Simon, W. and J.H. Gagnon, 'Sexual Scripts', *Society,* 22 (1984) 53–60.

Simon, W. and J.H. Gagnon, 'Sexual Scripts', in R. Parker and P. Aggleton (eds) *Culture, Society and Sexuality – A Reader*, London and Philadelphia: UCL Press, 1999, 29–38.

Sipilä, P., *Sukupuolitettu ihminen – kokonainen etiikka* (A Gendered Person – Wholesome Ethics), Tampere: Gaudeamus, 1998.

Tennov, D. *Love and Limerence: The Experience of Being in Love*, Chelsea, Michigan: Scarborough House, 1989.

Traeen, B. *Norwegian Adolescents' Sexuality in the Era of AIDS. Empirical Studies on Heterosexual Behaviour*, Oslo: National Institute for Alcohol and Drug Research, 1993.

Vance, C.S. (ed.) *Pleasure and Danger: Exploring Female Sexuality*, London: Pandora Press, 1989.

Vilkko, A. *Omaelämäkerta kohtaamispaikkana. Naisen elämän kerronta ja luenta* (Autobiography As Meeting Place. Telling and Reading about Women's Life), Helsinki: Suomalaisen Kirjallisuuden Seura, 1997.

Weeks, J. *Sexuality and its Discontents: Meanings, Myths and Modern Sexualities,* London: Routledge and Kegan Paul, 1985.

Weeks, J. *Sexuality*, Bungay, Suffolk: Ellis Horwood, 1986.

Weigert, A.J. *Mixed Emotions. Certain Steps Toward Understanding Ambivalence,* Albany, N.Y.: State University of New York Press, 1991.

Wikman, K.R.V. *Die Einleitung der Ehe* (Initiation to Marriage), Åbo: Acta Academiae Aboensis, Humaniora XI:1, 1937.

Yearbook of Population Research in Finland, XXXI, Helsinki: The Population Research Institute, 1993.

Appendix 1 Guidelines of the Writing Competition in Finland 1 April–30 September, 1992

Sexuality as an integral part of life

The purpose of the competition

The main purpose of this writing competition is to collect experiences and personal information relating to sexuality and their effects on life as a whole in Finland. The competition is open to anyone, not depending on age.

Sexuality forms part of the life of all people. It consists of phases which almost everyone enters into sometime during his or her life, To name a few of those phases: playing doctor and patient in childhood, growing up with problems in adolescence, going out with someone and gaining sexual experiences for the first time, establishing a long-term relationship or contracting a marriage, having sexual adventures, establishing new relationships, paying or getting paid for love, having difficulties in getting sexual gratification. facing the effects of ageing etc. The list could go on and on.

We would like you to write about the small things as well as the major changes of your life as concerns sexuality. Describe the events, situations, feelings and hopes you have gone through in as personal and as realistic way a as possible. Authenticity is much more important than clear handwriting or grammar. Write as if you were telling about your life to a trusted friend – be honest and outspoken. You may use fictitious names, but the people should be real.

When the winners of the competition have been decided, the writings are handed over to the research group examining human relations, sexual attitudes and sexual lifestyles in Finland. The leaders of this study are Professor Elina Haavio-Mannila and Dr Osmo Kontula in the University of Helsinki. The study is financed by the Academy of Finland.

The contents of the writings will be summarised and published in the form of a report at the end of 1993. Any information which might reveal the identity of the writer or the people mentioned will be removed at this stage. Treatment of the writings will be fully confidential and the researchers are bound by a pledge of secrecy. You may also remain anonymous when writing.

Sexual autobiography

The form of your sexual autobiography is free. However, your description should be versatile enough to give real information to the researchers. For example, you may write in the following way:

1. Describe your present life situation as accurately as possible. Describe your sexual life. Is it better or more disappointing than usual? Tell about the highlights as well as the everyday side of your life.
2. Describe your life so far: attitudes of your parents and childhood home toward sexuality; the most important events of your childhood and adolescence relating to sexuality, your first sexual experiences; sexuality in studies and at work; sexual experiences and relationships in adulthood; the meaning of sexuality changing with age; changes in hopes and ideas; crises and moments of happiness; adventures and incidents.
3. Assess your life: what are the central questions and the most important experiences in relation to sexuality? Are you satisfied with your sexual life? What is it that sexuality has given to you at its best? What have been your most traumatic experiences or greatest disappointments? How valuable have your experiences and feelings relating to sexuality been as a whole? What could you compare them with?
4. Think of the matters and events which have most affected your attitude toward and experiences of sexuality. What has life taught you? What would have you done differently? From whom have you received help in difficult times? What do you wish of other people?

The participants were asked to write at most 50 typed pages in Finnish or Swedish and include the following personal information: name, occupation, date and place of birth, address and telephone number. They were also asked to grant permission for future publication of excerpts of the autobiography in the research report. If permission was given, the participants were asked if the researchers should change the names in the story in order to prevent personal identification. People who wanted to use a pseudonym, could participate in the competition by sending their name and address in a separate envelope to the researchers. The three prizes were 3000 FIM, 2000 FIM and 1000 FIM (one euro is six FIM).

Appendix 2   List of Authors

Code (number, gender, and age)	Year of birth	Couple Relationship*	Occupation
001M29	1963	single	unemployed employee
002F77	1915	single	retired employee
003F29	1963	married	employee
004M37	1955	single	employee
005M25	1967	married	employee
006F50	1942	married	employee
007M31	1961	single	employee
008F48	1944	married	employee
010M?	?	married	employee
012M65	1927	married	retired employee
013M25	1967	married	employee
014F44	1948	LAT	employee
015F48	1944	married	home-staying housewife employee
016F25	1967	single	student
017F49	1943	married	employee
018F65	1927	LAT	employee
019M59	1933	married	employee
020F47	1945	LAT	employee
021F38	1954	cohabiting	employee
022M69	1923	LAT	retired employee
023F?	?	LAT	?
024F30	1962	cohabiting	employee
025F57	1935	married	retired worker
026F55	1937	single	retired employee
027M80	1912	single	retired worker
028F57	1935	single	employee
029F31	1961	married	employee
031F27	1965	married	home-staying housewife employee
032F43	1949	LAT	employee
033F53	1939	single	employee
034M61	1931	married	retired employee
035M34	1958	single	working for pay no information where
036F52	1940	LAT	working for pay no information where
037F40	1952	LAT	worker
038F28	1964	married	worker
039F45	1947	single	employee
040F26	1966	married	no information

Code (number, gender, and age)	Year of birth	Couple Relationship*	Occupation
041F21	1971	LAT	student
042F23	1969	married	student
043F26	1966	no information	
044M53	1939	married	employee
045M53	1939	cohabiting	employee
046F27	1965	single	employee
048M55	1937	married	retired employee
049F48	1944	single	unemployed employee
050F81	1911	single	retired without information on occupation
051F46	1946	married	employee
052F23	1969	cohabiting	working for pay no information where
053F54	1938	LAT	employee
054M36	1956	LAT	no information if working for pay
055F41	1951	married	employee
056M32	1960	cohabiting	worker
057F25	1967	cohabiting	student
058M44	1948	married	employee
060F38	1954	LAT	employee
061F55	1937	?	employee
062M39	1953	LAT	no information if working for pay
063F23	1969	LAT	student
064F53	1939	single	employee
065M44	1948	cohabiting	employee
067F25	1967	single	unemployed employee
068M50	1942	married	no information if working for pay
069F22	1970	LAT	no information if working for pay
070M40	1952	married	working for pay no information where
071M54	1938	single	employee
072F42	1950	LAT	employee
073M60	1932	married	retired worker
074F31	1961	LAT	employee
075F40	1952	single	student
076F62	1930	LAT	employee
077F36	1956	LAT	employee
078F30	1962	LAT	unemployed without information on occupation
079F43	1949	single	employee
080F23	1969	single	student
082M47	1945	married	unemployed employee
082F30	1962	married	home-staying housewife without information on occupation
083F37	1955	LAT	no information if working for pay
084M31	1961	LAT	unemployed employee

Code (number, gender, and age)	Year of birth	Couple Relationship*	Occupation
085F53	1939	single	worker
086F30	1962	single	employee
087F42	1950	LAT	home-staying housewife without information on occupation
088M39	1953	cohabiting	employee
089W20	1972	single	student
091M52	1940	LAT	employee
092F61	1931	married	retired worker
095F43	1949	married	worker
096F20	1972	cohabiting	worker
097F52	1940	married	farmer hostess
098F31	1961	single	student
099M62	1930	married	employee
100F17	1975	LAT	student
101F66	1926	married	retired without information on occupation
102F54	1938	LAT	employee
103F38	1954	cohabiting	home-staying housewife without information on occupation
104F38	1954	cohabiting	employee
105F63	1929	single	retired worker
106F39	1953	married	employee
107F42	1950	cohabiting	employee
108M32	1960	married	employee
109F21	1971	LAT	student
110M70	1922	married	retired employee
111F35	1957	LAT	employee
112F40	1952	single	no information if working for pay
113M54	1938	LAT	retired employee
114F39	1953	married	employee
115F29	1963	married	employee
116F31	1961	LAT	employee
117F72	1920	married	retired without information on occupation
118M48	1944	married	worker
119F46	1946	LAT	employee
120F30	1962	married	home-staying housewife without information on occupation
121F42	1950	single	unemployed without information on occupation
122M44	1948	married	employee
123M64	1928	married	retired worker
124M47	1945	married	home-staying housewife without information on occupation

Code (number, gender, and age)	Year of birth	Couple Relationship*	Occupation
125F34	1958	married	employee
126F73	1919	single	retired employee
128F25	1967	single	employee
129M45	1947	married	employee
130F47	1945	single	employee
131F28	1964	married	student
132F34	1958	single	student
134F49	1943	LAT	employee
135F32	1960	LAT	no information if working for pay
136F49	1943	single	employee
137M70	1922	married	retired employee
138M29	1963	single	employee
139M68	1924	married	retired employee
140F55	1937	married	employee
141F?	?	cohabiting	employee
142F25	1967	LAT	worker
143F22	1970	single	unemployed without information on occupation
144F35	1957	married	employee
145F31	1961	single	employee
146F33	1959	single	employee
147F41	1951	LAT	unemployed employee
148F36	1956	single	no information if working for pay
149F33	1959	LAT	employee
150F26	1966	cohabiting	worker
151F25	1967	married	employee
153M70	1922	married	retired employee
155M76	1916	married	retired worker
156M68	1924	single	retired employee
157F63	1929	single	retired employee
158M33	1959	married	student
159M55	1937	single	unemployed worker
160M48	1944	married	worker
161F50	1942	married	employee
162F22	1970	cohabiting	unemployed employee
163M50	1942	married	employee
164F80	1912	single	retired employee
165F69	1923	single	retired without information on occupation
166F30	1962	cohabiting	home-staying housewife without information on occupation
167F22	1970	single	student
168F24	1968	single	employee
169M50	1942	married	employee

Code (number, gender, and age)	Year of birth	Couple Relationship*	Occupation
170F51	1941	married	farmer hostess
171M71	1921	married	retired worker
172M46	1946	married	worker
173M46	1946	married	retired employee
174F68	1924	single	retired employee

Note: * LAT=living -apart-together

Index